Chesterton and the Philosophers

Chesterton and the Philosophers

Edited by

LANDON LOFTIN

WIPF & STOCK · Eugene, Oregon

CHESTERTON AND THE PHILOSOPHERS

Wipf & Stock
An Imprint of Wipf and Stock Publishers
199 W. 8th Ave., Suite 3
Eugene, OR 97401

www.wipfandstock.com

PAPERBACK ISBN: 979-8-3852-3099-0
HARDCOVER ISBN: 979-8-3852-3100-3
EBOOK ISBN: 979-8-3852-3101-0

VERSION NUMBER 02/19/26

Wonder is the feeling of a philosopher, and philosophy begins in wonder.

—Plato

It is through wonder that men now begin, and
originally began, to philosophize.

—Aristotle

Wonder is defined as a kind of desire for knowledge.

—Aquinas

The world will never starve for want of wonders; but only for want of wonder.

—Chesterton

I have attempted . . . to state the philosophy in which I have come to believe. I will not call it my philosophy; for I did not make it. God and humanity made it; and it made me.

—"Introduction in Defense of Everything Else," *Orthodoxy*

Contents

Editor's Note

CRITICS HAVE LONG DISAGREED about whether, or in what sense, G. K. Chesterton should be considered a philosopher. Gary Wills, for instance, is hesitant about that particular description: "Chesterton," he wrote, "was not a philosopher, nor did he want to be. He was a defender of philosophy, which is quite another thing."[1]

That Chesterton was a brilliant and enthusiastic defender of philosophy is amply illustrated by many of the quotations included in this book. But is Wills correct in saying that Chesterton was "not a philosopher"? Unsurprisingly, the answer depends on which of the many senses of the term "philosopher" he intends. There is a somewhat trivial sense in which *everyone* is a philosopher, since everyone has a philosophy (even if that philosophy consists in largely inarticulate and unexamined assumptions). And there is a slightly less trivial sense that excludes all but an elite few who can boast of formal academic achievements and professional standing. But the really interesting question is not whether Chesterton was a philosopher in either of these unduly restrictive senses, but whether he was a philosopher in the oldest, most common, and enduring sense: that is, "a friend or lover of truth." This Chesterton certainly was; and he not only loved truth, he pursued it and wrote about it with extraordinary insight and rhetorical skill.

Failure to recognize this for any reason (e.g., because he never earned a degree; because he made his living outside of the university; because he

1. Gary Wills, *Chesterton* (Doubleday, 2001), 107.

avoided the technical minutia that fills the pages of philosophical journals; because his style of argument was aphoristic—sometimes prioritizing pith over precision) is to hold him to a standard that would exclude many of the greatest and most influential figures in the history of Western philosophy, from Socrates to Nietzsche. This book, in any case, was conceived under the conviction that Stephen R. L. Clark—himself a formidable philosopher—was correct in his assessment of Chesterton as "an excellent philosopher of a non-academic sort."[2] My purpose in collecting and editing these essays is to stimulate the conversation about Chestertonian philosophy which has proceeded in fits and starts since Chesterton's day.

Thanks are due first and foremost to each of the contributors whose response to my call made this project possible. Thanks also go to the editors of *The Chesterton Review* who have allowed me to include a revised version of "Hume and Chesterton," here called "Hume's Faith and Chesterton's Doubt."[3] The crew at Vault Coffee deserve special mention as well. As always, I am indebted to my family, especially my wife, whose patience and support enables me to pursue my various interests. And finally, I want to thank Zach Manis, whose encouragement has proved, once again, to be invaluable. It is to Zach, my first and best philosophy teacher, that I dedicate this book.

2. Stephen R. L. Clark, *Thinking Backward, Looking Forward* (Templeton Foundation, 2006), vii.

3. See Volume 47, Issue 3/4, Fall/Winter 2021 of *The Chesterton Review*.

1

Chesterton on the Strengths and Limitations of Plato

Louis Markos

As a Catholic of a Thomistic bent, G. K. Chesterton tended to be more Aristotelian than Platonic in his outlook. Still, the shadow of Aristotle's great teacher looms large over the work of Chesterton, who heartily agreed with Plato in the ancient and ongoing debate between realism and nominalism. Chesterton believed, as did Plato, that the words we use point back to real things, to what Plato called the Forms or Ideas. Though Plato located his Forms in an abstract World of Being—it would take Augustine to move those Forms into their proper abode: the Mind of God—Chesterton understood the debt owed to Plato for turning the eyes of the Western world toward universal, transcendent, absolute standards of Goodness, Truth, and Beauty.

Plato got some things wrong, but he avoided the black pit of nominalism, of believing that concepts like the good, the true, and the beautiful were just names (*nomen*) and did not participate in the reality of the three transcendentals. Whether those nominalists lived in ancient Greece, medieval Europe, or the modern world, their skepticism in the face of Meaning posed a threat to philosophy and theology alike. For Chesterton, as for Plato, universals existed; they were real, fixed, and eternal. They made reason and logic possible, for they provided the necessary standards and starting points *from* which, not *for* which, arguments were made.

Chesterton, like Plato before him, believed in something counterintuitive: that the unseen things are often more real than the things we see. Both dwelled boldly in the land of paradox, but with one major difference. Plato did not know, as Chesterton did, that goodness, truth, and beauty once took on flesh in the form of the incarnate Son of God. In what follows, I will work my way through two of Chesterton's most important and representative works of nonfiction, *Orthodoxy* and *The Everlasting Man*, considering as I go both the influence of Plato and how Chesterton praised Plato's insights while seeking to transcend the limits of his knowledge.

Though Plato was not Chesterton's sole teacher in the art of paradox, he was quite adept at turning things on their head. The man on the street, then and now, views our earthly realm as real and concrete, and the heavenly realm as vague and indistinct. Not so Plato. For Plato, the things of our world were shadowy imitations of the real but unseen Forms. The Origin, the Cause, the Source were invisible and above. Truth, not facts, was primary. To this metaphysical paradox, Plato added several political ones. The best ruler, he argued, was not the politician or the general but the philosopher king—for only the philosopher sees and understands the divine standards against which true justice must be measured. Plato went further than that. He argued that the absolute tyrant is the most enslaved of men, for he obeys his base desires rather than the laws, his own perverse sense of justice rather than the Form of Justice.

Chesterton imitates such Platonic topsy-turvy when he argues, in chapter 2 of *Orthodoxy*, that the "madman is not the man who has lost his reason. The madman is the man who has lost everything except his reason."[1] The true maniac is not the religious man who grounds his reason in a transcendent God, but the materialist who thinks his narrow and groundless philosophy can explain all things. In truth, it explains nothing. "Like the sun at noonday, mysticism [the religious worldview] explains everything else by the blaze of its own victorious invisibility. Detached intellectualism [the materialist worldview] is . . . all moonshine; for it is light without heat, and it is secondary light, reflected from a dead world."[2]

In chapter 4, Chesterton extends this Platonic paradox, which privileges invisible over visible, mysticism over materialism, into a critique of theological liberalism. In his own inimitable way, however, he mingles his

1. G. K. Chesterton, *Orthodoxy* (Image, 1990), 19.

2. Chesterton, *Orthodoxy*, 29.

Platonic paradox with an anti-Platonic one that privileges democracy over aristocracy, the voice of the people over the voice of the expert.

> The man who quotes some German historian against the tradition of the Catholic Church . . . is strictly appealing to aristocracy. He is appealing to the superiority of one expert against the awful authority of a mob. It is quite easy to see why a legend is treated, and ought to be treated, more respectfully than a book of history. The legend is generally made by the majority of people in the village, who are sane. The book is generally written by the one man in the village who is mad.[3]

In Christianizing Plato, Chesterton also democratizes him. One can almost, but not quite, imagine Plato saying what Chesterton says a few sentences later about the deep connection between tradition and democracy: "Tradition may be defined as an extension of the franchise. Tradition means giving votes to the most obscure of all classes, our ancestors. It is the democracy of the dead. . . . Democracy tells us not to neglect a good man's opinion, even if he is our groom; tradition asks us not to neglect a good man's opinion, even if he is our father."[4]

Plato would have agreed with this in principle but would have been dubious about trusting the people and their opinions in such matters. There is a strong aristocratic air to Socrates and Plato, but then they did not know, as Chesterton did, about the indwelling Holy Spirit or about the incarnate Logos who is the true Light that enlightens every man coming into the world.[5] Because he knew these things, Chesterton could effect a Platonic topsy-turvy that located truth in a transcendent realm that was, paradoxically, more accessible to the simple and the meek than the rich and the proud. In that sense, Chesterton is more like Socrates than Plato: for the former was at his best when deflating the arrogance of the smug Athenian elites. Chesterton cut through the pretensions of modernism with a wit-whetted knife, but he always did it with Socratic humility and humor. In fact, Chesterton suggests, in the last sentence of *Orthodoxy*, that Jesus hid from us his mirth, for it was too grand and wild a thing for us to handle.

Still, though Chesterton speaks ever as the man of the people, trusting to fairy tales more than philosophical treatises, he is as firm as Plato in his insistence that without fixed standards, there can be no actual progress.

3. Chesterton, *Orthodoxy*, 48.
4. Chesterton, *Orthodoxy*, 48
5. Cf. John 1:9.

> Progress should mean that we are always changing the world to suit the vision. Progress does mean (just now) that we are always changing the vision. It should mean that we are slow but sure in bringing justice and mercy among men: it does mean that we are very swift in doubting the desirability of justice and mercy. . . . Progress should mean that we are always walking towards the New Jerusalem. It does mean that the New Jerusalem is always walking away from us. We are not altering the real to suit the ideal. We are altering the ideal: it is easier.[6]

Whether it is the aristocrats or the people, the obsessive experts or the carefree villagers, there must be those who remember and uphold philosophical ideals and traditional standards. The point at which Plato and Chesterton come back together is in chapter 7, with Chesterton offering a democratic, common-man version of Plato's call for philosopher kings to rule his perfect republic. "The one specially and peculiarly un-Christian idea is the idea of Carlyle—the idea that the man should rule who feels that he can rule. Whatever else is Christian, this is heathen. If our faith comments on government at all, its comment must be this—that the man should rule who does *not* think that he can rule. Carlyle's hero may say, 'I will be king'; but the Christian saint must say 'Nolo episcopari.'"[7]

Here we find Plato and Chesterton alike insisting that the best ruler is the one who does not want to rule, who does not seek for himself power or wealth or prestige. Plato's philosopher king does not want the job, for he would rather spend his time in contemplation; Chesterton's Christian ruler refuses, for, in his humility, he does not feel adequate to the job. Both understand the seriousness of the position to which they are called and so hesitate to take it on. And yet, that is the very reason they must be forced to do so. Their ego dampened, if not effaced, they will rule in accordance with objective standards outside themselves rather than subjective desires within.

Orthodoxy is Chesterton's spiritual autobiography of the long pilgrimage he took in search of that which is truly true and really real. It can be compared with Plato's *Apology*, in which Socrates recounts his own bumpy journey toward truth—a journey that won him many enemies along the way. *The Everlasting Man* is more like Plato's dialogues with the famous sophists of his day. Just as Plato's dialogues counter the philosophical, moral, and aesthetic relativism of the sophists, so Chesterton's Christian history of the world

6. Chesterton, *Orthodoxy*, 105–6.

7. "I do not wish to be bishoped." Chesterton, *Orthodoxy*, 119; emphasis original.

counters the materialistic, evolutionary worldview that runs throughout H. G. Wells' influential, bestselling *Outline of History.*

Though few realize it today, Wells' *Outline* played a central role in propagating the extraordinarily pervasive pseudoscientific myth of the caveman. To challenge the existence of these mythical missing links between the higher primates and man, Chesterton resorts to a kind of argument that is still strong in Descartes but which ultimately goes back to Plato. I speak of the argument of kind versus degree, qualitative versus quantitative.

For Descartes, the existence in our mind of the idea of infinity proves that an infinity beyond our world must exist. Though Locke would later argue that a person who knew only finite numbers could keep counting higher and higher until he found his way into infinity, Descartes knew better. The difference between infinity and finitude is qualitative, not quantitative; it marks a difference of kind rather than degree. Count as high as we like, we shall never reach infinity, for infinity is wholly other; it marks a leap, not a mere progression.

This kind of argumentation runs throughout Plato's theory of the Forms. We cannot, as Nietzsche thought, argue up (inductively) from a large set of different chairs and trees to the Forms of Chair and Tree (chair-ness; tree-ness). We must, instead, argue down (deductively) from the Forms that transcend our world to the various imitations that we encounter on earth. The eternal, timeless standards of Goodness, Truth, Beauty, and Justice that dwell in Plato's World of Being are qualitatively different than the lesser, relativistic versions of goodness, truth, beauty, and justice that we meet in our ever-shifting World of Becoming. The cause must be greater than the effect; water does not rise above its source.

In the spirit of Plato, Chesterton demonstrates how one of the few material proofs of the caveman's existence offers the strongest argument *against* his existence: the cave drawings of animals at Lascaux. The man who painted those animals, Chesterton insists in part 1, chapter 1, was a full human being. He was not a half-man or a half-ape; he was as much a man and an artist as any man or artist today. What the drawings teach us "is the simple truth that man does differ from the brutes in kind and not in degree; and the proof of it is here; that it sounds like a truism to say that the most primitive man drew a picture of a monkey and that it sounds like a joke to say that the most intelligent monkey drew a picture of a man. Something of division and disproportion has appeared; and it is unique. Art is the signature of man."[8]

In chapter 2, Chesterton makes his point with even greater panache. "[Art] belongs to man and to nothing else except man; that is a difference

8. G. K. Chesterton, *The Everlasting Man* (Image, 1955), 32.

of kind and not a difference of degree. A monkey does not draw clumsily and a man cleverly; a monkey does not begin the art of representation and a man carry it to perfection. A monkey does not do it at all; he does not begin to do it at all; he does not begin to begin to do it at all. A line of some kind is crossed before the first faint line can begin."[9] Art is not something that evolved from higher apes to lower men. The first man who took up a brush to paint an animal engaged in something of which the animal world knows nothing; a qualitative leap was made that continues to this day. For monkeys still do not begin to begin to begin to make art.

Only a prior commitment to a reductionistic Darwinism could make moderns miss the real meaning and implications of the cave drawings. But that is not surprising for, as Chesterton goes on to show in chapter 3, Wells and his heirs use the same evolutionary paradigm to make us ignore one of the clear lessons of ancient history. Far from demonstrating that the human race evolved slowly from caves to primitive tribal structures to small villages to cities, history presents us with a highly civilized, and highly decadent, Egypt and Babylon at the very dawn of recorded history. "The dawn of history reveals a humanity already civilised. Perhaps it reveals a civilisation already old. . . . If we want to get rid of half the nonsense about nomads and cave-men and the old man of the forest, we need only look steadily at the two solid and stupendous facts called Egypt and Babylon."[10] While the worldview of Darwin and Wells would have us believe that the story of history is a struggle upward from barbarism to civilization, "the real records available [show that] barbarism and civilisation were not successive stages in the progress of the world. They were conditions that existed side by side, as they still exist side by side."[11]

What has this argument to do with the influence of Plato? It is too often forgotten that Plato invented the enduring myth of Atlantis. In his *Timaeus* and *Critias*, Plato tells the story of an ancient, highly advanced civilization that grew proud and greedy and was destroyed by a great wave sent by the gods. Although Plato almost surely made up this myth, he clearly believed that there were great civilizations (Egypt, Crete, Athens, etc.) that predated his own by centuries, if not millennia. Plato does not tell a story of ethical evolution but of moral entropy.

Chesterton, like Plato, extends this anti-evolutionary aspect of history to take in the rise and fall of political systems. Moderns tend to see tyranny as old and democracy as new, with the latter evolving as a matter of course

9. Chesterton, *Everlasting Man*, 44.

10. Chesterton, *Everlasting Man*, 55.

11. Chesterton, *Everlasting Man*, 61.

out of the former. In *Republic* VIII, Plato shows how a democracy, when it devolves into mob rule, naturally gives way to tyranny. Chesterton, though he does not reference Plato directly, makes the same argument: "Despotism can be a development, often a late development and very often indeed the end of societies that have been highly democratic. A despotism may almost be defined as a tired democracy. As fatigue falls on a community, the citizens are less inclined for that eternal vigilance which has truly been called the price of liberty; and they prefer to arm only one single sentinel to watch the city while they sleep."[12]

As Chesterton moves forward to discuss the "evolution" of religion, he highlights the Jews as the one people group who refused to succumb to syncretism: that is, they did not combine their God (Yahweh) with Zeus or Jupiter or Ammon or Moloch, as all the other Mediterranean cultures did. To preserve the purity of Yahweh, they even forbade all images of him. This was a good and God-ordained thing, but it meant that the world would have to wait for Christianity to bring together reason and imagination, divine holiness and images, philosophy and religion, logic and myth. Chesterton does, however, concede some ancient glimmerings of this union.

> It is only as an afterthought, when such cults are decadent or on the defensive, that a few Neo-Platonists or a few Brahmins are found trying to rationalise them, and even then only by trying to allegorise them. But in reality the rivers of mythology and philosophy run parallel and do not mingle till they meet in the sea of Christendom. Simple secularists still talk as if the Church had introduced a sort of schism between reason and religion. The truth is that the Church was actually the first thing that ever tried to combine reason and religion. There had never before been any such union of the priests and the philosophers.[13]

Although I agree with Chesterton on this point, he would have done well to read his Plato more carefully. It is no exaggeration to say that Socrates/Plato invented philosophy by combining metaphysics with ethics. This can be seen in Plato's central dialogues, where he makes logical, practical arguments about the way one should live one's life and then drives his point home by telling a myth about beginnings or endings, creations or final judgments. Reason and imagination work side by side in Plato's dialogues as he spins purified myths to bolster his logical claims.

Still, as Chesterton moves from part 1, chapter 1 ("The Man in the Cave") to part 2, chapter 1 ("The God in the Cave"), from the cave drawings

12. Chesterton, *Everlasting Man*, 58.

13. Chesterton, *Everlasting Man*, 110.

in Lascaux to the Christ child born in a stable, which was likely a cave, he does offer an analysis that distinguishes carefully between the (religious, imaginative) shepherds and the (philosophical, rational) magi that come to the Christ child and the highest of the ancient philosophers (Pythagoras, Plato, and Confucius). In the shepherds, Chesterton hears the voices and the yearnings of the common folk, of those who, though they were in error about many things, "had not been wrong in believing that holy things could have a habitation and that divinity need not disdain the limits of time and space."[14] They were of those who loved and believed in myths, no matter how strange and irrational they might seem. How different those shepherds were

> than all those in the circle of cities round the Mediterranean who had become content with cold abstractions or cosmopolitan generalisations; than all those who were spinning thinner and thinner threads of thought out of the transcendentalism of Plato or the orientalism of Pythagoras. The place that the shepherds found was not an academy [like the school Plato established] or an abstract republic [as Plato builds in *Republic*]; it was not a place of myths allegorised or dissected or explained or explained away. It was a place of dreams come true. Since that hour no mythologies have been made in the world. Mythology is a search.[15]

Here, I believe, Chesterton's analysis of what is present and lacking in Plato bears fruit. There was something (someone) in that stable that exceeded the limits even of Plato's, and Pythagoras', robust imagination. Next to the reality of the Christ child, Plato's Forms and Pythagoras' mystical numbers dim into "cold abstractions" and "cosmopolitan generalisations." Plato's myths are certainly purer and more ethical than those of Homer or Hesiod or Aeschylus, but they are still attempts to allegorize and explain away rather than statements of reality that can enter, concrete and incarnate, into our World of Becoming.

What, then, of the magi? In these great philosophers from the East, Chesterton glimpses—as T. S. Eliot would glimpse in his autobiographical and apologetical "Journey of the Magi"—the zenith of ancient philosophy. "They [the magi] would stand for the same human ideal if their names had really been Confucius or Pythagoras or Plato. They were those who sought not tales but the truth of things; and since their thirst for truth was itself a thirst for God, they also have had their reward."[16] Here we see the full

14. Chesterton, *Everlasting Man*, 173.
15. Chesterton, *Everlasting Man*, 173.
16. Chesterton, *Everlasting Man*, 175.

magnanimity of Chesterton, who can recognize in Plato, Pythagoras, *and* Confucius a striving for truth and a yearning for reality.

Indeed, Chesterton claims boldly that had "Plato and Pythagoras and Aristotle stood for an instant in the light that came out of that little cave, they would have known that their own light was not universal. It is far from certain, indeed, that they did not know it already. Philosophy also, like mythology, has very much the air of a search."[17] The Platos and Pythagorases and Aristotles of the ancient world were on the right track, even as the uneducated lovers of myth were. That is why their twin searches ended at the same destination point: the God in the cave.

So Plato *did* get many things right, and yet, without the full revelation of Christianity, Chesterton argues, Pythagoras, Plato, and Aristotle, not to mention the Stoics and Neo-Platonists, would have been stuck in the kind of philosophical dead ends that remained, and still remain, in the East. Paganism alone, even the high paganism of Plato, could not have fully grown and matured apart from the God in the cave.

> If classic paganism had lingered until now, a number of things might well have lingered with it; and they would look very like what we call the religions of the East. There would still be Pythagoreans teaching reincarnation, as there are still Hindus teaching reincarnation. There would still be Stoics making a religion out of reason and virtue, as there are still Confucians making a religion out of reason and virtue. There would still be Neo-Platonists studying transcendental truths, the meaning of which was mysterious to other people and disputed even amongst themselves; as the Buddhists still study a transcendentalism mysterious to others and disputed among themselves.[18]

And with those, Chesterton adds, there would have been dark magic and bloody sacrifices and sacred orgies. Plato's search was a good and correct one, but it was not enough on its own. Apart from the complete marriage of reason and imagination, philosophy and religion effected by the incarnation and the church, the world would have been condemned to cold abstractions on the one hand and divine madness on the other.

What then was Chesterton's overall assessment of Plato? To answer that, I must return to the opening paragraphs of this essay where I argued that Chesterton shared the philosophical realism of Plato. In part 1, chapter 6 of *The Everlasting Man*, Chesterton offers his final word on Plato's

17. Chesterton, *Everlasting Man*, 177.

18. Chesterton, *Everlasting Man*, 236–37.

strengths and limitations, on what he got right and what he missed. He also shows, helpfully, why he was more an Aristotelian than a Platonist.

> The two great philosophers of antiquity do indeed appear to us as defenders of sane and even of sacred ideas; their maxims often read like the answers to sceptical questions too completely answered to be always recorded. Aristotle annihilated a hundred anarchists and nature-worshipping cranks by the fundamental statement that man is a political animal. Plato in some sense anticipated the Catholic realism, as attacked by the heretical nominalism, by insisting on the equally fundamental fact that ideas are realities; that ideas exist just as men exist. Plato however seemed sometimes almost to fancy that ideas exist as men do not exist; or that the men need hardly be considered where they conflict with the ideas. He had something of the social sentiment that we call Fabian in his ideal of fitting the citizen to the city, like an imaginary head to an ideal hat; and great and glorious as he remains, he has been the father of all faddists. Aristotle anticipated more fully the sacramental sanity that was to combine the body and the soul of things.[19]

Plato was right to stand for realism against the nominalism of the sophists, thus providing the church with philosophical weapons to defeat the resurgent nominalists of the Middle Ages. His firm commitment to the "fact that ideas are realities," that they are as real and substantial as the people we meet on the street, anchored Western philosophy for over two millennia.

And yet, sadly, though Plato bequeathed this legacy to the church, his loyal adherence to the real existence of the Forms tended to overshadow the reality of people. The lives of real men and women became less important than the working out of pure ideas—as seen in his *Republic*. Rather than fit his ideal republic to the deep and enduring nature of man, he attempts to adjust man's nature so that it will embody the ideal abstractions he fashions for his perfect city. For Chesterton, Plato's excessive idealism made him the father of such faddist groups as the socialist Fabians who sought to slowly refashion the social, political, and economic structures of Britain. One of those Fabians was none other than H. G. Wells; two others, George Bernard Shaw and Bertrand Russell, debated publicly with Chesterton, as did Wells, on the issues of the day.

As a counter to Plato's idealism, Chesterton hails Aristotle's more practical philosophy that sought to balance idealism and realism, the spirit

19. Chesterton, *Everlasting Man*, 125–26.

and the flesh. There is in Aristotle's philosophy a slight intimation of man's incarnational nature, for his hylomorphic view of the intimate relationship between body and soul comes close to approximating the Christian view that we are not souls trapped in bodies but enfleshed souls. It is significant that Aristotle, unlike Pythagoras and Plato (at least the Plato of the myths), rejected reincarnation as incompatible with our body-soul union. For Chesterton, Aristotle's hylomorphism is sacramental, for it points in its own way to the incarnation, something that rarely happens in Plato's writings—where the soul seems eager to cast off its bondage to the flesh.

Chesterton the Catholic Thomist favored Aristotle over Plato, but that does not mean that he did not acknowledge his enormous debt, and the debt of Western Christendom, to Plato's rejection of any evolutionary paradigm that confuses kind and degree, his seeking after transcendent truths, and his affirmation of Goodness, Truth, and Beauty as real and essential things. Chesterton loved nothing more than to follow arguments wherever they led, and, in that, he modeled himself on both Socrates and Plato.

BIBLIOGRAPHY

Chesterton, G. K. *The Everlasting Man*. New York: Image, 1955.

———. *Orthodoxy*. New York: Image, 1990.

Plato. *Plato: The Collected Dialogues, Including the Letters*. Edited by Edith Hamilton and Huntington Cairns. Princeton, NJ: Princeton University Press, 1961.

The best reason for a revival of philosophy is that unless a man has a philosophy certain horrible things will happen to him. He will be practical; he will be progressive; he will cultivate efficiency; he will trust in evolution; he will do the work that lies nearest; he will devote himself to deeds, not words. Thus struck down by blow after blow of blind stupidity and random fate, he will stagger on to a miserable death with no comfort but a series of catchwords. . . . Those things are simply substitutes for thoughts. In some cases they are the tags and tail-ends of somebody else's thinking. That means that a man who refuses to have his own philosophy will not even have the advantages of a brute beast, and be left to his own instincts. He will only have the used-up scraps of somebody else's philosophy; which the beasts do not have to inherit; hence their happiness.

—"The Revival of Philosophy—Why?" *The Common Man*

The modern habit of saying "Every man has a different philosophy; this is my philosophy and it suits me"; the habit of saying this is mere weak-mindedness. A cosmic philosophy is not constructed to fit a man; a cosmic philosophy is constructed to fit a cosmos. A man can no more possess a private religion than he can possess a private sun and moon.

—"Introduction to the Book of Job"

2

Philosophical Parallels

Chesterton and Aristotle

Wojciech Załuski

Though Chesterton's outlook may be roughly described as "Aristotelian," he did not accept every aspect of Aristotle's philosophy. Without attempting to determine the relative weight of his agreements or disagreements with Aristotle, I will explore both similarities and differences in their thought. What is beyond doubt, though, is that Aristotle is a philosopher for whom Chesterton had great sympathy, and that a large part of this sympathy is indirect: It flows through St. Thomas Aquinas, Chesterton's absolutely beloved philosopher. Chesterton saw the greatness of Aristotle through the lens of Aquinas, whom he held in higher regard: "Aristotle," he said, "would never have recovered his own greatness but for the miracle that created the more magnanimous man."[1]

Of course, regarding one obvious issue—the nature of God—Chesterton strongly disagreed with Aristotle. Even here, however, the disagreement is not fundamental. For Aristotle was not an atheist, and especially not a radical, fighting naturalist, which was a species of philosopher particularly irritating to Chesterton. But the fact that Aristotle did not anticipate the

1. G. K. Chesterton, *The Autobiography of G. K. Chesterton* (Sheed and Ward, 1936), 236.

Christian vision of God—the vision of God as Love—affected Chesterton's attitude toward him. So despite Chesterton's sympathy for Aristotle, he could never embrace him as he embraced Aquinas; their stance toward the world was too different, precisely because of their differing visions of God.

CONVERGENCES

Populism

The meaning of "populism" has undergone a strange transformation in recent decades. It has become a derogatory term that is used to describe an emotion-driven, xenophobic, and divisive approach to politics which is contrary to the spirit of liberal democracy. However, its original meaning was entirely different. "Populism" originally referred to a political position with two key components, the first of which involves trust in the rational capabilities of so-called "common" or "ordinary" people. Indeed, many populists have gone on to reject the distinction between "ordinary" and "extraordinary" people, affirming instead that all people are equal, not only in terms of dignity, but also in terms of their capacity for political participation. In its first component, then, populism is deeply democratic: It expresses skepticism toward the pretensions of the so-called "elites" who claim superiority over the masses. The second component of populism is a practical outworking of the first. It is a call for the creation of social and economic conditions that enable all citizens to exercise their capacity for political participation. These conditions involve an equitable (though not necessarily equal) distribution of private property, particularly land. This call—which is at the heart of distributivism—was vigorously defended by all the major classical populists of the early twentieth century, including Chesterton himself, and Hilaire Belloc.[2] Populists believe that only under these conditions can society become truly democratic, which is to say that

2. Some eminent thinkers from the second half of the twentieth century subscribed to this view, such as Christopher Lasch (see *The Revolt of the Elites and the Betrayal of Democracy*) and Richard Weaver (*Ideas Have Consequences*). Lasch makes a compelling case for the argument that democracy functions best when there is a rough equality of conditions, although he appears to be more influenced by American pragmatism, particularly John Dewey, than by Chesterton or Hilaire Belloc. Richard Weaver, on the other hand, defends private property as "the last metaphysical right"—the right that teaches us the virtue of responsibility and promotes the growth of personality by helping us express our being. He is closer to Chesterton and Belloc than Lasch in that he is more overtly metaphysical (theistic). However, there is a certain note of aristocratic elitism in his approach which is absent in both Chesterton and Belloc, as well as in Lasch.

political power can be spread equally among all citizens only if most of them belong to the middle class—the class of economically independent citizens. If these conditions are not met (that is, if deep economic stratification sets in) then democracy becomes a mere façade; the real power becomes vested in the most affluent and the political system turns into an oligarchy.[3] But the fault of oligarchy is not only in diminishing the political power of the least affluent citizens. Its other, perhaps more pernicious, effect is that it deludes the elites into thinking that they are superior to the lower classes. This breeds arrogance among the elites and undermines the sentiment of unity among citizens.

Let us now consider whether these two components of populism can be discerned in Aristotle's political ideal. It will be easier to start with the second component (i.e., the social and political dominance of the middle class). In *Politics*, Aristotle explicitly states that the best citizens are those from the middle class, neither too rich nor too poor. These, he argues, should rule the state:

> Now in all states there are three elements: one class is very rich, another very poor, and a third is a mean. It is admitted that moderation and the mean are best, and therefore it will be clearly best to possess the gifts of fortune in moderation; for in that condition of life men are most ready to follow rational principle. But he who greatly excels in beauty, strength, birth, or wealth, or on the other hand who is very poor, or very weak, and very much disgraced, finds it difficult to follow rational principle. Of these two the one sort grow into violent and great criminals, the others into rogues and petty rascals. . . . Again, the middle class is least likely to shrink from rule, or to be over-ambitious for it; both of which are injuries to the state. Again, those who have too much of the goods of fortune, strength, wealth, and friends, and the like are neither willing nor able to submit to authority. . . . On the other hand, the poor, who are in the opposite extreme, are too degraded. So that the one class cannot obey, and can only rule despotically; the other knows not how to command and must be ruled like slaves. Thus arises a city, not of freemen, but of masters and slaves, the one despising, the other envying; and nothing can be more fatal to friendship and good fellowship in states like this.[4]

3. Moderate stratification is acceptable because distributivism is not a doctrine of a classless society.

4. Aristotle, *Politics*, trans. B. Jowett (Batoche, 1999), 4.11.1295b.

This well-known passage could easily serve as the basis of a manifesto for classical populism. If, as seems likely, Chesterton was familiar with it, he almost certainly approved. But the question of whether the first component of populism—namely, trust in the common man—can be ascribed to Aristotle is more complex. Among other reasons, he was an empiricist, and his emphasis on the role of senses in human cognition would have made it difficult to dismiss the opinions of ordinary people. After all, human beings are fairly equal in their sensual perception of reality; as he put it in his *Metaphysics*:

> The investigation of the truth is in one way hard, in another easy. An indication of this is found in the fact that no one is able to attain the truth adequately, while, on the other hand, we do not collectively fail, but every one says something true about the nature of things, and while individually we contribute little or nothing to the truth, by the union of all a considerable amount is amassed. Therefore, since the truth seems to be like the proverbial door, which no one can fail to hit, in this respect it must be easy, but the fact that we can have a whole truth and not the particular part we aim at shows the difficulty of it.[5]

Epistemological rationalism—a view of human cognition that downplays the role of the senses—tends to support intellectual elitism. This is one reason why Chesterton admired Aristotle who, in contrast to the abstractions of pure Platonism or idealism, restored the "authority of the Sense." Of course, Chesterton's point is not just epistemological: It is an ontological affirmation of the material world and its implications, both anthropological and political. These are seen in the "earth-bound common sense" that Chesterton rightly attributes to Aristotle.[6] But this view implies that the mind is not purely receptive: It is active, and its activity, open to all people, "consists in following so far as the will chooses to follow, the light outside that does really shine upon real landscapes. That is what gives the indefinably virile and even adventurous quality to this view of life. . . . The essence of the Thomist common sense is that two agencies are at work: reality and the recognition of reality; and their meeting is a sort of marriage."[7]

Aristotle's respect for the opinions of the common man is also confirmed by the fact that he systematically collected popular sayings and proverbs. According to Carlo Natali's classic account of Aristotle's life,

5. Aristotle, *Metaphysics*, trans. W. D. Ross (e-artnow, 2023), 2(a).1.993a30-b.

6. G. K. Chesterton, *St. Thomas Aquinas*, in *St. Thomas Aquinas, St. Francis of Assisi* (Ignatius, 2002), 37.

7. Chesterton, *St. Thomas Aquinas*, 169–70.

> research into proverbs is also a facet of the attention given by Aristotle to common opinion and to the *phainomena*, those impressions and beliefs that seem evidently true to various people. A theoretical study must take ample account of these facts, as Aristotle tells us in his *Metaphysics* . . ."the theoretical study of the truth is in a way difficult and in a way easy. An indication of this is the fact that nobody is able to reach the truth satisfactorily, nor completely misses it; but each one says something true about nature, and while individually they contribute nothing, or not much, to the truth, from the conjunction of all we get a considerable amount. 'Who could fail to hit the doors?' as the proverb goes."[8]

Aristotle was undoubtedly more elitist than Chesterton (who, to be clear, was not elitist at all). While Aristotle appreciated common sense and, by extension, the common man, he believed that some people were better fit for intellectual work than others (not to mention his infamous claim that some people are "natural" slaves). His political views cannot, therefore, be classified as "populism" in the strict sense of the term; yet, it seems that his political philosophy is closer to populism (in the positive, Chestertonian sense) than any other ancient Greek political doctrine.

Affirmation of the Empirical World

As previously noted, Chesterton wrote enthusiastically about the Aristotelian realism of the *Summa Theologiae*. He praises Aquinas's philosophical realism, especially his affirmation of the external world—that is, of *Ens* or Being. As Chesterton argued, affirming or rejecting the external world is one of the first "decisions" a philosopher must make when constructing a picture of reality. (We can call it a "decision" because there are no arguments that are compelling enough to force either choice.) In making this decision, Aquinas looked not only to the revealed Truth, but also to Aristotle, his philosophical master: "In all the work of St. Thomas the world of positive creation is perpetually present."[9] According to Chesterton, Aristotle's empirical realism played a crucial role in the recovery of the true spirit of Christianity. And this attests to a deep affinity between Aristotelianism and Christianity; as Chesterton put it: "[Aquinas'] business was to defend the faith against the abuse of Aristotle, and he boldly did it by supporting the

8. Carlo Natali, *Aristotle: His Life and School* (Princeton University Press, 2013), 25.

9. Chesterton, *St. Thomas Aquinas*, 79.

use of Aristotle."[10] Thus, Aristotle did not need to be distorted in order to adapt his work for Christian purposes; the adaptation occurred naturally once the full implications of Christian truth were embraced:

> There really was a new reason for regarding the senses, and the sensation of the body, and the experience of the common man, with reverence at which great Aristotle would have stared, and no man in the ancient world could have begun to understand. . . . Plato might despise the flesh, but God had not despised it. . . . After the Incarnation had become the idea that is central to our civilization, it was inevitable that there should be a return to materialism, in the sense of the serious value of matter and the making of the body. When once Christ had risen, it was inevitable that Aristotle should rise again.[11]

This, according to Chesterton, was nothing short of miraculous: "It was Aquinas who baptized Aristotle, when Aristotle could not have baptized Aquinas; it was a purely Christian miracle which raised the great pagan from the dead."[12]

DIVERGENCES

Magnanimity

The religion of humility and gratitude is one of Chesterton's central themes. This religion constitutes one of the deepest messages of the Christian faith: the idea that we have an infinite debt toward God, for all that we have has been given to us out of love, without any merit on our part. In the following passages, Chesterton presents this religion as it was embodied in the life of St. Francis:

> It is not only true that the less a man thinks of himself, the more he thinks of his good luck and of all the gifts of God. It is also true that he sees more of the things themselves when he sees more of their origin; for their origin is a part of them and indeed the most important part of them. Thus they become more extraordinary by being explained.[13]

10. Chesterton, *St. Thomas Aquinas*, 84.

11. Chesterton, *St. Thomas Aquinas*, 109.

12. Chesterton, *St. Thomas Aquinas*, 107.

13. G. K. Chesterton, *St. Francis of Assisi*, in *St. Thomas Aquinas, St. Francis of Assisi* (Ignatius, 2002), 248–49.

> All these profound matters must be suggested in short and imperfect phrases; and the shortest statement of one aspect of this illumination is to say that it is the discovery of infinite debt. . . . It is the highest and holiest of the paradoxes that the man who really knows he cannot pay his debt will be ever paying it. He will be forever giving back what he cannot give back, and cannot be expected to give back. He will be always throwing things away into a bottomless pit of unfathomable thanks.[14]

This sort of attitude is entirely absent in Aristotle's thought. And this is another reason—rather than Aristotle's uncolorful personality—that Chesterton could not have felt the deep emotional connection to the work of Aristotle that he felt toward that of Aquinas.

This difference in their attitudes toward the world underpins Chesterton's reservations about Aristotle's ethical ideal of the magnanimous man. This man of "great soul" (*megalopsychos*) demands great honors, is truly worthy of them, and is fully aware of his worthiness; few things strike him as impressive or remarkable; he admires little, praises no one, and accepts honor with moderate joy because he knows he deserves it. At the same time, he does not hold grudges against those who insult him—he is not vindictive and easily forgets the injuries he has sustained. He values beautiful things over useful ones. He speaks the truth openly, not for the sake of appearances but because he loves the truth. He prefers to give rather than to take, so as not to feel indebted to anyone. Now, what was Chesterton's attitude toward this ideal? On the one hand, Chesterton acknowledges some dignity in it; he even invokes it in his portrayal of his friend and intellectual adversary, George Bernard Shaw:

> It is not easy to dispute violently with a man for twenty years, about sex, about sin, about sacraments, about personal points of honour, about all the most sacred or delicate essentials of existence, without sometimes being irritated or feeling that he hits unfair blows or employs discreditable ingenuities. And I can testify that I have never read a reply by Bernard Shaw that did not leave me in a better and not a worse temper or frame of mind; which did not seem to come out of inexhaustible fountains of fair-mindedness and intellectual geniality; which did not savour somehow of that native largeness which the philosopher attributed to the Magnanimous Man.[15]

14. Chesterton, *St. Francis of Assisi*, 252.
15. Chesterton, *Autobiography*, 235–36.

However, this ideal is inferior to the Christian one, as Chesterton made clear when he said that "Aristotle had described the magnanimous man, who is great and knows that he is great. But Aristotle would never have recovered his own greatness, but for the miracle that created the more magnanimous man, who is great and knows that he is small."[16] Furthermore, Chesterton insisted that if he could only preach one sermon, it would be against the sin of pride, to which magnanimity, in the Aristotelian sense, may easily lead. Though, strictly speaking, magnanimity is not the same thing as pride. The vice of pride [*superbia*] gets its name from the fact that "a man . . . aims higher [*super*] than he is"; Aquinas defined it as "an inordinate desire for one's own excellence" (*inordinatus appetitus propriae excellentiae*).[17] As a result, proud people believe themselves to be greater than they actually are. Understood in this way, pride opposes both magnanimity and humility: It opposes humility because it rejects subjection to God, and it opposes magnanimity because it seeks greatness in an immoderate way.[18]

Polemics—The Nature of Virtue

The Aristotelian account of virtue assumes that virtue is a mean between two correlated extremes (i.e., the excess and the deficiency in a passion or action to which the virtue refers[19]), and is therefore radically different from them. This account has been criticized on many grounds, but, to my knowledge, no philosopher before Chesterton questioned its most fundamental assumption: that virtues are radically opposed to their correlated extremes.[20] According to Chesterton's account, virtue holds together two apparently opposite extremes in an ethically creative tension. Virtue is therefore a paradoxical synthesis of extremes. I will not attempt to provide a critical examination of both accounts, but will limit myself to presenting Chesterton's argument, supplemented with some general comments.[21]

16. Chesterton, *St. Thomas Aquinas*, 84.

17. Thomas Aquinas, *Summa Theologiae* II-II, q. 162, art. 1, in Fathers of the English Dominican Province (trans.), *Summa Theologiae: Complete English Edition in Five Volumes* (Christian Classics, 1981).

18. Cf. Aquinas, *Summa Theologiae* II-II, q. 162, art. 2.

19. Of moral virtues, only justice has as its object actions (more specifically: actions by which we deal with external things in interpersonal relations); the object of the other moral virtues are passions.

20. However, there is some similarity between Chesterton's account and Richard Weaver's, though, of course, Weaver's works are later than Chesterton's; cf. *Ideas Have Consequences* (University of Chicago Press, 1948), 119.

21. I have made such an attempt in an article: "Virtue as a Synthesis of Extremes vs.

Chesterton's account can be summed up in five crucial points. First, he argues that virtue is not "in a balance" but "in a conflict": It arises as a result of "the collision of two passions apparently opposite . . . of the still crash of two impetuous emotions."[22] According to this view, the two passions whose collision gives rise to a virtue "were not really inconsistent; but they were such that it was hard to hold simultaneously."[23] Second, Chesterton claims that this account makes virtue more attractive because the opposing passions are preserved "at the top of their energy,"[24] whereas, on the Aristotelian account, virtue risks being reduced to a mediocre compromise. Third, Chesterton contrasts these views historically and religiously, claiming that the idea of virtue as balance is the idea of the pagans, whereas the idea of virtue as paradoxical synthesis is the idea of Christendom. Fourth, Chesterton, like Aristotle, presents his account as applying to the structure and essence of all virtues. Fifth, he analyzes in greater length the following virtues: courage, modesty (humility), charity, faith, and hope. On his account, courage is a paradoxical combination of a strong attachment to life and a disdain of death;[25] modesty is a paradoxical combination of high self-esteem ("thinking too much of one's self") and low self-esteem ("thinking too little of one's self");[26] charity, in one of its aspects, is a paradoxical combination of forgivingness (toward the agent) and unforgivingness (toward the deed), or "wrath and love" (i.e., wrath toward the deed and love toward the doer). As for the other two theological virtues: Faith is a paradoxical synthesis of strong belief and the awareness of inscrutable mystery; and hope is a paradoxical synthesis of having grounds for despair while looking serenely toward the future.[27] All of these, for Chesterton, exemplify the paradoxical structure of virtue: not a safe moderation between extremes, but a full-hearted embrace of opposites held together in creative, often heroic, tension. What should we make of this account? Several comments come to mind.

First, it is possible that Chesterton has misinterpreted Aristotle's account of virtue. The Aristotelian virtue, on Chesterton's interpretation, is "a

---

Virtue as a Mean Between Extremes. A Comparison of Chesterton's Account of Virtue with Aristotle's," in Liesbeth Huppes-Cluysenaer and Nuno M. M. S. Coelho (eds.), *Aristotle on Emotions in Law and Politics* (Springer, 2018), 297–311. Some parts of this section have been borrowed (with substantial modifications) from this article.

22. G. K. Chesterton, *Orthodoxy* (Simon & Brown, 2010), 85–86.

23. Chesterton, *Orthodoxy*, 85.

24. Chesterton, *Orthodoxy*, 88.

25. Chesterton, *Orthodoxy*, 85–86.

26. Chesterton, *Orthodoxy*, 86.

27. G. K. Chesterton, *Heretics* (Wilder, 2009), 80–81.

mixture of two things" and "a dilution of two things; neither is present in its full strength or contributes its full colour."[28] Thus, Chesterton suggests that, according to the Aristotelian account, the mean is a mediocrity—a compromise between extremes. But virtue, as understood by Aristotle, does not recommend mediocrity; quite the contrary, it recommends extremity in the pursuit of moral perfection; as Aristotle explicitly wrote about virtue:

> It is a mean state between two vices, that which depends on excess and that which depends on defect; and again it is a mean because the vices respectively fall short of or exceed what is right in both passions and actions, while virtue both finds and chooses that which is intermediate. Hence in respect of its substance and the definition which states its essence virtue is a mean, with regard to what is best and right an extreme.[29]

Furthermore, virtues understood in the Aristotelian fashion need not result in "mediocrity"; there seems to be nothing "mediocre" about courage or generosity as Aristotle understood them. However, Chesterton's account is not undermined by his misinterpretation of Aristotle's. Even if the objection of mediocrity does not apply, Aristotle's account may still be subject to a less evocative critique. The former account implies that virtue is extreme in an ethical sense, but not an emotional one; the latter implies that virtue is an extreme in both senses (since it is a synthesis of extremes, it preserves them both "at the top of their energy," as Chesterton put it in the previously quoted passage).

Secondly, the claim that each virtue can be interpreted as a synthesis of extremes does not seem entirely convincing. It is not easy to interpret virtues other than those Chesterton insightfully analyzed in his "un-Aristotelian" manner. The list of virtues that might be interpreted in the Chestertonian manner could perhaps be expanded to include romantic love (assuming, contentiously, that it qualifies as a virtue) and toleration. The former could be construed as the result of the "impetuous collision" of two "apparently inconsistent" emotions or attitudes: the desire to possess the other person and respect for their autonomy. Toleration, on the other hand, might be seen not as a moderate attachment to one's views (as it could interpreted on the Aristotelian account) but as the result of the "impetuous collision" of a strong attachment to one's views and an awareness of one's fallibility or, alternatively, as a synthesis of two opposing attitudes: disapproval of another person's view and respect for that person. Toleration does seem more

28. Chesterton, *Heretics*, 86.

29. Aristotle, *Nicomachean Ethics* 1107a2–7, in Richard McKeon, ed., *Introduction to Aristotle*, trans. W. D. Ross (Modern Library, 1947).

attractive under this interpretation than on the Aristotelian one, which arguably sees it as merely a moderate (neither too strong nor too weak) attachment to one's views.

Thirdly, it is unclear whether the Chestertonian account makes sense only within the Christian worldview, or whether it can be upheld even from a naturalistic perspective. On the one hand, it is clear that to accept, for example, the Chestertonian view of modesty, one must abandon the view of "merely rational sages."[30] On this view, certain combinations of attitudes—such as being both proud and humble—are not merely paradoxical (as they are within the Christian worldview), but are simply inconsistent and therefore unthinkable. This is because, on the Chestertonian account, the grounds for both pride and humility are explicitly theological. The same point applies to theological virtues. On the other hand, in the case of courage, Chesterton's view seems plausible even if one rejects a broadly Christian framework. Chesterton appears to have acknowledged this himself, noting the positive practical consequence of combining the two opposing passions or attitudes constituting courage: a strong attachment to life and a disdain for death.

> "He that will lose his life, the same shall save it," is not a piece of mysticism for saints and heroes. It is a piece of everyday advice for sailors and mountaineers. . . . This paradox is the whole principle of courage; even of quite early or quite brutal courage. A man cut off by the sea may save his life if he will risk it on the precipice. He can only get away from death by continually stepping within an inch of it. A soldier surrounded by enemies, if he is to cut his way out, needs to combine a strong desire for living with a strange carelessness about dying. He must not merely cling to life, for then he will be a coward, and will not escape. He must not merely wait for death, for then he will be a suicide, and will not escape.[31]

The relationship between the Chestertonian account and Christian doctrine could, therefore, be described as follows: The Chestertonian account implies Christian doctrine in the analysis of some virtues—modesty, faith, hope, but not in the analysis of courage, tolerance, or romantic love. One might also argue that charity, understood as a combination of forgivingness (toward the doer) and unforgivingness (toward the deed), though discovered by Christianity, does not necessarily imply specifically Christian assumptions. It should also be noted that, contrary to what Chesterton seems to

30. Chesterton, *Orthodoxy*, 87.

31. Chesterton, *Orthodoxy*, 85.

have suggested, Christianity does not necessarily require the account of virtue as a synthesis of extremes. To support this claim, one could point to the historical fact that many great Christian philosophers (including Aquinas) did not accept it. Accordingly, Chesterton's assertion that his account of virtue is "Christian" must be qualified: While Christian doctrine certainly inspired him to propose the account of virtue as a synthesis of extremes, it does not necessarily entail it.[32] Consequently, Christian doctrine accommodates both accounts of virtue—the Aristotelian and the Chestertonian.

I will not attempt to answer the question of which account of virtue—the Chestertonian or the Aristotelian—is more convincing. Chesterton claimed that the Aristotelian account recommends mediocrity, but, as I have argued, this claim is based on a misreading of *Nicomachean Ethics*. Therefore, the choice between cultivating, for example, the virtue of courage in the Chestertonian sense—as a synthesis of strong attachment to life and disdain for death—or in the Aristotelian sense—as the mean between cowardice and rashness—depends on which conception one finds more compelling or illuminating in capturing the moral and psychological depth of that virtue. Both accounts seem ethically attractive, but since they are incompatible, one cannot develop the same virtue in both senses (courage in the Chestertonian sense would likely be seen as rashness from the Aristotelian standpoint). All in all, it is a testimony to Chesterton's intellectual stature that he proposed an account of virtue that can function as a genuine and attractive alternative to Aristotle's.

BIBLIOGRAPHY

Aquinas, Thomas. *Summa Theologiae: Complete English Edition in Five Volumes*. Translated by Fathers of the English Dominican Province. Westminster, MD: Christian Classics, 1981.

Aristotle. *Metaphysics*. Translated by W.D. Ross. New York: e-artnow, 2023.

———. *Nicomachean Ethics*. In *Introduction to Aristotle*, edited by Richard McKeon, translated by W.D. Ross, 308–545. New York: Modern Library, 1947.

———. *Politics*. Translated by B. Jowett. Kitchener: Batoche, 1999.

Barker, Ernest, ed. *The Social Contract: Essays by Locke, Hume, and Rousseau*. Oxford: Oxford University Press, 1956.

Chesterton, G. K. *The Autobiography of G. K. Chesterton*. New York: Sheed and Ward, 1936.

———. *Heretics*. New York: Wilder, 2009.

32. This remark only stresses Chesterton's originality, though it was not his intention to be original: He believed himself to be making explicit what was already implicit in the tradition of Christian ethics.

———. *In Defense of Sanity: The Best Essays of G. K. Chesterton*. Selected by D. Ahlquist, J. Pearce, A. Mackey. San Francisco: Ignatius, 2011.

———. *Orthodoxy*. New York: Simon and Brown, 2010.

———. *St. Thomas Aquinas* and *St. Francis of Assisi*. San Francisco: Ignatius, 2002.

Lasch, Christopher. *The Revolt of the Elites and the Betrayal of Democracy*. New York: Norton, 1996.

Natali, Carlo. *Aristotle: His Life and School*. Princeton: Princeton University Press, 2013.

Weaver, R. M. *Ideas Have Consequences*. Chicago: The University of Chicago Press, 1948.

Załuski, W. "Virtue as a Synthesis of Extremes vs. Virtue as a Mean Between Extremes. A Comparison of Chesterton's Account of Virtue with Aristotle's." In *Aristotle on Emotions in Law and Politics*, edited by Liesbeth Huppes-Cluysenaer and Nuno M. M. S. Coelho, 297–311. Berlin: Springer, 2018.

Philosophy is not the concern of those who pass through Divinity and Greats, but of those who pass through birth and death. Nearly all the most awful and abstruse statements can be put in words of one syllable, from "A child is born" to "A soul is damned." If the ordinary man may not discuss existence, why should he be asked to conduct it?

—"The Philosopher," *George Bernard Shaw*

Philosophy is merely thought that has been thought out. It is often a great bore. But man has no alternative, except between being influenced by thought that has been thought out and being influenced by thought that has not been thought out. The latter is what we commonly call culture and enlightenment today. But man is always influenced by thought of some kind, his own or somebody else's; that of somebody he trusts or that of somebody he never heard of, thought at first, second or third hand; thought from exploded legends or unverified rumours; but always something with the shadow of a system of values and a reason for preference. A man does test everything by something. The question here is whether he has ever tested the test.

—"The Revival of Philosophy—Why?" *The Common Man*

3

"Beauty and Terror Are Very Real Things"

Philip Irving Mitchell

> Behind all these things is the fact that beauty and terror are very real things and related to a real spiritual world; and to touch them at all, even in doubt or fancy, is to stir the deep things of the soul. We all understand that and the pagans understood it. . . . [Pagans] had an attitude towards their gods which is quite queer and puzzling to men in the Christian era. There seems to be an admitted conflict between the god and the man; but everybody seems to be doubtful about which is the hero and which is the villain.
>
> —"Man and Mythologies," *The Everlasting Man*

Both Augustine of Hippo and G. K. Chesterton were prolific controversialists. While one wrote during the rise of Christendom, the other did so during the beginning of its dissolution. In an emerging Christian order, Augustine answered the objections of pagan intellectuals, including those thinkers who embraced Roman history as a lost ideal, whereas Chesterton's interlocutors defended an array of theories from higher criticism to evolutionary anthropology, comparative religion, and materialist views of history.

Both writers confront readers with a fundamental question: Is there anything in human experience that is permanent and irreducibly transcendent?

Charles Taylor has described the change from a premodern, sacred world to a modern, desacralized one as where once the self was open to indistinguishable moral, mental, and supernatural forces, now the self is closed, even "buffered," against a metaphysical cosmos.[1] This fundamental shift stands between Augustine and Chesterton. Both writers evoked the metaphysical weight, or what might be termed the "real presence," not only of the supernatural, but also of the historical and indeed of the human, and both saw Christ the incarnate God-man as history's fulfillment. Yet Chesterton's *Everlasting Man* needed to step beyond Augustine's *City of God*: Chesterton had to defend that human freedom which Augustine could assume, for in Chesterton's world, history was judged in terms of material forces moving forward by deterministic causes. It is that shared struggle that the concept of presence helps unfold in both writers.

PRESENCE IN HISTORY

George Steiner once asserted that "real presences"—that is the transcendentals of the good, true, and beautiful—are to be taken on trust if our experience of them is not to be explained away. Though they cannot be proved, they are a testament to that reality which transcends the purely material and are thus also a kind of Pascalian wager on God.[2] Steiner was not addressing philosophy of history, but his insights apply, and for something greater than a calculated intellectual risk on intangible realities. Arguably, the transcendentals are ubiquitous in human experience and repeatedly manifest themselves as phenomena, even in our experience of the past. In the twentieth century, philosophy of history's concerns with narrative arose out of a failure to find a covering law that guaranteed an objective, scientific historiography—one that could explain on predictable, material grounds the causes of all events. History, it was argued, is more a matter of the logic and evidence provided by a plottable sequence of events.[3] More recently, this

1. Charles Taylor, *A Secular Age* (Harvard University Press, 2007), 7–14.

2. George Steiner, *Real Presences* (University of Chicago Press, 1991), 143–47, 215–20, 225, 229–30. Such trust is also inherently social, for aesthetics practice courtesy and hospitality if they are to be shared with others, especially across space and time. See also 148, 152, 155–56, 165–66, 175–76.

3. See Paul Ricoeur, *Time and Narrative* 1, trans. Kathleen McLaughlin and David Pellauer (University of Chicago Press, 1984). Ricoeur's magisterial survey looks at how the covering law of Karl Hempel gave way before various objections from the disposition of the historian, only to be followed by William Dray's stress on weak models of

turn towards historical narrative has also been found wanting, for some fear that the past can never be said to be with us in any tangible manner—that between us and any direct experience of the concrete past there is always some filter of language and presupposition. Recent explorations of presence in history, then, hope to recover the *actuality* of the past as experienced today, and this includes some sense of the true, good, and beautiful.

Presence, for the purpose of this essay, can be defined as that phenomenal reality which makes itself bodily and imaginatively felt in experience as other than the self and yet is nevertheless pressing upon the self in some complex fashion.[4] Presence is often personal, even noumenal, or at least uncanny, and because it involves the transcendental, it evokes the metaphysical weight of persons, the past, and even the gods. Not all who employ the term "presence" would extend it this far, nor are all concerned with whether it communicates the actual past. Some assume that the experience of historical presence is brief and epiphanic: sublime and unrepeatable, disruptive, or if mediated by language, poetic and ritualistic.[5] None of these views is traditionally religious.[6] On the other hand, Catholic historian Rob-

---

explanation that do not need "laws," then by G. H. Von Wright's recognition that quasi-causal explanations need teleology, then by defenses of historical narrative by the likes of Arthur Danto (narratival sentences), W. B. Gaille (followability), and Hayden White (typology of various emplotments).

4. In its widest usage in phenomenological thought, "presence" approaches or is synonymous with "givenness." It considers not only how there-ness is now here, but how it, in presenting itself, calls for a response from us. See Jean-Luc Marion, *Reduction and Givenness: Investigations of Husserl, Heidegger, and Phenomenology*, trans. Thomas A. Carlson (Northwestern University Press, 1998), 22–39, 51–66. In this paper, I am focusing on that which is not always obviously present to moderns, or at least classical philosophical naturalists.

5. Frank Ankersmit argues for an unmediated experience of the past in moments when the past's difference becomes remarkably present with us; see chapter 8 of *Sublime Historical Experience* (Stanford University Press, 2005) and chapter 8 of *Meaning, Truth, and Reference in Historical Representation* (Cornell University Press, 2012). Eelco Runia makes a similar claim for the ruptures from the past, when its "metonymic" (i.e., associative) echoes that have remained implicit become formative of our revised self-understanding. See chapters 3 and 4 of *Moved by the Past: Discontinuity and Historical Mutation* (Columbia University Press, 2014). And Hans Ulrich Gumbrecht stresses the revelatory quality of presence that is not language but that which language can help mediate, especially in its formalized, bodily patterning. See chapter 4 of *Production of Presence: What Meaning Cannot Convey* (Stanford University Press, 2004).

6. Gumbrecht does make overtures: While not a Heideggerian, Gumbrecht follows Heidegger in seeing truth as a disclosure of Being, and as disclosure, holds that it (as an event) may be received differently in different eras; thus the Reformation debate over the real presence does have some applicability to contemporary pursuits, while a contemporary theologian like Catherine Pickstock can be brought into conversation with Zen Buddhism and Noh theater (*Production*, 28–32, 65–77, 146–52).

ert A. Orsi seeks to describe the experience of people with the supernatural in an immanent, bodily, and densely interpersonal fashion. In something like the *histoire des mentalités*, Orsi treats presence as equivocal, for it may manifest as both the supernal and infernal, as blessing and abuse, and he stresses that historical presence thus remains narratable.[7] Approaches to presence share the belief that something is experienceable which phenomenally transcends not only banal and casual materialism, but also narrative as reduced to a linguistic system. What Orsi's method adds is why a discussion of presence must also address the supernatural, and since Augustine and Chesterton each treated the supernatural and human seriously in their historiography, any account of them must narrate faithfully the matter of many kinds of presence.[8] For Augustine's audience, the weight of the presence of the gods resided in a *civitas*, while, for Chesterton's, the presence of human creativity and freedom itself was being questioned in light of material and evolutionary views of persons and their societies. For Augustine the past made itself present in both Roman tradition and in Jewish and Christian Scripture while, for Chesterton, that presence was felt foremost in human exceptionalism amid the biological and mythological records of anthropology and cultural history. Likewise, both books bring to the forefront the question of whether divine blessing and judgment can be discovered within history—and find answers in a recapitulative structure centered on Christ.

THE SPLENDOR AND WEIGHT OF THE WORLD

The first time I read *The City of God*, I was in graduate school and quite tempted to skim the sections on Augustine's angelology, for they seemed like unnecessary asides in an already baggy political theology. I was, of course, deeply wrong; they are not tangents. Still, I suspect my experience is not atypical. As moderns, we do not fully understand Augustine, certainly not with sympathy, unless we sense that people in the ancient world felt prosperity and misfortune as the presence of divine action, and as twenty-first-century persons, we should second-guess our relativistic propensity

7. Robert A. Orsi, *History and Presence* (Harvard University Press, 2016), 6–9, 29–30, 38–42, 57–65.

8. I will use the terms "presences," "powers," and "gods" interchangeably throughout, as well as the more precise Christian terms of "God," "angels," and "demons." I will also use "presence" (and the cognates "metaphysical weight" and "gravity") to address ways that history is felt to be present, as well as the phenomenal impact of human exceptionalism. The ambiguity is somewhat native to the literature, and Augustine and Chesterton both assume that the presence of history and of persons follow from divine presence.

to read this past as only anthropological. Augustine's supernatural descriptions were not primarily a tactic of social power. We would better conceive of his historical or mythic examples as the *gravitas* in a religious tragedy or as deeply felt as the problem of evil, for they are not so much theoretical counterexamples as experienced counter-presences.

Writing in the fifth century, Augustine lived when an established Christianity had begun to displace the older pagan civil and religious order, yet that order was alive enough to be a challenge. In such a world, the mythic, theatrical, and poetic had been intertwined with the civil in temples and monuments, and even as the Christian imperial government had begun to dismantle this, their presence was still real and liable to stir debates, even riots on both sides.[9] If theatrics could be said to "give delight to impure demons," the pagan theological poets could nevertheless offer true overtures to God and creation.[10] The old gods could still be felt as near, even as sources of inspiration; thus, Augustine sought to explain what historical purpose they had served in the divine plan: "The gods were permitted to exercise a certain amount of power, not in order to demonstrate their might but only so that they might be convicted of being present."[11] This presence was a key to all pagan and Christian life, for the city's happiness was not separate from the felicity brought about by true worship. The Roman gods possessed the numinous, as did in a fuller fashion the one God of Judaism and Christianity. Augustine's political theory and philosophy of history were finally impossible without an open cosmos and a rival naming of the powers.

In the late classical world, ancient heritage too was felt as presence when tradition was known as continuous or at least as recovered. For example, the polymath of the Roman Republic, Marcus Terentius Varro, represented a historical center and revered authority for the educated pagan elite.[12] Augustine could quote with approval Cicero's praise of Varro: "When we were wandering and roaming like strangers in our own city, it was as though your books led us back to our home, so we could at last know who we were and where we were." Cicero admired Varro's scope which ranged across history, law, jurisdiction, and human and divine causation, and Augustine could value this because Varro was an upstanding man of his city.[13]

9. Augustine, *The City of God Against the Pagans*, trans. R.W. Dyson (Cambridge University Press, 1998), 6.7; Peter Brown, *Augustine of Hippo: A Biography*, New Edition (University of California Press, 2000.

10. Augustine, *City of God* 18.12, 18.14.

11. Augustine, *City of God* 3.7, p. 101.

12. Gerard O'Daly, *Augustine's City of God: A Reader's Guide* (Oxford University Press, 1999), 101–4.

13. Augustine, *City of God* 6.3.

But Varro also troubled Augustine. He did not believe the myths any more than Varro did, but their obscenity indicated that a powerful, corrupting reality was present, and that Varro observed sacrifices to such gods and excused the lewd stories that accompanied them indicated to Augustine that they were hardly benign, even for a noble person.

As Augustine sought to answer the charge that Rome was sacked by the Goths (in 410) because the Christian imperium no longer sacrificed to the old gods, he pointed out that in the past even a virtuous Roman could not count on deliverance. No power rescued the general Marcus Regulus who, unable to secure a return of Carthaginian prisoners, returned to Carthage himself to be tortured to death, when "these gods were worshipped precisely so that they might render this life prosperous!"[14] Likewise, the gods were supposed to have been the center of a healthy *civitas*: "Why did the gods of Rome fail to ensure that their votaries were set free from their worst practices?" Shouldn't the gods have sent prophets to correct the people or provide clear moral instruction in their spectacles? Augustine compared the state to "great bands of robbers." Victory is only one Roman deity among a great "swarm, not, indeed, of gods, but of demons," and can possess no inner tranquility or lasting happiness.[15] In such a mob of powers, Augustine sneered, should not the Roman pretext for invasion, that of "Foreign Iniquity," also be a goddess of sorts?[16] Yet Augustine was not about simply dismissing these civic ideals as pretexts, nor disproving them as superstitions, but arguing that their power had another source and purpose.[17] The moral repugnance that the pagan myths brought was visceral, and he sought to name the source of that vulgar presence in the still very present past. Thus, he did not merely *demonize* his enemies in the modern sense.

Instead, Augustine restructured the entire question: God's presence is everywhere. What is the one true and sovereign God doing in history and how much of his plan may we know?[18] Augustine held history to be the tension of two cities and their glories: the City of God being redeemed and the City of Humanity fallen and tragic.[19] Rather than a mixture of conflicting

14. Augustine, *City of God* 1.15. This famous story may be apocryphal, though near to the identity of many intellectual pagans: David Vincent Meconi, "Book 1: The Crumbling and Consecration of Rome," in *The Cambridge Companion to Augustine's City of God*, ed. David Vincent Meconi (Cambridge University Press, 2021), 29–30.

15. Augustine, *City of God* 4.3–4, esp. 4.16.

16. Augustine, *City of God* 4.15.

17. Augustine, *City of God* 3.4; also 3.10.

18. Augustine, *City of God* 1.29; also 5.13–17, 19.

19. For Augustine, perfect peace is awaiting us in heaven, while imperfect peace is not possible without an ordered *civitas*: "Justice is present in each man when he obeys

gods, Augustine held that the one true God chose Rome for a season to be blessed with those who sought the health of their *patria*, and though most were driven by "lust for glory," even this retarded greater evil by working for the common good. He understood that there were public truths hidden here that, when uncovered, would reconfigure how his audience saw their shared history and thus themselves.[20] So Augustine sought to trigger epiphanic moments when their history was felt anew.

While Augustine's interlocutors still attested to divine presences, Chesterton's lived in a closed universe that dismissed the presence of the gods as evolved vestigial behavior and psychological projection. In the first half of the twentieth century, the masters of suspicion—Darwin, Marx, Freud, and Nietzsche—dominated conceptions of human nature. "They suggest everywhere the grey gradation of twilight, because they believe it is the twilight of the gods. I propose to maintain that whether or no it is the twilight of the gods, it is not the daylight of men."[21] *Everlasting Man* points to human freedom made apparent in prehistoric art and early myth and culture. Only with this acknowledged could one recognize the presence of the powers, for having lost freedom, moderns stood in danger of losing presence. Evolutionary arguments could empty humans of metaphysical status, so Chesterton worked to help people see their early history and personhood anew.

For Chesterton, humanity's splendor is embodied in dramatic forms which reveal its exceptionalism. It is adventure that uncovers human freedom,[22] and his characteristic approach was to make the familiar strange, only that we might see the familiar for its fullness.[23] The world has to be known afresh, as both natural and supernatural, "and anybody who really understands that question will know that it always has been and always will be a religious question; or at any rate a philosophical and metaphysical question."[24] Chesterton's use of Pascalian opposites sought to awaken a perception of human presence, ordinary and yet extraordinary if allowed its nobility, comedy, and tragedy. As he pointed out more than once, the

---

God, when the mind rules the body, and when the reason governs the vices which oppose it," and such can only happen as a person begs the true God for forgiveness and grace. *City of God* 19.27.

20. Augustine, as a Latin North African, had been trained in Roman education and civilization, so Roman history was both his history and not quite his history. He would need that training to address the influx of pagan *intelligentsia* into North Africa after Rome was sacked. Brown, *Augustine of Hippo*, 290, 298–310, 458–60.

21. G. K. Chesterton, *The Everlasting Man. Collected Works* 2 (Ignatius, 1986), 147.

22. See G. K. Chesterton, *Orthodoxy. Collected Works* 1 (Ignatius, 1986), ch. 9.

23. Chesterton, *Everlasting Man*, 143–45, 155–57.

24. Chesterton, *Everlasting Man*, 157.

human being is not quite at home in the world, yet still strangely belongs: "Alone among the animals, he is shaken with the beautiful madness called laughter; as if he had caught sight of some secret in the very shape of the universe hidden from the universe itself." Only the human "feels the need of averting his thought from the root realities of his own bodily being; of hiding them as in the presence of some higher possibility which creates the mystery of shame."[25] Chesterton refused a desacralized cosmos that reduced the human self to so many impersonal forces, and his superlative, theatrical language confronted the reader with what was already there—human uniqueness. As he noted, the sudden appearance of mind in the human species "has all the appearance of a transaction outside of time."[26]

What can be known of prehistoric humans reveals them as creative rather than subhuman. As soon as we know anything of them, they are already like us. The popular view of prehistoric humanity deserves agnosticism, for the earliest evidence is already organized, recognizably human in behavior, and religious as much as artistic. Chesterton made the same point about the first evidence of culture: "The dawn of history reveals a humanity already civilized," already old and developed,[27] and as such, comparable with the modern world. It imparts an unmistakable presence of past personhood; creativity being a manifestation of exceptionalism; and human history setting out this uniqueness, if we will but receive it.[28] Early history already discloses civilization, and this does not easily reduce to anthropological, evolutionary, or economic development. Chesterton admitted the past's brutality and corruption but insisted that being modern was no guarantee of their absence. Mythology, likewise, is an expression of creativity, and what it tells of the universe and of the powers is evidence of the numinous, of a moral and providential presence in the world. The various tales told of the gods possess whimsy, even in the grotesque, and following Andrew Lang's *The Making of Religion*, Chesterton saw the ineffable God as one aspect of this gravity, namely the Sky-Father whom numerous cultures acknowledge even as they seemingly desire to forget him.[29] Because the supreme God is set apart, he is a keenly felt absence, "a void" yet "not a negation," and, thus, "the presence of the absence of God" carries with it

25. Chesterton, *Everlasting Man*, 168.
26. Chesterton, *Everlasting Man*, 170.
27. Chesterton, *Everlasting Man*, 188.
28. Chesterton, *Everlasting Man*, 166–67, 177.
29. Chesterton, *Everlasting Man*, 220–22.

a sense that the gods are a kind of literary suppression, artistic tales which hide the reality of the high God.[30]

THE FIDELITY OF NARRATIVES

While Augustine tended to see the immoral myths as the haunt of demons, only when given over to magic and the demonic did Chesterton hold myth as a sign of civilizational corruption. Understandably, Christians, as monotheists, have a history of treating other religious powers/presences as either demonic powers or as expressions of an intuitive, universal desire for the true God.[31] *City of God*'s thorough examination of angels and demons was not tangential to late classical philosophy. Augustine's Platonic opponents Apuleius and Porphyry treated demons as mediators in a hierarchical cosmos,[32] and Augustine not only had to answer the reported miracles of pagan gods, but also push back against Porphyry's counter-oracles contradicting Christ.[33] In turn, the angelic let Augustine acknowledge positive presence misnamed.[34] He accepted the biblical language of "gods" as either angels or human rulers[35] and conceded that Varro's gods, who are friends of the wise, are sometimes better identified as angels, at least by the Christian community able to see the truth.[36] Angels are not creators of anything, though perhaps they serve as mediators in the development of things,[37] and they do mediate miracles.[38]

However we as moderns may seek to explain or explain away their presence, Augustine lived in a world where miracles could happen and were variously present to human experience.[39] In *City of God*, he stressed that he

30. Chesterton, *Everlasting Man*, 224–25.

31. Orsi, *History and Presence*, 32–34.

32. Augustine, *City of God* 8.14, pp. 332–33.

33. Augustine, *City of God* 19.23, pp. 954–55, 957–58; 21.6, 1055–56.

34. Augustine, *City of God* 8.25.

35. Augustine, *City of God* 9.23.

36. Augustine, *City of God* 19.3, p. 918.

37. Augustine, *City of God* 12.26.

38. Augustine, *City of God* 10.7–8, 10.12–20.

39. While Augustine had seemed to say in *On True Religion* that miracles such as those of the apostles were no longer necessary since the church was now established, in *On Christian Belief* he would stress that in his *Retractions* he had meant the ceasing of phenomena such as *glossolalia*, not physical miracles, which he himself had experienced. See Augustine, *On True Religion*, trans. Edmund Hill (New City, 2005), 24.47; Augustine, *Retractions*, trans. Mary Inez Bogan (Catholic University Press of America, 1968), 1.13.7.

suspended judgment about them unless he had experienced them or subjected accounts to scrutiny and confirmation. On this basis, he recounted at least twenty-one recent miracles, including several he witnessed.[40] He was especially concerned to publicize these for the church's benefit as well as God's glory. In one episode, he recalled a brother and sister, well known in Hippo, who experienced convulsions from their infancy. Paulus, the brother, clinging to the reliquary of Stephen the martyr, experienced a healing, and stunned, presented himself to Augustine:

> Who at that point could restrain himself from praising God? The whole Church was filled in every part with voices crying out in thanksgiving. They ran to where I was sitting, waiting for the procession to begin: they rushed in one after another, each one telling me, as if it were something new, what the one before had already said. I was giving my own joyful thanks to God when the young man himself came in with several others. He fell at my knees, and then rose to receive my kiss. We went into the congregation; the church was full, and resounding with shouts of joy: "Thanks be to God! Praise be to God!" No one was silent; the cries came from all sides.[41]

Understandably, all this seems beside the point for many modern philosophers of history, yet its narratival impact is hard to deny. Whenever an entity has presence, it calls to us. Its immediacy makes claims upon those in its vicinity, and reported presence can take on a similar gravity when narrated. What Augustine's accounts remind us is that, regardless of whether we believe them, such narratives do carry weight; they have metaphysical attestation. *Presence presents, rather than represents*, and rather than an epistemic wager that language can point to an actual past, narrative may be a response to the past's call, a response which can strive for fidelity to phenomena that is experienced even by the contemporary reader.[42]

Simple testimony was not open to Chesterton in the same, direct manner, though he certainly understood the power of story, including those of miracles.[43] He took as a principle that "Nature is always looking

40. Augustine, *City of God* 22.7–8.

41. Augustine, *City of God* 22.8, 1132–33.

42. Charles Taylor, *The Language Animal: The Full Shape of the Human Linguistic Capacity* (Harvard University Press, 2016), 79.

43. *The Ball and the Cross* ends with a miracle that converts an atheistic rationalist, while in *Magic*, devils at the Conjuror's bequest perform deeds that divide the play's characters. Likewise, in *Orthodoxy*, Chesterton owned simply that miracles were not only desirable but possible, and there was no need to dismiss so many accounts of them, unless one was already committed to a faith that refused even their possibility in the

for the supernatural."[44] Thus, he thought that the neo-pagan resurgence was more a rival to Christianity than all the contemporary reductionist theories because it had a vital sense of the world's transcendent realities, even if it too remained a fragmentary, faulty nexus of beliefs.[45] Chesterton located in paganism an aesthetic yearning for both the beautiful and the grotesque. Magical tales transcend abstraction or allegory with a natural mysticism that seeks "transcendental truths," that is the "shadows of things seen through the veil."[46] "If an Asiatic god has three heads and seven arms, there is at least in it an idea of material incarnation bringing an unknown power nearer to us, and not farther away."[47]

Chesterton's fourfold taxonomy of religion (i.e., God, the gods, the demons, and the philosophers) is analogous to Augustine's naming of the powers.[48] Chesterton was attempting a holistic description of humanity's experience with supernatural presence: The ineffable and the aesthetic are not the full story; the turn to cruelty and the placation of the demons address the inhuman search for power through magic, while the philosophers (Socrates, Confucius, Buddha, Akhenaten), even when engaging the mystical, are rivals with institutional priests, for the philosophical turn to pattern can be several steps removed from the pragmatics of religion: "Mysticism concerns something transcending experience; religion seeks glimpses of a better good or worse evil than experience can give," and system-building is more private and particular, longing for order amidst mystery.[49]

When Chesterton does recount the horrible side of the pagan past, he finds in magic a terrible pragmatism, "a sort of secret and perverse feeling that the darker powers would really do things."[50] Since the supreme God

---

world. *Orthodoxy*, 331–32.

44. Chesterton, *Everlasting Man*, 261–62.

45. Chesterton, *Everlasting Man*, 218–19.

46. Chesterton, *Everlasting Man*, 234–37. Because the myths attach such stories to their local geography, the local gods represent a loyalty to the experience of the divine in place (see 239).

47. Chesterton, *Everlasting Man*, 215. Chesterton in his *Avowals and Denials* (1934), chapter 13, "On Man: Heir of the Ages," summarizes historian Christopher Dawson on historical development of religion and therefore the human experience of the spiritual. Chesterton held that we do not entirely disregard these earlier strata; they remain part of human makeup.

48. Chesterton, *Everlasting Man*, 219.

49. Chesterton, *Everlasting Man*, 264.

50. Chesterton, *Everlasting Man*, 250. His association of demonic activity like human sacrifice and cannibalism with higher civilization—with art for art's sake even—opened a more complex view of non-Western civilizations than simple Eurocentric praise or guilt.

was judged too distant for the mundane, people performed the degrading acts that malevolent beings required.[51] Here, Chesterton makes his characteristic move towards dramatic narrative and contrasts the good paganism of the Roman household gods with the wicked paganism of Carthage's child sacrifice to demons: Rome fought from humane repugnance at the worship of Moloch and, thus, for more than political expedience, and the Latin prognostications had a deeper understanding than any modern historical analysis, for "the modern historian who can see nothing in it but a success of strategy concluding a rivalry in commerce" is missing not only a wide swath of human behavior but its fundamental motivations.[52] In the story Chesterton tells, this humane Roman paganism eventually aged into a tired imperialism, which depleted myth, offered a philosophy of despair, and multiplied the dark magic of secret societies. Roman society faded once its belief was compromised. "This religion was not quite a reality" anymore. Rome, possessed with the demons of the mystery cults, broke down the family and descended into relativism. The imperial world was soon bored, decadent, and depleted, all before Christ's coming.[53]

Such narratives can be charged with the excesses which critical academic history sought to eliminate. Chesterton was aware of the abuses of Romantic historiography, yet he thought the modern historical tome was blind on principle to anything heroic or grand in the past. Positions like Marxism, Hegelianism, or other systems of determinism or relativism *spoil the story* because they distort human freedom and personhood which transcend material creaturely existence.[54] As a corrective, he recommended a sympathetic entry into a culture's folkways and defended history that expands the imagination and increases the stock of moral models. Despite the scope of *Everlasting Man*, Chesterton privileged local history, arguing that invested positions opened up aspects too easily overlooked.[55] At their best, Chesterton's adventure motifs refused to empty out the fullness of historical existence, and thus sought a measure of fidelity to reality.[56]

51. Chesterton, *Everlasting Man*, 251–52.

52. Chesterton, *Everlasting Man*, 278. See also 269–75.

53. Chesterton, *Everlasting Man*, 290–95.

54. Chesterton, *Everlasting Man*, 377–79.

55. G. K. Chesterton, "Need for Historical Humility," in *Collected Works* 33 (Ignatius, 1986), 607–10; "The Teaching of History," in *Collected Works* 32 (Ignatius, 1986), 317–18.

56. Chesterton was infamously spotty with his sources. He depended upon his prodigious memory, which nevertheless often misquoted poetry he loved. The same must be said of some key history. Chesterton can be charged (and at times rightly) with pushing the past into his chosen genres of heroic adventure. But in *Appendices I* and

THE WEIGHT OF THE CENTER

If Augustine reimagined late Roman identity, and if Chesterton opened that past as possessing metaphysical possibilities, both writers recognized that the powers were a key fact of human existence, and both insisted that this was bound up with God in Christ. In the ancient world, every city had its gods—the body politic was only a body with right *pietas*. Augustine noted how service, divine and otherwise, is revealed in what one sacrifices and to whom. Thus, the various Latin terms for "worship" extended beyond just how one regards the gods. Whereas *laeteia* is reserved for the service due the divine, *cultus* can extend to the educational and memorial cultivated in public life, and *religio* concerns the piety due to others. There is a *laeteia* that grounds every *cultus*, which is also present in the responsibility of many loyalties.[57] The weight of this felt history in the *civitas* is where the powers reside and, thus, where true sacrifices must be made.[58]

Except now, Augustine stressed, Christ is the final sacrifice, so no other sacrifices are needed.[59] Christ the *Principium* has become flesh so that true citizens of the City of God may be found faithful and experience the fullness of his presence here and now, betokened by miracles, and in the future in perfect beatitude. On pilgrimage, his people shall "see how great a love they owe to their spiritual fatherland" in comparison with any city "greatly loved by its citizens for the sake of earthly glory."[60] The question of polity is not simply one of philosophy or public order, but of right relations to the past and to the *numena*. Christ as the supreme sacrifice is the Mediator, the Logos made flesh, and thereby the center of the *polis*, of the universe, and of all history.[61] While some treat humans as the middle of the ladder of being,

II he is willing to make caveats to real scientists and real historians. Chesterton admits that a populist work like *Everlasting Man* does not mean to undervalue real prehistoric evidence or more technical historical studies (404–7).

57. Augustine, *City of God* 10.1.

58. A people or commonwealth are defined by what they love (*City of God* 19.24). Chesterton will say as much in *Orthodoxy*: "Morality did not begin by one man saying to another, 'I will not hit you if you do not hit me'; there is no trace of such a transaction. There *is* a trace of both men having said, 'We must not hit each other in the holy place.' They gained their morality by guarding their religion. They did not cultivate courage. They fought for the shrine, and found they had become courageous. They did not cultivate cleanliness. They purified themselves for the altar, and found that they were clean." *Orthodoxy*, 271; emphasis original.

59. Augustine, *City of God* 10.20.

60. Augustine, *City of God* 5.16, pp. 216–17.

61. Augustine, *City of God* 10.20, 10–23–24. Not surprisingly, Augustine continued to offer a defense of Christ's sacrifice in book 19 against Porphyry's charges (See also 19.23, esp. p. 959).

and others like Seneca award the wise the place of mediation,[62] Augustine argued that only one who touched the spiritual and the temporal by his very dual natures could satisfy mortal desires for eternal blessedness:

> By this love a way was opened for men to come to him who was so distant from men—as distant as the immortal is from the mortal, as the immutable is from the mutable, as the righteous is from the ungodly, as the blessed is from the wretched. And because He had imbued our nature with the desire for blessedness and immortality, He, remaining blessed even while assuming mortality, taught us to despise what we fear by undergoing it Himself, so that He might bestow upon us what we long for.[63]

Though a Platonist like Porphyry denied any means by which history could impart wisdom, Augustine insisted that this universal history in Christ explained past, present, and the coming future, bringing light to both the individual person and to the body social,[64] and in holding so, Augustine recognized that the history of one's city and one's world was as deeply felt as any eternal matter. We are not only what we know, but also what we love, a truth based in the Trinity.[65] Augustine's providential history of type-antetype, traced over the last half of *City of God*, opposed ancient histories that shrugged before Nemesis, Fortuna, or some plurality of unpredictable causes, as well as any Roman imperial vision of destiny based on the gods.[66] Augustine paralleled Roman with biblical history to establish the latter's antiquity of heritage and as providential proof of its predictions: "In that City of ours however, it was by prophecy—that is by the divine voice speaking through men—that such things were commended to the people."[67] Sacred history, then, prefigures Christ and church, now "being fulfilled in all things."[68] History is most fully present in Christ. For Augustine, the *civitas* and its founding sacrifice hold together in the Incarnate God-Man, and temporal history's course and destiny are weighty and not illusory. To experience each other as persons is to likewise feel the weight of our shared history which both divides and unites us, as God intended.[69]

62. Augustine, *City of God* 9.14, pp. 376–77.

63. Augustine, *City of God* 10.29, p. 436.

64. Augustine, *City of God* 10.32, p. 446.

65. Augustine, *City of God* 11.26–28.

66. Charles Cochrane, *Christianity and Classical Culture: A Study of Thought and Action from Augustus to Augustine* (Liberty Fund, 2003), ch. 12.

67. Augustine, *City of God* 18.42, p. 882.

68. Augustine, *City of God* 16.2.

69. Augustine, *City of God* p. 537.

Much like Augustine's typological history, Chesterton saw Christ as recapitulating all prehistory, comparative religion, philosophy, and civic destiny. Christ's birth, accompanied by shepherds and magi, answered the lost Roman agricultural ideal and the philosophers' aspirations.[70] It is a history with weighty presence. Christmas overwhelms human categories: It "surprises us from behind" and can "take us off our guard," and by its arrival in our experience comes "winged levity" and a mildness that imparts "something more human than humanity."[71] The incarnation offers a plentitude: "Its unique note is the striking of many notes: of humility, of gaiety, of gratitude, of mystical fear, but also of vigilance and of drama.[72] Thus, it makes present historical truth that demands continual unpacking: "Endless expositions have not come to the end of it, or even the beginning."[73] Fundamentally, Chesterton urged his audience to read the Gospels as *new* and not overlaid with modernist portraits of Jesus.[74] As news, they "puzzle us and perhaps terrify us." The realism of the narratives "are precisely the descriptions of the supernatural," of that which is unsettling and threatening, and calls forth "stark straining incredulity."[75] Jesus' life is purposeful, dramatic, and drives towards his sublime end, for in the cross the gathering of all history—all the myths and philosophers—is buried and raised anew in himself.[76] "It is enough to say that the materialists have to prove the impossibility of miracles against the testimony of all mankind," and not just against Jesus' own cultural context.[77] For Chesterton, the Gospels present rather than represent, their immediacy claiming all who hear them.

The Everlasting Man was written in part as a rejoinder to H. G. Wells' *Outline of History*, which had given only a few pages to Jesus as a kind of Semitic mystic.[78] Wells had wanted his populist work to help educate a transnational identity, a sense of being human that would encourage geopolitical peace.[79] In answer, and not unlike Augustine, Chesterton treated

70. Chesterton, *Everlasting Man*, 305–7, 309–10.

71. Chesterton, *Everlasting Man*, 316–17.

72. Chesterton, *Everlasting Man*, 312.

73. Chesterton, *Everlasting Man*, 344–45. Likewise, Christ's claim to divinity makes comparative religious study unfruitful; his singularity outstrips them (see also 334).

74. Chesterton, *Everlasting Man*, 328–29.

75. Chesterton, *Everlasting Man*, 324, 330.

76. Chesterton, *Everlasting Man*, 341–45, 378.

77. Chesterton, *Everlasting Man*, 327.

78. Chesterton could be grateful for much of Wells' history even while complaining of its lack of proportion. See *Everlasting Man*, 394.

79. H. G. Wells, *An Outline of History: Being a Plain History of Life and Mankind* (Cassel and Co., 1920), v–vi.

Christ's divinity and humanity as a fecund plentitude: "Omnipotence and impotence, or divinity and infancy, do definitely make a sort of epigram which a million repetitions cannot turn into a platitude."[80] And thus part 2 of *Everlasting Man* gives three chapters over to Christ before turning to Christian history. In similar fashion, Chesterton treated the church's birth and its history as transcending naturalistic explanations; indeed, as engaged in spiritual warfare. There is an exclusiveness to the truth that unites and divides: "Unless we understand the presence of that enemy, we shall not only miss the point of Christianity, but even miss the point of Christmas." Christianity is a rebellion against the powers, "a revolution against the prince of the world."[81]

Humanity has told itself tales about supernatural reality, yet these myths were never meant to reveal dogmatic certainties. The church, on the other hand, keeps acting as an emissary of a message.[82] The emergence of Christianity, set against a pagan background, "had all the character of a unique thing and even a supernatural thing."[83] And for Chesterton this was a principle of continual reinvention within continuity, incarnating the faith anew even when the church appeared empty and hollow. The church could only have divine origins, "out of the mind of God, mature and mighty and armed for judgment and for war," and the church's many-sided nature was thus made manifest in its responses to heresies.[84] Its continual power made present a demand upon each human identity. Paradoxically, it remained global by its very exclusive call.

For those who fear that theology is a Rubicon that philosophy dare not cross, perhaps there is still room to cross, learn, and return with some lessons.[85] *The City of God* and *The Everlasting Man* confront us with the question of whether the narratives of history can be told apart from the transcendentals, and whether the center of history has such gravity that it pulls us toward something or someone. Both their works ask us whether a past presence—an event or a person—can call forth a faithful narrative structure, and they ask us to consider an open cosmos of presence: supernal, infernal, and traditional. Above all, they confront us with the presence of the God-Man in space and

80. Chesterton, *Everlasting Man*, 303.

81. Chesterton, *Everlasting Man*, 312–15.

82. Chesterton, *Everlasting Man*, 397–99.

83. Chesterton, *Everlasting Man*, 382.

84. Chesterton, *Everlasting Man*, 363.

85. After Emmanuel Falque's title and metaphor: *Crossing the Rubicon: The Borderlands of Philosophy and Theology*, trans. Reuben Shank (Fordham University Press, 2016).

time, a transcendent weight experienced by both Augustine and Chesterton, and no honest philosophy of history need deny it.

BIBLIOGRAPHY

Ankersmit, Frank. *Meaning, Truth, and Reference: In Historical Representation*. Ithaca, NY: Cornell University Press, 2012.

———. *Sublime Historical Experience*. Redwood City: Stanford University Press, 2005.

Augustine. *The City of God Against the Pagans*. Translated by R. W. Dyson. New York: Cambridge University Press, 1998.

———. *On Christian Belief*. Translated by Edmund Hill. New York: New City, 2005.

———. *The Retractions*. Translated by Mary Inez Bogan. Washington, DC: Catholic University Press of America, 1968.

Brown, Peter. *Augustine of Hippo: A Biography*. New Edition. Berkeley: University of California Press, 2000.

Chesterton, G. K. *Avowals and Denials*. London: Dodd and Mead, 1935.

———. *The Ball and the Cross*. In *Collected Works* 7. San Francisco: Ignatius, 1986.

———. *The Everlasting Man*. In *Collected Works* 2. San Francisco: Ignatius, 1986.

———. "Magic." In *Collected Works* 11. San Francisco: Ignatius, 1986.

———. "Need for Historical Humility." In *Collected Works* 33. San Francisco: Ignatius, 1986.

———. *Orthodoxy*. In *Collected Works* 1. San Francisco: Ignatius, 1986.

———. *St. Thomas Aquinas*. In *Collected Works* 2. San Francisco: Ignatius, 1986.

———. "The Teaching of History." In *Collected Works* 32. San Francisco: Ignatius, 1986.

Cochrane, Charles. *Christianity and Classical Culture: A Study of Thought and Action from Augustus to Augustine*. Indianapolis: Liberty Fund, 2003.

Falque, Emmanuel. *Crossing the Rubicon: The Borderlands of Philosophy and Theology*. Translated by Reuben Shank. New York: Fordham University Press, 2016.

Gumbrecht, Hans Ulrich. *Production of Presence: What Meaning Cannot Convey*. Redwood City: Stanford University Press, 2004.

Marion, Jean-Luc. *Reduction and Givenness: Investigations of Husserl, Heidegger, and Phenomenology*. Translated by Thomas A. Carlson. Evanston, IL: Northwestern University Press, 1998.

Meconi, David Vincent, ed. *The Cambridge Companion to Augustine's City of God*. New York: Cambridge University Press, 2021.

O'Daly, Gerard. *Augustine's City of God: A Reader's Guide*. New York: Oxford University Press, 1999.

Orsi, Robert A. *History and Presence*. Cambridge, MA: Harvard University Press, 2016.

Ricoeur, Paul. *Time and Narrative* 1. Translated by Kathleen McLaughlin and David Pellauer. Chicago: University of Chicago Press, 1984.

Runia, Eelco. *Moved by the Past: Discontinuity and Historical Mutation*. New York: Columbia University Press, 2014.

Steiner, George. *Real Presences*. Chicago: University of Chicago Press, 1991.

Taylor, Charles. *The Language Animal: The Full Shape of the Human Linguistic Capacity*. Cambridge, MA: Harvard University Press, 2016.

———. *A Secular Age*. Cambridge, MA: Harvard University Press, 2007.

Wells, H. G. *An Outline of History: Being a Plain History of Life and Mankind*. New York: Cassel and Co., 1920.

All through history, there have been broad conceptions of the aims of life, tests of morality which masses of men have held and applied with certainty; but in the modern world these various systems have been abandoned and what is left of them is nothing but debris—a collection of broken bits, the ruins of past philosophies. There are some, like myself, who hold a mystical philosophy, a belief that behind human experience there are realities, powers of good and evil, and the final test for things is their influence for good or evil. The good power intends us to be happy and we are justified in being happy, but the real question is not whether we are happy, but whether, behind the things wherein we seek our happiness, lies the power of good. Are they parts of the good or of the evil?

—"The Need of a Philosophy," *The Philosopher*

It is felt by many that strong philosophical conviction, while it does not (as they perceive) produce that sluggish and fundamentally frivolous condition which we call bigotry, does produce a certain concentration, exaggeration, and moral impatience, which we may agree to call fanaticism. They say, in brief, that ideas are dangerous things. . . . Ideas are dangerous, but the man to whom they are least dangerous is the man of ideas. He is acquainted with ideas, and moves among them like a lion-tamer. Ideas are dangerous, but the man to whom they are most dangerous is the man of no ideas. The man of no ideas will find the first idea fly to his head like wine to the head of a teetotaller. . . . Religious and philosophical beliefs are, indeed, as dangerous as fire, and nothing can take from them that beauty of danger. But there is only one way of really guarding ourselves against the excessive danger of them, and that is to be steeped in philosophy and soaked in religion.

—"Concluding Remarks on the Importance of Orthodoxy," *Heretics*

4

The Angelic Doctors

Chesterton and Aquinas

Peter Kreeft

PUTTING AN "AND" BETWEEN Chesterton and Aquinas is unlike putting an "and" between Chesterton and any other philosopher, simply because Chesterton was a Thomist. Most modern philosophers were to him pretty much as the Sophists were to Socrates. And all his important references to Aquinas are in one book, the only one he ever wrote about any philosopher, *Saint Thomas Aquinas, the "Dumb Ox."* I shall quote almost exclusively from that book, for everything he has to say explicitly about Aquinas is in there, although many of Aquinas' principles are scattered throughout his other books, especially *Orthodoxy*, which is his masterpiece and also his most philosophical book.

I shall also use his words rather than my own, quoting rather than summarizing, because Chesterton says more in fewer and more memorable words than any philosopher who ever lived. (I think Pascal and Nietzsche come the closest to Chesterton's mastery of aphorism. Their style is surprisingly similar even though their content is as dissimilar as possible.) Summarizing Chesterton in other words than his own is like muffling a bell by depositing loads of snow on it.

The significance of Chesterton's unusual subtitle, "*The Dumb Ox*," manifests his love of both irony and humor. Like philosophy itself, these two great things are founded on the contrast between appearance and reality. The irony in the subtitle, of course, is based on the confusion between the two meanings of "dumb": "stupid" and "silent." Aquinas was probably the most sheerly intelligent philosopher who ever lived, but his humility manifested itself in a habit of silence. When his fellow students called him "the dumb ox," conflating the two meanings, he did not respond or defend himself to refute that incredibly inaccurate label, but his teacher St. Albert the Great, the greatest scientist of his age, did.

Even in the literally millions of words he wrote in his short career, we sense a great surrounding silence. Most words come out of other words; his come from the silence. Most modern minds remind us of sharp, quick little paper shredders; his reminds us of enormous underground caverns filled with quiet light. (*The Quiet Light*, by the way, is the fitting title of an excellent novel about Aquinas' life by Louis DeWohl.)

Gilson said of *Saint Thomas Aquinas, the "Dumb Ox"* (and many other, lesser Thomists, like myself, agree):

> I consider it as being without comparison the best book ever written on St. Thomas. Nothing short of genius can account for such an achievement. . . . Readers who have spent twenty or thirty years in studying St. Thomas . . . cannot fail to perceive that the so-called "wit" of Chesterton has put their scholarship to shame. He has guessed all that which we had tried to demonstrate, and he has said all that which they were more or less clumsily attempting to express in academic formulas.[1]

And Chesterton never even graduated from university.

The book is not perfect and not even wholly fair, especially in his last chapter, for the comparisons between Aquinas and his opponents are not only oversimplified (which is forgivable in a popular book) but also quite unfair (which is not forgivable) to Plato, Luther, the Puritans, and even Augustine, all of whom he sees as almost Manichees. Yet he gets the main point profoundly right and burns that "big picture" into our our consciousness: the sacramentalism, the incarnationalism, the creationism, the holism, the Catholic "both/ands" versus the Platonic, Protestant, and Puritan "either/ors": Faith vs. reason, grace vs. nature, soul vs. body, intellect vs. senses and imagination, and the eternal vs. the temporal.

1. Quoted in Joseph Pieper's *Guide to Thomas Aquinas* (University of Notre Dame Press, 1962), 6–7.

Only two of its eight chapters (VI and VII) focus on Aquinas' philosophy, and this is a plus rather than a minus, because one of the reasons he gets the philosophy so right is that he situates it within three other contexts or dimensions of Aquinas: his personality and life, his theology, and his sanctity. In his preface he says that "the biography is an introduction to the philosophy, and that the philosophy is an introduction to the theology and that I can only carry the reader just beyond the first stage of the story."[2] The biography, the philosophy, and the theology are all part of merely the "first stage." "Anyone writing so small a book about so big a man must leave out something."[3] That is, of course, his sanctity. Chesterton is here implying that the profoundest thing Aquinas ever said was the three words he replied to God when God asked him what he wanted as his reward for writing so well about Him: *Nisi te, Domine* ("Only Thyself, Lord"). This is simply the best possible answer to the most important possible question: "What is the meaning of life?"

Within this "sketchy" treatment of philosophy, I shall pick out distinct but related points worthy of our notice and gratitude. I order them systematically along philosophy's conventional divisions: Method, logic, metaphysics, cosmology, anthropology, epistemology, and ethics. (Politics, our modern idolatry and obsession, is here ignored, as it will be in Heaven, for the same reason it always is between lovers.)

(1) The first aspect of philosophy, the one presupposed in all the others, is method. Socrates, Descartes, Kant, Hegel, Husserl and the "phenomenologists," James and the "pragmatists," and also the "analytic philosophers" all invented new methods for doing philosophy. What is Aquinas' method, according to Chesterton? It is that of Thomas Reid and G.E. Moore: Beginning with common sense.

Chesterton says: "The fact that Thomism is the philosophy of common sense is itself a matter of common sense."[4] "Since the modern world began in the sixteenth century, nobody's system of philosophy has really corresponded with everyone's sense of reality, to what, if left to themselves, common men would call common sense."[5] Even Descartes observed, in his *Discourse on Method*, that there is no idea so absurd that it has not been held by some philosopher.

There is no self-contradiction in common sense, or between common sense and common life and activity. Chesterton notes that "Of nearly all

2. G. K. Chesterton, *St. Thomas Aquinas* (Ignatius, 1986), 2.
3. Chesterton, *St. Thomas Aquinas*, 99.
4. Chesterton, *St. Thomas Aquinas*, 77.
5. Chesterton, *St. Thomas Aquinas*, 78.

other philosophies it is strictly true that their followers work in spite of them or do not work at all. No sceptics work sceptically; no fatalists work fatalistically . . . No materialist who thinks his mind was made up for him by mud and blood and heredity has any hesitation in making up his mind. No sceptic who believes that truth is subjective has any hesitation about treating it as objective."[6]

Thus Aquinas' logic is commonsensical, not Hegelian or Deconstructionist (Derridaian): "For St. Thomas Aquinas," Chesterton says, "it is impossible that contradictions should exist together."[7] The reason for this is simple: "St. Thomas was sane and Hegel was mad."[8] "The philosophy of St. Thomas stands founded on the universal common conviction that eggs are eggs."[9] This conviction cannot be undone; we cannot rip out our logical motherboard.

The method of commonsense logic centers on syllogisms, the easiest and most obvious form of argument, and they are the habitual structure of St. Thomas' writing, especially in the *Summa*. His arguments are often elaborate webs of syllogisms, as a geodesic dome is an elaborate web of triangles. Modern philosophers like Bacon, Hobbes, Hume, Mill, and Derrida are positively allergic to syllogisms. But Chesterton says:

> I have never understood why there is supposed to be something crabbed or antique about a syllogism; still less can I understand what anybody means by talking as if induction ["I am mortal and you are mortal and they are mortal, therefore probably all men are mortal"] had somehow taken the place of deduction ["All men are mortal and we are men, therefore we are mortal"]. The whole point of deduction is that true premises produce a true conclusion. What is called induction seems simply to mean collecting a larger number of true premises.[10]

This is one of the many ways in which Aquinas is a "both-and" thinker: Like Socrates, he uses both induction and deduction, both logical form and empirical content, thus transcending the great modern divide between Rationalists and Empiricists.

Style may be classified as part of method. Chesterton's style is famous for paradox, but his paradoxes are all commonsensical. They seem upside down to us only because we are upside down, standing on our heads, eyes in the

6. Chesterton, *St. Thomas Aquinas*, 103.
7. Chesterton, *St. Thomas Aquinas*, 78.
8. Chesterton, *St. Thomas Aquinas*, 78.
9. Chesterton, *St. Thomas Aquinas*, 79.
10. Chesterton, *St. Thomas Aquinas*, 82.

earth, nose to the grindstone, and feet kicking against the heavens, as Chesterton puts it elsewhere. Chesterton is the little boy in "The Emperor's New Clothes." All he has to do is tell the simple truth simply, and it seems shocking.

Here is Chesterton's parody of scholarly style in his own commonsensical style and apt analogies:

> Long words go rattling by us like long railway trains. We know they are carrying thousands who are too tired or too indolent to walk and think for themselves. It is a good exercise to try . . . to express any opinion one holds in words of one syllable. If you say "The social utility of the indeterminate sentence is recognized by all criminologists as a part of our sociological evolution towards a more humane and scientific view of punishment," you can go on talking like that for hours with hardly a movement of the gray matter inside your skull. But if you begin "I wish Jones to go to gaol and Brown to say when Jones shall come out," you will discover, with a thrill of horror, that you are obliged to think.[11]

(2) The first issues of content, as distinct from method, are issues of metaphysics. Metaphysics is simply that division of philosophy which deals with being, or existence itself, that which is common to everything real. For as Aquinas says, the first philosophical idea, even in the mind of a small child, is that something exists. Chesterton notes that

> The whole system of St. Thomas hangs on one huge yet simple idea, which does actually cover everything there is and everything there could possibly be. He represents this cosmic conception by the word *Ens* . . . Unfortunately there is no satisfying translation of the word *Ens* . . . when the translator says in English "being," we are aware of a rather different atmosphere . . . the word "being" as it comes to the modern Englishman, through modern associations, has a sort of hazy atmosphere that is not in the short and sharp Latin word. Perhaps it reminds him of fantastic professors in fiction who wave their hands and say, "Thus do we mount to the ineffable heights of pure and radiant Being"; or, worse still, of actual professors in real life who say, "All being is Becoming, and is the evolution of Not-being by the law of its Being" . . . it has a wild and wooly sort of sound, as if only very vague people used it . . . Now the Latin word *Ens* has a sound like the English word *End.* It is final and even abrupt. It is nothing but itself.[12]

11. G. K. Chesterton, *Orthodoxy* (Image, 1959), 129.
12. Chesterton, *St. Thomas Aquinas*, 82.

The first principle of Aquinas' logic, the law of non-contradiction, is based on this first idea of his metaphysics, for "it is instantly apparent, even to the child, that . . . a thing cannot be and not be, that there is a false and [a] true."[13] What a liberation from confusion and complexity to certainty and simplicity! The truth of truth and the falsehood of falsehood! Not everything is a grey fog. Even grey is made of black and white. Concepts may be infinitely varied and multi-colored, but propositions are either true or false—including this one! So the principle is assumed even when it is denied.

Chesterton calls our attention to the fact that Aquinas ignores the primary problem that bedevils classical modern philosophers from Descartes through Hegel, namely the "critical problem" of the justification or validation of human reason itself. This is because he begins not with epistemology, like all the moderns, but with metaphysics, like all the pre-moderns. Chesterton explains why Thomas

> . . . does not deal at all with what many now think the main . . . question: whether we can prove that the primary act of recognition of any reality is real. The answer is that St. Thomas recognized instantly, what so many modern skeptics have begun to suspect rather laboriously, that a man must either answer that question in the affirmative or else never answer any question at all . . . I suppose it is true in a sense that a man can be a fundamental skeptic, but he cannot be anything else, certainly not a defender of fundamental skepticism.[14]

Descartes insists that we begin with epistemology rather than metaphysics, that we examine our epistemological tools before we build our metaphysical house, and Chesterton approves Aquinas' denial of this priority, which is why "St. Thomas's work has a constructive quality about it absent from all cosmic systems after him. For he is already building a house, while the newer speculators are quarrelling about whether they can even make the tools that will make the house."[15]

Faith and reason are both prior or primordial for, as Chesterton says, "it is all idle to talk of the alternative of reason and faith. It is an act of faith to assert that our thoughts have any relation to reason at all."[16] As Gilson argues in *Thomistic Realism and the problem of Knowledge*, all proofs of proof itself, or reasons for reason itself, must always beg the question, that is, they must assume the very conclusion they seek to prove. If *all* the prisoners (acts

13. Chesterton, *St. Thomas Aquinas*, 91.
14. Chesterton, *St. Thomas Aquinas*, 79.
15. Chesterton, *St. Thomas Aquinas*, 79.
16. Chesterton, *Orthodoxy*, 29.

of human reasonings) are on trial, by what right do any of the accused (the reasonings and arguments of the modern "critical" philosopher) leap up into the judges bench? If we are to put reason itself on trial, we have no judge.

So we begin with metaphysics. "If the morbid Renaissance intellectual (Hamlet) is supposed to say, 'To be or not to be—that is the question,' then the massive medieval does certainly reply in a voice of thunder, 'To be—that is the answer.'"[17] "To this question 'Is there anything?' St. Thomas begins by answering 'Yes.' If he began by answering 'No,' it would not be the beginning but the end. That is what some of us would call common sense."[18]

We might call this beginning "mystical." (Indeed, Wittgenstein does, in *Philosophical Investigations.*) Chesterton, like Wittgenstein, says that "There is at the back of our lives an abyss of light more blinding and unfathomable than any abyss of darkness; and it is the abyss of darkness; and it is the abyss of actuality, of existence, of the fact that things truly are . . . it is unthinkable, yet we cannot unthink it."[19]

This is a "mysticism" of the most simple, ordinary experience:

> I invented a rudimentary and makeshift mystical theory of my own. It was substantially this: that even more existence, reduced to its most primary limits, was extraordinary enough to be exciting. Anything was magnificent as compared with nothing . . . We should dig for this submerged sunrise of wonder so that a man sitting in a chair might suddenly understand that he was actually alive, and be happy.[20]

Chesterton, like Aquinas, says that "Being" is the best word for what God is for two reasons: first, because it is God's own essence (He is not caused or contingent; He cannot not-be.) and second, because it is God's own name for Himself: "The Arabs have a phrase about the hundred names of God (all of which are also in the Bible, by the way); but they also inherit the tradition of a tremendous name unspeakable because it expresses Being itself . . . His own name, which can only be written I AM."[21]

(3) So much for being, and metaphysics. What, then, of becoming, and cosmology? The feature common to everything in the universe, everything created, is that "they are largely in a state of change, from being one thing to being another" and "that is because what we see is not the fullness of

17. Chesterton, *St. Thomas Aquinas*, 58.

18. Chesterton, *St. Thomas Aquinas*, 80.

19. G. K. Chesterton, *Chaucer* (Ignatius, 1991), 172–73.

20. G. K. Chesterton, *The Autobiography of G. K. Chesterton* (Sheed and Ward, 1936), 90–91.

21. Chesterton, *St. Thomas Aquinas*, 62.

being . . . Ice is melted into cold water and cold water is heated into hot water; it cannot be all three at once . . . But the fullness of being (God) is everything that it can be . . . Things change because they are not complete."[22]

The feature of all creation that Chesterton emphasizes most dramatically is its contingency: "the world does not explain itself, and cannot do so merely by continuing to expand itself . . . it is absurd for the Evolutionist to complain that it is unthinkable for an admittedly unthinkable God to make everything out of nothing and then pretend that it is more thinkable that nothing should turn itself into everything."[23]

> Until we realize that things might not be, we cannot realize that things are . . . we discover that the rhinoceros does exist and then take pleasure in the fact that he looks as if he didn't . . . Any man in the street is a Great Might Not Have Been . . . If a man saw the world upside down, with all the trees and towers hanging head downward as in a pool, one effect would be to emphasize the idea of dependence . . . He would be thankful to God Almighty that it had not been dropped . . . He who has seen the whole world hanging on a hair of the mercy of God has seen the truth . . . He who has seen the vision of his city upside-down has seen it the right way up.[24]

Chesterton also emphasizes another universal feature of all creatures: their teleology, final causality, or directionality. Acorns become oaks because that is their goal and their destiny—and that is their goal because oaks have more being. Everything seeks fuller being; everything in its own way moves toward the fullness of being, every creature not only depends on God, as its First Cause, but also seeks God, as its Final End. It not only moves by energy, from a push from behind but also in a certain direction, by a pull from ahead.

This is a version of "the argument for God from design." For "it is impossible even to say that a change is for the better unless the best exists."[25] "If there has been from the beginning anything that can possibly be called a Purpose, it must reside in something that has the essential elements of a Person. There cannot be an intention hovering in the air all by itself, any

22. Chesterton, *St. Thomas Aquinas*, 92.
23. Chesterton, *St. Thomas Aquinas*, 95.
24. Chesterton, *Orthodoxy*, 62.
25. Chesterton, *St. Thomas Aquinas*, 96.

more than a memory that nobody remembers."[26] "I had always felt life first as a story; and if there is a story there is a story-teller."[27]

The cosmos contains universals (forms) as well as particulars (concrete material things): "the Nominalist declared that things differ too much to be really classified, so that they are only labelled. Aquinas was a firm but moderate Realist, and therefore held that there really are general qualities; as that human beings are human, amid other paradoxes . . . H. G. Wells had an alarming fit of Nominalist philosophy and poured forth book after book to argue that everything is unique and untypical, as that a man is so much an individual that he is not even a man."[28] "Thus when Mr. Wells says, 'All chairs are quite different', he utters . . . a contradiction in terms. If all chairs were quite different, you could not call them 'all chairs.'"[29]

I find Aristotle the most neglected philosopher by other philosophers in modern times and the hardest to teach: my students "get" his ethics but not his cosmology, mainly because they do not understand the meaning of or even believe in the existence of this key term. Essentially, it means "ontological essence," not "methodological category." Chesterton gives us the best explanation I have ever seen of the concept of "form," perhaps the key philosophical term for both Aristotle and Aquinas:

> It is not really very difficult to learn the meaning of the main terms [of Aquinas's philosophy]; but their medieval meaning is sometimes the exact opposite of their modern meaning. The obvious example is in the pivotal word "form." We say nowadays, "I wrote a formal apology to the Dean," or "The proceedings of the Tip-Cat Club were purely formal." But we mean they were purely fictitious; and St. Thomas, had he been a member of the Tip-Cat Club, would have meant just the opposite. He would have meant that the proceedings dealt with the very heart and soul and secret of the whole being of the Tip-Cat Club; and that the apology to the Dean was so essentially apologetic that it tore the very heart out in tears of true contrition. For "formal" in Thomist language means actual, or possessing the real decisive quality that makes a thing itself. Roughly, when he describes a thing as made of Form and Matter, he very rightly recognizes that Matter is the more mysterious and indefinite and featureless element, and that what stamps anything with its own identity is its Form. Matter, so to speak, is not so much the solid as the

26. Chesterton, *St. Thomas Aquinas*, 97.
27. Chesterton, *Orthodoxy*, 59.
28. Chesterton, *St. Thomas Aquinas*, 95.
29. Chesterton, *Orthodoxy*, 31.

> liquid or gaseous thing in the cosmos . . . But the form is the fact; it is that which makes a brick a brick . . . Every artist knows that the form is not superficial but fundamental; that the form is the foundation. Every sculptor knows that the form of the statue is not the outside of the statue but the inside of the statue.[30]

(4) One quotation (as usual in Chesterton, a concrete image rather than an abstract concept) is so central that it can stand for the fundamental concept of Aquinas' philosophical anthropology: "Man is not a balloon going up into the sky nor a mole burrowing merely in the earth, but rather a thing like a tree, whose roots are fed from the earth while its highest branches seem to rise almost to the stars."[31]

(5) This "psychosomatic unity" or "hylomorphism" (literally, "matter-form-ism") is the foundation of his epistemology. On the one hand, Chesterton quotes Aquinas' empiricist starting point, that "everything that is in the intellect has been in the senses . . . [T]he Neo-Platonists all tended to the view that the mind was lit entirely from within; St. Thomas insisted that it was lit by five windows, that we call the windows of the senses."[32] On the other hand, the intellect understands the form, the universal, while the senses only deliver the particulars to this x-ray machine. (Remember, the form is not the outer shape but the inner essence.)

Aquinas' epistemology is firmly objectivist and Realist, not subjectivist and Idealist:

> The strangeness of things, which is the light in all poetry, and indeed in all art, is really connected with their otherness, or what is called their objectivity. What is subjective must be stale; it is exactly what is objective that is in this imaginative manner strange. In this the great contemplative is the complete contrary of that false contemplative . . . who looks only into his own soul.[33]

On the other hand, he is no materialist:

> According to Aquinas, the object becomes a part of the mind; nay, according to Aquinas the mind actually becomes the object. But . . . it only becomes the object and does not create the object. In other words, the object . . . does exist outside the mind, or in the absence of the mind. And therefore it enlarges the mind of which it becomes a part. The mind conquers a new province like

30. Chesterton, *St. Thomas Aquinas*, 95.
31. Chesterton, *St. Thomas Aquinas*, 90.
32. Chesterton, *St. Thomas Aquinas*, 88.
33. Chesterton, *St. Thomas Aquinas*, 102.

> an emperor; but only because the mind has answered the bell like a servant.[34]

Chesterton notices this habitual pattern in Aquinas of avoiding opposite popular errors, for, as he says in *Orthodoxy*, "is always simple to fall; there are an infinity of angles at which one falls, only one at which one stands."[35] As in Aristotle, there is usually a "golden mean" between two opposite extremes, which is not a compromise, but a "both-and" between two goods or truths instead of an "either-or"; an "on the one hand" and an "on the other hand," as in the habitually used particles "men" and "de" in ancient Greek.

> This view avoids both pitfalls . . . The mind is not merely receptive in the sense that it absorbs sensations like so much blotting-paper; on that sort of softness has been based all that cowardly materialism which conceives man as wholly servile to his environment. On the other hand, the mind is not purely creative in the sense that it paints pictures on the windows and then mistakes them for a landscape outside . . . In other words, the essence of the Thomist common sense is that two agencies are at work: reality and the recognition of reality, and their meeting is a sort of marriage . . . the external fact fertilizes the internal intelligence.[36]

This is the exact opposite of Kant's "Copernican Revolution in Philosophy" according to which everything we perceive or understand is the result of the internal intelligence, which is universal (the same in all) but subjective (not independent of our thinking, not a "thing in itself"). For Kant, the mind forms its object, so that what we consciously know we have already unconsciously made. For Aquinas, as for common sense (again!), it is the reverse: The object forms the mind. In other words, Aquinas restores the natural relationship between the epistemological male and the epistemological female, which Kant reverses. In other words, Kant's philosophy is epistemological transgenderism.

(6) Aquinas is probably less original and revolutionary (but also more detailed) in his ethics than in the other dimensions of his philosophy; and the traditional themes that Chesterton emphasizes throughout his writings are not only typically Thomistic but typically Catholic, for instance:

34. Chesterton, *St. Thomas Aquinas*, 103.

35. Chesterton, *Orthodoxy*, 103.

36. Chesterton, *St. Thomas Aquinas*, 102–3.

(a) The fact that moral values are objective and absolute: "Right is right, even if nobody does it. Wrong is wrong, even if everybody is wrong . . . Men spoke of the sinner breaking the law, but it was the law that broke him."[37]

(b) The fact that morality gets its absoluteness from its origin, which is not human but divine: "Morality did not begin by one man saying to another, 'I will not hit you if you do not hit me'. There is no trace of such a transaction. There is a trace of both men having said, 'We must not hit each other in the holy place.'"[38]

(c) The fact that conscience is not a feeling: "The (modern) critic instinctively avoids the admission that Hamlet's was a struggle between duty and inclination, and tries to substitute a struggle between consciousness and subconsciousness. He gives Hamlet a complex to avoid giving him a conscience."[39]

(d) The fact that moral law is the friend, not the enemy, of freedom and happiness: "Doctrine and discipline may be walls, but they are the walls of a playground."[40]

(e) The fact that virtues are positive, not negative: "virtue is not the absence of vices . . . Virtue is a vivid and separate thing, like a pain or a particular smell. . .as white is a colour, not an absence of a colour. It is a shining thing, as fierce as red and as shining as black."[41]

(f) The fact that justice is foundational, as childhood is foundational. Thus he explains why children love fairy tales where the villains are punished, because "children are innocent and love justice, while most of us are wicked and naturally prefer mercy."[42]

(g) The fact that humility is not small-minded but great-minded: "Humility is the mother of giants. One sees great things from the valley, only small things from the peak."[43]

37. G. K. Chesterton, *The Illustrated London News*, May 11, 1907.

38. Chesterton, *Orthodoxy*, 67.

39. Chesterton, "Hamlet and the Psycho-Analyst," in *Fancies vs. Fads*.

40. Chesterton, *Orthodoxy*, 153.

41. G. K. Chesterton, "A Piece of Chalk," in *Tremendous Trifles*.

42. G. K. Chesterton, "On Household Gods and Goblins," in *The Illustrated London News*, July 7, 1906.

43. G. K. Chesterton, "The Hammer of God," in *The Innocence of Father Brown* (Cassell, 1913), 256.

There is much, much more. These are only a few samples. But they are samples of a banquet of words fit for Heaven. Like the music of Palestrina, it is difficult to believe that its author was only a man and not an angel. Like Aquinas, Chesterton should be called an "angelic doctor." Why did he understand Aquinas so well? Because "it takes one to know one," or, in other words, this is an example of "knowledge by connaturality."

Someone once said that Chestertonianisms are like potato chips: you cannot eat only one. But the addiction to them is not narrowing but broadening because it is an addiction not just to cleverness or even just to humor, but to truth, goodness, and beauty, and above all the union of these three divine attributes in nearly everything Chesterton says. I sense that same unity in Aquinas even though the irony, the paradox, the humor, and the one-liners are not there. Aquinas' style is as spare and straight as Chesterton's is colorful and slant (Chesterton obeyed Emily Dickinson's advice to "tell the truth, but tell is slant.") We need both, and therefore God, in His wisdom and generosity, gave us both. Praise the very great and very happy divine Mind who gave us both of these large and happy human minds.

BIBLIOGRAPHY

Chesterton, G. K. *Chaucer*. San Francisco: Ignatius, 1991.

———. *Orthodoxy*. New York: Image, 1959.

———. *St. Thomas Aquinas: The "Dumb Ox."* San Francisco: Ignatius, 1986.

———. *The Autobiography of G. K. Chesterton*. London: Sheed and Ward, 1936.

———. "Tom Jones." Chesterton Digital Library. https://library.chesterton.org/all-things-considered-6816/.

———. "A Piece of Chalk." Chesterton Digital Library. https://library.chesterton.org/a-piece-of-chalk-24987/.

———. *The Innocence of Father Brown*. London: Cassell, 1913.

———. *Fancies vs. Fads*. London: Methuen, 1923.

Pieper, Josef. *Guide to Thomas Aquinas*. Translated by Richard Winston and Clara Winston. South Bend, IN: University of Notre Dame Press, 1962.

The modern world is not evil; in some ways the modern world is far too good. It is full of wild and wasted virtues. When a religious scheme is shattered (as Christianity was shattered at the Reformation), it is not merely the vices that are let loose. The vices are, indeed, let loose, and they wander and do damage. But the virtues are let loose also; and the virtues wander more wildly, and the virtues do more terrible damage. The modern world is full of the old Christian virtues gone mad. The virtues have gone mad because they have been isolated from each other and are wandering alone. Thus some scientists care for truth; and their truth is pitiless. Thus some humanitarians only care for pity; and their pity (I am sorry to say) is often untruthful.

—"The Suicide of Thought," *Orthodoxy*

But what we suffer from to-day is humility in the wrong place. Modesty has moved from the organ of ambition. Modesty has settled upon the organ of conviction; where it was never meant to be. A man was meant to be doubtful about himself, but undoubting about the truth; this has been exactly reversed . . . Thus we should be wrong if we had said hastily that there is no humility typical of our time. The truth is that there is a real humility typical of our time . . . The old humility was a spur that prevented a man from stopping; not a nail in his boot that prevented him from going on. For the old humility made a man doubtful about his efforts, which might make him work harder. But the new humility makes a man doubtful about his aims, which will make him stop working altogether. [. . .]

We are on the road to producing a race of men too mentally modest to believe in the multiplication table. We are in danger of seeing philosophers who doubt the law of gravity as being a mere fancy of their own. Scoffers of old time were too proud to be convinced; but these are too humble to be convinced. The meek do inherit the earth; but the modern sceptics are too meek even to claim their inheritance.

—"The Suicide of Thought," *Orthodoxy*

5

Faith, Reason, and Madness

Julian Ahlquist

René Descartes is widely regarded as the founder of modern philosophy and lays claim to what is perhaps the most famous philosophical quote in history: "*Cogito ergo sum*" ("I think, therefore I am"). He was, moreover, a key figure in the development of the modern scientific method and made notable contributions to mathematics, including the Cartesian coordinate system, which bears the adjectival form of his name. Though few philosophers would consciously follow in his epistemological footsteps, some of the fundamental assumptions that were built into Descartes' method would come to pervade the thought of most of his modern successors, even those who ultimately adopted philosophies that Descartes would abhor.

G. K. Chesterton mentions Descartes a few times in passing, often in benign ways. He cites Descartes, for instance, as an example of a great natural philosopher who, contrary to atheist expectation, believed in miracles, and says that "Descartes the Catholic" was more a philosopher of rationalist science than "[Francis] Bacon the Protestant."[1] However, when looking at Chesterton's criticism of earlier thinkers whom Descartes resembles (such as Plato and even Augustine) as well as Chesterton's endorsement of thinkers who contrast with Descartes (such as Aristotle and especially Aquinas),

1. G. K. Chesterton, "If They Had Believed," in *The Thing* (Sheed and Ward, 1929), 239.

the real differences become, as Descartes might say, "clear and distinct." It might even be argued that Chesterton considers Descartes' philosophy to be a major source of madness in the modern world.

Descartes' thought arose out of frustration with the state of philosophy in his time, which he saw as a complicated mess inherited from the medieval Scholastics—a philosophy that was littered with errors, especially regarding the natural world, which were being refuted by ongoing scientific discoveries. While Chesterton loved aspects of medieval Scholasticism, especially its Thomist school, he would also admit that some of its later representatives "took everything that was worst in Scholasticism and made it worse. They continued to count the steps of logic; but every step of logic took them further from common sense."[2] Some of the Scholastic philosophers were aware of this problem, notably the controversial Franciscan philosopher William of Ockham, famous for "Ockham's Razor"—an idea which can be roughly summarized as follows: "The simplest possible explanation for something is the best explanation." Ironically, subsequent Ockhamists, in their attempt to simplify Scholastic thought, made it even more confusing. They also influenced Martin Luther and other Protestants to leave the Catholic Church, believing Christianity likewise needed to be trimmed down by eliminating superfluous Catholic doctrines to return it to a more elementary state like the early church (or what they thought it was). Ultimately, neither the late Scholastics nor the Protestants could agree on how to wield Ockham's Razor. Many Protestants sought to cut away philosophy altogether, embracing only what the faith would reveal (extreme "fideism"). Even many Catholics during the Renaissance were inspired with a growing skepticism about natural reason. This lack of both philosophical and theological harmony led to increasing social disunity and widespread violence (like the Thirty Years' War).

It was in the midst of this chaos that Descartes found himself, and he was, for better or for worse, inspired by a dream to mitigate these divisions. Though theological agreements might be a long way off, some unity in philosophy might be possible if a method for adjudicating disputes—something like a philosophical analogue to the scientific method—could be devised. Descartes attempted to devise such a method in two of his most famous works: *Meditations on First Philosophy* and *Discourse on Method*. In these texts, Descartes tried to abolish all existing philosophy and carefully rebuild it from the ground up, as one might demolish a decrepit building to construct a new one in its place instead of inefficiently repairing each of its countless flaws. To do this, Descartes came up with "methodic doubt," which involved a

2. G. K. Chesterton, *St. Thomas Aquinas* (Dover, 2009), 125.

systematic examination of all his beliefs and a provisional rejection of any that could possibly be doubted. His ultimate goal was to rebuild his philosophy on an unshakable foundation of self-evident and indubitable truths. Like axioms in a mathematical proof, these truths would guarantee the truth of anything that could be validly deduced from them. Descartes did not want to doubt everything for doubt's sake, but to doubt as much as possible to find what he could not doubt. His paradoxical aim was to use skepticism to defeat skepticism and achieve certainty of the highest degree.

There is something in this Cartesian venture that Chesterton would applaud, for he too recognized that "all argument begins with an assumption; that is, with something that you do not doubt."[3] But unlike Descartes, Chesterton understood that *any* assumption can, in principle, be doubted. Also, unlike Descartes, Chesterton maintained that just because you *can* doubt an assumption, it doesn't follow that you *should*: "You can, of course, if you like, doubt the assumption at the beginning of your argument, but in that case you are beginning a different argument with another assumption at the beginning of it."[4]

Though Descartes was a professing Christian, he seemed intent on eliminating the need for "faith" when it came to philosophy. Chesterton, on the other hand, aimed to maintain a balance between faith and reason: "Reason is itself a matter of faith," he said. "It is an act of faith to assert that our thoughts have any relation to reality at all."[5] Descartes, in contrast, wished to create a system of reason that was so clear and undeniably true that no faith was needed at all to fill the gaps. Though Descartes' view persists in many modern minds, often taking the form of "only believing in things you can prove," Chesterton argues that everyone must take *something* on faith, for "you can never prove your first statement or it would not be your first."[6] Chesterton thus repudiates that modern maxim, for an infinite regress of statements to prove other statements is impossible. Descartes agreed, but he differs from Chesterton in his conviction that some statements are beyond the possibility of doubt, and that a wholly undoubtable philosophy could be built on that foundation. According to Chesterton, this modern aversion to mystery is something logicians in general, especially mathematicians, are prone to, even though the project is doomed to failure and leads those who relentlessly pursue it into a kind of madness. In contrast, Chesterton writes:

3. G. K. Chesterton, "Philosophy of the Schoolroom" (June 22, 1907).
4. Chesterton, "Philosophy of the Schoolroom."
5. G. K. Chesterton, "The Suicide of Thought" (1908).
6. Chesterton, "Philosophy of the Schoolroom."

"Mysticism keeps men sane. As long as you have mystery you have health; when you destroy mystery you create morbidity."[7]

Again, Chesterton says that a kind of faith is necessary to trust that one's reasoning works in the first place, for you cannot rely on logic to show that logic is reliable without offending logic by begging the question. Hence, Chesterton maintains that a certain nonlogical—indeed, poetic—attitude is needed in the human mind: "The poet only asks to get his head into the heavens. It is the logician who seeks to get the heavens into his head. And it is his head that splits."[8] While Descartes wanted to have his beginning premise be utterly unmysterious so that the conclusions that follow from it would share in its absolutely certain nature, Chesterton would counter with this paradox: "The whole secret of mysticism is this: that man can understand everything by the help of what he does not understand." Doing otherwise, he says, will actually cause the logician to do all kinds of hopeless mental acrobatics that will end up mudding things even more than before: "The morbid logician seeks to make everything lucid, and succeeds in making everything mysterious. The mystic allows one thing to be mysterious, and everything else becomes lucid."[9] Chesterton would thus declare that this hunt for the indubitable truth that Descartes sought was logically and psychologically doomed from the start.

In any case, armed with his innovative method of doubt, Descartes went into an isolated cottage on a wintry day and did not emerge until he had systematically rejected almost everything he once believed and reconstructed all of philosophy anew in his head. Reflecting on this event in his *Meditations*, he wrote that the first victims of methodic doubt were beliefs that depended upon his senses. This was because he had sometimes believed the sensations in his dreams were real: If his sensory impressions had deceived him in the past, he reasoned, their present truthfulness could not be guaranteed; hence, as methodic doubt demands, beliefs that depend on sensation must be rejected *as if they were false*. In this we find another example of the connection that Chesterton implicitly makes between methodic doubt and a form of characteristically modern madness: "Every sane man," he says, "believes that the world around him and the people in it are real, and not his

7. Chesterton, "The Maniac."
8. Chesterton, "The Maniac."
9. Chesterton, "The Maniac."

own delusion or dream."[10] Chesterton explains how not believing in your senses is as bad as *only* believing in your senses:

> The man who cannot believe his senses, and the man who cannot believe anything else, are both insane, but their insanity is proved not by any error in their argument, but by the manifest mistake of their whole lives. They have both locked themselves up in two boxes, painted inside with the sun and stars; they are both unable to get out, the one into the health and happiness of heaven, the other even into the health and happiness of the earth.[11]

But instead of coming to his senses, Descartes pressed onward, rejecting the deliverances of science (since scientific claims are founded on sensory data) and even mathematics (recalling past miscalculations). Indeed, Descartes became so paranoid about the possibility of error that he really began fearing that he might be a madman trapped in a world of hallucinations, or that there might really be an entity (whether it was God or a demon or an "evil genius") who had the power to deceive him at every turn. And yet, Descartes kept thinking all the same.

After putting himself under a sort of philosophical sensory deprivation, Descartes turned inward to examine his own mental world. This move would prove to be characteristic of other modern rationalists who rejected the assumption that our minds start as blank slates, but come naturally equipped with *a priori* ideas. However, this tradition of thought did not begin in the modern era. Two thousand years before, Plato had argued that the physical world was a sort of simulation, and that each material object was merely a "shadow" or representation of an immaterial idea that could somehow be contemplated by itself apart from sense perception.

Overall, Chesterton gives Plato mixed reviews: "Plato was right, but not quite right."[12] He differed from "the Platonists, or at least the Neo-Platonists, [who] all tended to the view that the mind was lit entirely from within"[13]—an assumption which Descartes himself adopted. But Chesterton thought the much saner option is found in someone like "Aristotle[,] who took things as he found them, just as Aquinas accepted things as God created them,"[14] for when it came to the mind, an Aristotelian, including Aquinas, "insisted that it was lit by five windows, that we call the windows

10. Chesterton, "Philosophy of the Schoolroom."
11. Chesterton, "The Maniac."
12. Chesterton, "A Meditation on the Manichees."
13. Chesterton, "The Permanent Philosophy," in *St. Thomas Aquinas*.
14. Chesterton, "The Aristotelian Revolution," in *St. Thomas Aquinas*.

of the senses,"[15] and said, "I am not ashamed to say that I find my reason fed by my senses; that I owe a great deal of what I think to what I see and smell and taste and handle; and that so far as my reason is concerned, I feel obliged to treat all this reality as real."[16] Chesterton elaborates that Aquinas "seems fairly certain that the difference between chalk and cheese, or pigs and pelicans, is not a mere illusion,"[17] but "pretty much what we all feel it to be. It may be said that this is mere common sense; the common sense that pigs are pigs; to that extent related to the earthbound Aristotelian common sense."[18] Chesterton would therefore take issue with Descartes' grave departure from such common sense. Relatedly, Chesterton criticizes how he heard a rationalist once say that when a child looks out a window and sees grass, "the child does not see any grass at all; but only a sort of green mist reflected in a tiny mirror of the human eye"[19]—a sentiment similar to the Cartesian notion regarding the unreliability of the senses, but to which Chesterton responds: "This piece of rationalism has always struck me as almost insanely irrational. If he is not sure of the existence of the grass, which he sees through the glass of a window, how on earth can he be sure of the existence of the retina, which he sees through the glass of a microscope? If sight deceives, why can it not go on deceiving?"[20]

Chesterton would therefore reject Descartes' skepticism of the senses as a self-defeating position: To claim we cannot trust the senses is already to rely on them in distinguishing truth from delusion. With that said, Chesterton admits that there is a kind of "deceitfulness of things which has had so sad an effect on so many sages," but explains that "if things deceive us, it is by being more real than they seem."[21] In terms of Aristotelian and Thomistic metaphysics, "If they seem to have a relative unreality (so to speak) it is because they are potential and not actual; they are unfulfilled, like packets of seeds or boxes of fireworks," which only give us a limited glimpse that "does not satisfy us" until those things come to ontological fruition.[22] In contrast to the Platonic and Cartesian theories, Chesterton says: "In the Thomist, the energy of the mind forces the imagination outwards, but because the images it seeks are real things," rather than "things not to be found by staring

15. Chesterton, "The Permanent Philosophy."
16. Chesterton, "On Two Friars," in *St. Thomas Aquinas*.
17. Chesterton, "On Two Friars."
18. Chesterton, "On Two Friars."
19. Chesterton, "The Permanent Philosophy."
20. Chesterton, "The Permanent Philosophy."
21. Chesterton, "The Permanent Philosophy."
22. Chesterton, "The Permanent Philosophy."

inwards at the mind. The flower is a vision because it is not only a vision. Or, if you will, it is a vision because it is not a dream."[23] For certain Platonists, as well as this stage in Descartes' thinking, it is more like a false vision, or even a demonic nightmare.

Descartes' grim intellectual search for a glimmer of enduring truth while trying to outmaneuver a hypothetical diabolical deceiver is reminiscent of something else in Plato, namely, his famous "allegory of the cave." Plato's cave depicts the material universe as a dark cavern where enchained prisoners are forced to stare at shadow-puppets that they believe comprise the entirety of reality. Only the wisest and most courageous can break out, struggle to the surface, and see the world aboveground, which symbolizes the happier immaterial realm. Descartes' meditations not only suggest such epistemological imprisonment but also something darker. The early heresy of Gnosticism and later variants, like Manichaeism and Albigensianism, have roots in this aspect of Platonism. While these heresies differed slightly here and there, they all, broadly speaking, believed the material world was a prison from which the mind must escape.[24] While Plato had said the divine craftsman of the world (i.e., the "*Demiurge*") was a good entity, he admitted that he could not explain why this god would submerge our souls in the chaos of materiality, let alone manufacture this deceptive cosmos in the first place. In contrast, the Gnostics, Manichees, and Albigensians were somewhat more consistent in their antimaterial views, claiming this "Demiurge" was actually an evil being (either a demon or evil god, coexistent with a good god who created our souls before they were trapped in matter). Descartes was pondering eerily similar thoughts, speculating that the divine itself (or some similarly powerful being) was the source of his misperceptions. Chesterton, following Aquinas, had a special hatred for this gnostic doctrine. We can therefore easily imagine him admonishing Descartes to stop entertaining (if not succumbing to) such heterodox tendencies.

Notably, St. Augustine had once been a Manichee, and though he eventually converted to Christianity, he remained a sort of Platonist. But Augustine pushed back against extreme forms of Platonism which claimed that knowledge was impossible, seeing no way to tell whether we were being deceived at any given moment. In doing so, Augustine formulated a

23. Chesterton, "The Sequel to St. Thomas."

24. Notably, they practiced ritual murder of their fellow heretics when such souls were perceived to be purified adequately to die and escape into a purely incorporeal paradise.

predecessor to Descartes' most famous contention: "If I am deceived, then I exist, for if I do not exist, I cannot be deceived."[25] Following Augustine's lead, Descartes would famously declare that he had finally found certainty about his own existence in the aforementioned "*cogito*" argument: "I think, therefore I am." Upon this rock, Descartes built the rest of his philosophy—or so he tried.

As it turned out, various later modern philosophers who also tried their hand at methodic doubt did not agree with Descartes' assessment of the *cogito*'s indubitability. Chesterton notes, for example, that some radical evolutionists think things are constantly changing to such a degree that there is never a moment where anything is coherently stable enough to be anything in particular, which means that "there is no such thing as a thing," which further means that "you cannot think if there are no things to think about."[26] Here he mentions Descartes directly, saying, "Descartes said, 'I think; therefore I am.' The philosophic evolutionist reverses and negatives the epigram. He says, 'I am not; therefore I cannot think.'"[27] Chesterton did not embrace such radical skepticism because he was content to embrace a dose of dogmatism that makes productive argument possible. "Every argument," says Chesterton, "begins with an infallible dogma."[28] The *cogito* was Descartes' dogma, one which he thought indisputable, contrary to Chesterton, who says that "infallible dogma can only be disputed by falling back on some other infallible dogma."[29] For Descartes, this deeper dogma may perhaps be belief in methodic doubt itself. Could the dogmatic heart of Descartes' philosophy (and most modern philosophy, thanks to him) be the idea that "if something can be doubted, it must be rejected *as if it were false*?" Furthermore, if someone can doubt methodic doubt, should it too be rejected *as if it were false*? Is there some yet deeper dogma that would uphold it in the Cartesian-inspired mind? Chesterton, at the very least, would reject all those as being the supreme principle and would again subscribe to Aristotle and Aquinas, both of whom said the most fundamental knowledge is not an awareness of *self* but of *being*. In other words, it does not all start with "I think, therefore I am," but even more modestly: "There is existence." For a child, Chesterton says, "Long before he knows that grass is grass, or self is self, he knows that something is something. Perhaps it would be best to say very emphatically (with a blow on the table), 'There is

25. Paraphrased from Augustine's *City of God* 11.26.
26. Chesterton, "The Suicide of Thought."
27. Chesterton, "The Suicide of Thought."
28. Chesterton, "Philosophy of the Schoolroom."
29. Chesterton, "Philosophy of the Schoolroom."

an Is.'"[30] Moreover, preceding even the rise of self-consciousness, the child understands that "being is different from non-being." This is also known as the principle of noncontradiction; that is, as Chesterton puts it, "that a thing cannot be and not be. Henceforth, in common or popular language, there is a false and true."[31] Put yet another way, as far as the most basic fact goes, "Aquinas has affirmed that our first sense of fact is a fact; and he cannot go back on it without falsehood."[32] Despite this, even though Chesterton would see the Thomistic foundation of knowledge as more fitting than the Cartesian one, it seems he still would, once again, argue that it can be doubted since he, unlike Descartes, thinks a man has the power to doubt anything if he so chooses, for Chesterton observes how some skeptics "maintain that there is something that is both Yes and No. I do not know whether they pronounce it Yo."[33] Acknowledging that noncontradiction is not even immune to skepticism, Chesterton would have thus regrettably informed Descartes that neither is the holy *cogito*.

With Descartes at least convinced of his own existence due to the mere fact that he was thinking, he had now, at least provisionally, attained the position of a "solipsist." He firmly believed in himself, but nothing else. Again, even Descartes still thought everything he was grasping with his senses might be a mad fantasy unintentionally produced by his mind (or, again, intentionally by a demon), including everything in his memory, including his parents. Chesterton would remark that this mindset is worse than that of a materialist:

> There is a sceptic far more terrible than he who believes that everything began in matter. It is possible to meet the sceptic who believes that everything began in himself. He doubts not the existence of angels or devils, but the existence of men and cows. For him his own friends are a mythology made up by himself. He created his own father and his own mother.[34]

Chesterton argues this offense against common sense often manifests in the contradictory way a solipsist lives. For example, he knew of a skeptical solipsist who was surprised how there were not more solipsists in the world, despite how, if the man was right and consistent, this should be no surprise at all since no one else would exist. Descartes exhibited similar inconsistency,

30. Chesterton, "The Permanent Philosophy."
31. Chesterton, "The Permanent Philosophy."
32. Chesterton, "The Permanent Philosophy."
33. Chesterton, "The Permanent Philosophy."
34. Chesterton, "The Maniac."

writing how, despite disbelieving in the world outside of his head, he would still conform to local laws, his religion, and commonly accepted opinion in general, despite theoretically thinking there were no such things to conform to. Moreover, Chesterton says that solipsism "has in it something decidedly attractive to the somewhat mystical egoism of our day."[35] The fact that Descartes intended to base all philosophy on the existence of the "self" (the "ego") rather than the less self-centered notion of "being" in general helped inspire subsequent modern philosophers to do the same, ultimately fostering a radical individualism in the world that Chesterton abhors. "Ugly individualistic philosophy," Chesterton remarks, "is one of the commonest signs of a rotter,"[36] breeding overconfidence in one's own abilities, the dismissal of everything else (including wiser minds), and eventual incompetence in everything a person does to the point of complete self-delusion.

Feeling sure of his own existence, Descartes' next aim was to figure out *what* he was. He readily dismissed the idea that he was a "man" (i.e., a "rational animal") simply because he could doubt it. After all, "animality" implies physical existence—something pertaining to the senses—and should therefore, at this stage, be treated as fictional. Instead, building on the *cogito*, Descartes came to the supposedly undeniable conclusion that he was merely a "thinking thing"; that is, a "mind" or "soul" or, in this case, a "pure intellect." In other words, Descartes was denying he had a body and instead identified as an incorporeal spirit. Chesterton would wholeheartedly denounce this anthropology, as would Aristotle and Aquinas, for it was a view common to Platonists, Gnostics, Manichees, and Albigensians, all of whom preached that the body, being material, is not really part of us but only an inconvenient vessel that our soul was currently locked into. Chesterton notes how such heretical thinking necessitates condemning the Christian doctrine of the resurrection, in which body and soul are reunited at the end of time (a nightmare for Platonists and the aforementioned heretics). Chesterton emphasizes how this unorthodox tendency has continually resurfaced throughout history, due partly to overemphasis on early church asceticism: "The earlier Christian ages had been excessively anti-corporeal and too near the danger-line of Manichean mysticism."[37] He even states, "Granted all the grandeur of Augustine's contribution to Christianity, there was in a sense a more subtle danger in Augustine the Platonist than even in

35. Chesterton, "The Maniac."
36. Chesterton, "The Maniac."
37. Chesterton, "The Aristotelian Revolution."

Augustine the Manichee."[38] Chesterton would likely acknowledge that this subtle danger came to bloom once again when Descartes identified himself as a mind with no body. "There are a good many Manicheans among the Moderns,"[39] Chesterton claims, and in stark opposition to such stark mind-body dualism, Chesterton declares, "A corpse is not a man; but also a ghost is not a man. The earlier school of Augustine and even of Anselm had rather neglected this, treating the soul as the only necessary treasure, wrapped for a time in a negligible napkin."[40] Chesterton again favors Aquinas the Aristotelian on this matter: "St. Thomas stood up stoutly for the fact that a man's body is his body as his mind is his mind; and that he can only be a balance and union of the two," for man is "lower than the angels" and "higher than the animals."[41] Hence, to lose this balance in our minds, as Descartes did, would simply mean to become mentally imbalanced.

From "I think, therefore I am" to "I am a thinking thing," Descartes continued on by means of another supposedly infallible inference to belief in the existence of God. Descartes came to believe that he had an innate idea about a thing that lacked nothing, which stood in contrast to his ignorant self. Therefore, Descartes concluded that he was not himself equipped to create such an idea and had to receive it from something else that lacked nothing, which had to be "God" by definition (a surprising Thomistic appeal to "causal sufficiency," though hardly indubitable). Descartes concluded not only that God exists, but that his existence was beyond the possibility of rational doubt. Following Aquinas, who said God's existence was not so obvious, Chesterton said that "the ordinary man has always been sane" and "has always left himself free to doubt his gods."[42]

Now that his foundation of knowledge included knowledge about the existence and nature of God, Descartes was prepared to readmit many of the beliefs that his method had forced him, for a time, to reject. God cannot be a deceiver, since deception implies imperfection, and a perfect God lacks nothing. Therefore, Descartes inferred that God must have made Descartes' mind reliable—it is not God's fault that he has sometimes fallen into error, nor a fault in the nature of his mind (which God created), but because Descartes himself, with his own free will, has made rash judgments about things that were not "clear and distinct." He believed some things when he should have simply suspended judgment until they became such (what

38. Chesterton, "The Aristotelian Revolution."
39. Chesterton, "A Meditation on the Manichees."
40. Chesterton, "On Two Friars."
41. Chesterton, "On Two Friars."
42. Chesterton, "The Maniac."

exactly he meant by "clear and distinct" was not clear and distinct). Thus, in a plot twist, Descartes reversed his original position and declared that *his senses do not deceive him* since they are the handiwork of a good God, and that it was Descartes' own hasty interpretation of sensory data that had led him astray. While Chesterton would congratulate him on having regained his senses, he would criticize the supposedly undeniable reasoning process Descartes used to get there, for Chesterton says about the skeptic that "obviously there can be no positive proof given to him that he is not in a dream, for the simple reason that no proof can be offered that might not be offered in a dream" and "that I, at any given moment, am not in a dream, is unproved and unprovable. That anything exists except myself is unproved and unprovable."[43] Moreover, now that Descartes believed his senses again, he could also reaffirm the existence of the material world, which included his body, yet retained a sort of Platonic and Manichean residue, ultimately concluding like an engineer that the body was a mostly self-automated machine which his soul minimally pilots from somewhere in his brain. This robotic vision of the human being inspired later philosophers to use Ockham's Razor to eliminate the soul altogether, turning man into a fully functioning automaton with only the illusion of a mental self. In other words, contrary to Descartes' intention, he helped pave the way for later materialists who denied the existence of the self. This is why a friend once said, with Chestertonian sentiment: "After Descartes lost his body, the world lost its mind."

In the end, Descartes went from extreme skepticism to extreme certainty about many things, and Chesterton objected to both swings of this Cartesian pendulum. Descartes, in his mind, not only used skepticism to destroy skepticism but also used methodic doubt to destroy methodic doubt, for he first rejected doubtful things *as if they were false*, as methodic doubt dictates, but then later accepted many of them as certainly true and concluded that it is, in fact, wrong to judge doubtful things as if they were false. Chesterton may, perhaps, have appreciated this self-destructive paradox of the Cartesian methodology, but he did not see Descartes' move from radical skepticism to total certainty as the only, much less best, option.

I have focused here on matters Chesterton and Descartes would disagree about, primarily because of Chesterton's rather consistently critical view of the tradition of modern philosophy of which Descartes is the father. Defenders of Descartes, however, would say it is worth mentioning that methodic doubt (as well as Ockham's Razor before that) helped modern

43. Chesterton, "Philosophy of the Schoolroom."

scientists refrain from accepting arbitrary scientific claims too readily and instead test them more rigorously to arrive at more accurate conclusions about nature, resulting in greater advancements in science. Presumably, Chesterton would not object to this, but while many moderns might use this as proof that Cartesian skepticism was not a mistake, Chesterton would instead surely argue that, despite any benefits it has produced, it was mixed with enough error that it also set much of the world on a path toward insanity (as one might see, for example, in the archetype of the "mad scientist"). Moreover, it could be argued that Chesterton may have thought what Luther did to theology, Descartes did to philosophy. Both took Ockham's Razor to each of their targets with a disdain for established tradition, cutting away what they did not like, and galvanizing others to do the same, but, despite expectation, everyone, with their own individualistic idiosyncrasies, disagreed on how to do this right. The result was the modern disunity within both faith and reason. For this, Chesterton partially blames Luther's extreme Platonic and Augustinian influences characteristic of early church excesses, as he reasonably might do the very same for Descartes, who possessed those same tendencies. While Luther emphasized faith too much, Descartes emphasized it too little, yet both possessed gnostic and Manichean traits of the anti-Aristotelian and anti-Thomistic sort, which, again, Chesterton finds catastrophic. Contrary to their intentions, Luther's rejection of Catholic doctrine led many to reject Christian doctrine as a whole, and Descartes' rejection of the body led many to reject the soul. Not only would Chesterton therefore stress the importance of affirming both faith and reason but also both mind and body. Without such balance, Chesterton believes one can descend into irrational fideism, self-refuting skepticism, disembodied immaterialism, or mindless materialism, none of which align with common sense. Descartes perhaps never quite went mad in the end, but Chesterton would say he would have succeeded if he had really stuck to his hyper-rationalistic process. Descartes held on to his faith in some things at the back of his mind, while the same cannot always be said about some of those whom he inspired. On a more poetic note, however, many years after his death when there was a mishap during the transfer of Descartes' bones to another site, his skull was separated from his body. Its location is uncertain. At least in a literal way that Chesterton would no doubt appreciate . . . Descartes lost his head.

BIBLIOGRAPHY

Chesterton, G. K. *The Collected Works of G. K. Chesterton. Vol. 27: The Daily News, 1901–1907*. Edited by Lawrence J. Clancy. San Francisco: Ignatius, 1986.

———. "If They Had Believed." In The Thing. London: Sheed and Ward, 1929.

———. *Orthodoxy*. Chesterton Digital Library. https://library.chesterton.org/orthodoxy-62734/.

———. "The Suicide of Thought." Chesterton Digital Library. https://library.chesterton.org/orthodoxy-62734/.

———. "Philosophy for the Schoolroom." Chesterton Digital Library. https://www.chesterton.org/philosophy-for-the-schoolroom/.

———. *St. Thomas Aquinas*. Mineola, NY: Dover, 2009.

Some people fear that philosophy will bore or bewilder them; because they think it is not only a string of long words, but a tangle of complicated notions. These people miss the whole point of the modern situation. These are exactly the evils that exist already; mostly for want of a philosophy. The politicians and the papers are always using long words. It is not a complete consolation that they use them wrong. The political and social relations are already hopelessly complicated. They are far more complicated than any page of medieval metaphysics; the only difference is that the medievalist could trace out the tangle and follow the complications; and the moderns cannot. The chief practical things of today, like finance and political corruption, are frightfully complicated. We are content to tolerate them because we are content to misunderstand them, not to understand them. The business world needs metaphysics—to simplify it.

—"The Revival of Philosophy—Why?" *The Common Man*

It is foolish, generally speaking, for a philosopher to set fire to another philosopher in Smithfield Market because they do not agree in their theory of the universe. That was done very frequently in the last decadence of the Middle Ages, and it failed altogether in its object. But there is one thing that is infinitely more absurd and unpractical than burning a man for his philosophy. This is the habit of saying that his philosophy does not matter.

—"Introduction in Defense of Everything Else," *Orthodoxy*

6

Monsters in Search of Truth

Chesterton and Pascal

David P. Deavel

CHESTERTON AND PASCAL MIGHT seem an unlikely pairing at first glance. Pascal was himself a Jansenist for a time, and the scourge of the movement's most famous opponents, the Jesuits. Chesterton was a scourge of all forms of philosophical determinism, particularly the early modern theological schools that were, in Chesterton's view, reducible to it: Calvinism and Jansenism. Chesterton admired the early Jesuits and lamented the Jansenists' scrupulosity about cultural matters. "Nobody now is sorry," he wrote, "that the Jansenists failed to destroy all the dramas in France."[1] He observed that modern Protestants have tried to claim Pascal as one of their own "without taking the trouble to discover that any number of the things that Pascal denounced are things that any modern man would defend. For instance, Pascal blamed the infamous Jesuits for saying that a girl might in some conditions marry against the wish of her parents."[2] But Chesterton defended the Jesuit understanding that moral rules may well have exceptions that even the great Pascal had not discovered.

1. G. K. Chesterton, *The Thing*, in *The Collected Works of G. K. Chesterton* 3, introduction and notes by James J. Thompson Jr. (Ignatius, 1990), 189.

2. Chesterton, *The Thing*, 208.

Chesterton did consider Pascal great, even if different from himself. In *The Everlasting Man*, Chesterton used Pascal as an example of the Catholic Christian capacity to include geniuses of all sorts, noting that "men like Bossuet and Pascal could be as stern and logical as any Calvinist or Utilitarian."[3] He admired these characteristics in Pascal even if he thought they had fallen out of balance amid his ecclesial battles. "Why do people insist," Chesterton asked in his great biography of St. Thomas Aquinas, "on meeting the large and far-reaching mind of Pascal at its narrowest point; the point at which it was sharpened into a spike by the spite of the Jansenists against the Jesuits?"[4]

Despite apparent differences in philosophical and theological temperament, the two share some very important traits. Chesterton's biographer Maisie Ward observed that one of her main sources for Chesterton's early life was an exercise book "deliberately used for the development of a philosophy of life" that "is as important in studying Chesterton as the *Pensées* would be for a student of Pascal." Indeed, the teenaged Chesterton "is here already a master of phrase in a sense which makes a comparison with Pascal especially apt. For he often packs so much meaning into a brilliant sentence or two" that Ward thought it "worth while, in dealing especially with some of the less remembered books, to pull out a few of these sentences for quotation apart from their context."[5] A style with the capacity to distill large amounts of meaning and truth certainly unites these two. There have been a variety of collections of Chestertonian lines that stand beside the *Pensées* in their propensity to provoke or give birth to thoughts.

Yet it is not merely in style that the two are similar. Both were universal minds that saw all questions coming together on two luminous subjects: God and man. The order in which I have chosen to list these follows the order of being and importance. Yet in the order of knowledge, it is probably better to list them as man and God. For though God might be more intimate to me than I am to myself, as Augustine observed, the human condition after the events in the garden of Eden is one in which man is a strange and paradoxical creature made in the image of a God who seems hidden—though it may well be the case that we are hiding from God as the first human couple were reported to do.

It was on these two central topics—the oddity of man and the approach to God of a human race alienated from knowledge and true relationship

3. G. K. Chesterton, *The Everlasting Man* (Ignatius, 1995), 178.

4. G. K. Chesterton, *St. Thomas Aquinas*, in *The Collected Works of G. K. Chesterton* 2 (Ignatius, 1986), 527.

5. Maisie Ward, *Gilbert Keith Chesterton* (Sheed and Ward, 1943), xiv–xv.

with him—that Pascal and Chesterton are most fruitfully compared. Their approaches to our monstrous situation and to the hiddenness of God are in tension, but not ultimately contradictory. Both saw the odd and freakish nature of man and what it meant for man the monster to find a God who makes himself hard to find.

PASCAL ON MAN THE MONSTER

"What a chimera then is man!" writes Pascal. "What a novelty! What a monster, what a chaos, what a contradiction, what a prodigy! Judge of all things, imbecile worm of the earth; depositary of truth, a sink of uncertainty and error; the pride and refuse of the universe!"[6] We have both transcendent greatness and a desire to know all, yet we are mired in sins and passions that blind us to truth and a nature that is itself neither one thing nor the other.

For Pascal, we fall between the two stools of simplicity that are the infinite and the nothing:

> For in fact what is man in nature? A Nothing in comparison with the Infinite, an All in comparison with the Nothing, a mean between nothing and everything. Since he is infinitely removed from comprehending the extremes, the end of things and their beginning are hopelessly hidden from him in an impenetrable secret; he is equally capable of seeing the Nothing from which he was made, and the Infinite in which he is swallowed up.[7]

Because of this middling human nature, the scientist Pascal observes, we believe that we can find understanding by a close examination of nature, but the reality is that even scientific exploration of created reality bumps up against the "double infinity" that is at the heart of reality. We discover "that all the sciences are infinite in the extent of their researches" and "infinite in the multitude and fineness of their premises; for it is clear that those which are put forward as ultimate are not self-supporting, but are based on others which, again, having others for their support, do not permit of finality."[8]

Even abstracting from these questions of the limits of infinity and nothing at the edges, the world is itself one giant interlocking mystery, of which we can only know a few parts, presenting a problem for man who

6. Blaise Pascal, *Pensées*, translated by W. F. Trotter (Random House, 1941), 143 (434). In these notes, I will cite the page number first and then give the number of the thought in parentheses. Trotter followed the order used in Leon Brunschwig's edition (1894).

7. Pascal, *Pensées*, 23 (72).

8. Pascal, *Pensées*, 24 (72).

pretends to knowledge. "If man made himself the first object of study," Pascal writes, "he would see how incapable he is of going further. How can a part know the whole? But he may perhaps aspire to know at least the parts to which he bears some proportion. But the parts of the world are all so related and linked to one another, that I believe it impossible to know one without the other and without the whole."[9] Since our world is an immense chain of natural cause and effect, to not know "the whole" or "the parts in detail" means our capacity for true knowledge of the world is small at best.[10]

What makes knowledge supremely difficult is our twofold constructed nature. While God and angels are simple, we humans are "composed of two different natures, different in kind, soul and body." Our intellect is spiritual, to be sure, and capable of knowledge, yet it is united to a body. And thus we are limited by all sorts of bodily conditions, including "extreme youth and extreme age" that "hinder the mind." Pascal explains that "our true state . . . what makes us incapable of certain knowledge and of absolute ignorance" is this in-between nature, incapable of seizing on the full truth solidly. "When we think to attach ourselves to any point and to fasten to it, it wavers and leaves us; and if we follow it, it eludes our grasp, slips past us, and vanishes forever. Nothing stays for us. This is our natural condition, and yet most contrary to our inclination; we burn with desire to find solid ground and an ultimate sure foundation whereon to build a tower reaching to the Infinite."[11]

This twofold nature, which makes us much like the brutes (or animals) and also like the angels, is a strange, monstrous situation, one that we tend to want to forget and pretend we are one or the other.

> It is dangerous to make man see too clearly his equality with the brutes without showing him his greatness. It is also dangerous to make him see his greatness too clearly, apart from his vileness. It is still more dangerous to leave him in ignorance of both. But it is very advantageous to show him both. Man must not think he is on a level either with the brutes or the angels, nor must he be ignorant of both sides of his nature; but he must know both.[12]

While we might think it better for us to be less aware of the brutish side, Pascal's belief is that this is worse: "Man is neither angel nor brute, and he who would act the angel acts the brute."[13]

9. Pascal, *Pensées*, 26 (72).
10. Pascal, *Pensées*, 27 (72).
11. Pascal, *Pensées*, 27 (72).
12. Pascal, *Pensées*, 132 (418).
13. Pascal, *Pensées*, 118 (358).

Chesterton, too, thought of man as a monster. There is no doubt that he agreed with Pascal's dictum concerning man's most brutish behavior coming from pretensions to angelic life. He certainly believed that the angelic pretension to being a creature of pure reason was itself dangerous. In *Orthodoxy*, he diagnosed the problem with such "maniacs" as leaving behind imagination and relying solely on logic: "Imagination does not breed insanity. Exactly what does breed insanity is reason. Poets do not go mad; but chess-players do."[14] Like chess players, critics too tend to insanity, Chesterton says, observing that "though St. John the Evangelist saw many strange monsters in his vision, he saw no creature so wild as one of his own commentators."[15] Those focusing on reason to the exclusion of other faculties failed to understand the limits of reason mapped out by Pascal—they truly believe they can comprehend the whole: "The poet only asks to get his head into the heavens. It is the logician who seeks to get the heavens in his head."[16]

Yet Chesterton saw also that the monster that is man is a spectacle because of his positive qualities. In his exploration of human nature, its origin, and its destiny in *The Everlasting Man*, he advised twentieth-century readers, many of whom had formally theorized that man is nothing more than a brute, to take a closer look at man, for: "It is exactly when we do regard man as an animal that we know he is not an animal. It is precisely when we do try to picture him as a sort of horse on its hind legs, that we suddenly realise that he must be something as miraculous as the winged horse that towered up into the clouds of heaven."[17] It is not merely that man desires a tower rising up to the Infinite; it is that man, despite his weakness among the brutes, seems capable of realizing it.

Chesterton observes a whole series of ways in which human beings do not fit in with the other brutes who share the earth with them, demonstrating the odd and chimerical nature of which Pascal spoke.

> The simplest truth about man is that he is a very strange being; almost in the sense of being a stranger on the earth. In all sobriety, he has much more of the external appearance of one bringing alien habits from another land than of a mere growth of this one. He has an unfair advantage and an unfair disadvantage. He cannot sleep in his own skin; he cannot trust his own instincts. He is at once a creator moving miraculous hands and fingers and a kind of cripple. He is wrapped in artificial bandages called

14. G. K. Chesterton, *Orthodoxy* (Ignatius, 1995), 21.
15. Chesterton, *Orthodoxy*, 21–22.
16. Chesterton, *Orthodoxy*, 22.
17. Chesterton, *Everlasting Man*, 17.

> clothes; he is propped on artificial crutches called furniture. His mind has the same doubtful liberties and the same wild limitations. Alone among the animals, he is shaken with the beautiful madness called laughter; as if he had caught sight of some secret in the very shape of the universe hidden from the universe itself. Alone among the animals he feels the need of averting his thought from the root realities of his own bodily being; of hiding them as in the presence of some higher possibility which creates the mystery of shame. Whether we praise these things as natural to man or abuse them as artificial in nature, they remain in the same sense unique.[18]

Chesterton's focus on man's monstrosity covers not merely self-evident limitations but godlike abilities. And even some of the limitations seem to be hints of a hidden ability. Though humans are indeed weighed down by their inability to know with the kind of certainty that we would like, just as Pascal puts it to us, Chesterton implies that there is a kind of intuition present in man that allows him to perceive the reality in the universe that is hidden from all other creatures.

What demonstrates his godlike nature is that he is not merely another creature; he is also one who can create. "It is the simple truth," Chesterton writes, "that man does differ from the brutes in kind and not in degree; and the proof of it is here; that it sounds like a truism to say that the most primitive man drew a picture of a monkey and that it sounds like a joke to say that the most intelligent monkey drew a picture of a man." For Chesterton, "Art is the signature of man."[19]

Neither angel nor brute, Chesterton's focus is different and more positive: "Man is the microcosm; man is the measure of all things; man is the image of God."[20]

THE HIDDEN GOD

Man the monster has hints and allegations of the God who is beyond the physical world that sometimes seems impersonal. Chesterton's observation that the strangeness of man is in part because he perceives a secret at the heart of the universe or a perception of higher realities that causes us to feel shame is a nod toward the kind of hints present: suggestive and affecting

18. Chesterton, *Everlasting Man*, 36.
19. Chesterton, *Everlasting Man*, 34.
20. Chesterton, *Everlasting Man*, 35.

us at levels intellectual and moral. And yet, they are only hints. Pascal and Chesterton agree on this reality.

Pascal writes: "All appearance indicates neither a total exclusion nor a manifest presence of divinity, but the presence of a God who hides Himself. Everything bears this character."[21] Further, the attempt to find God through an examination of nature is rejected by Pascal as not effective for most people. In the section on the means of belief, he records his reaction to those who have written of the matter of coming to belief by reason:

> I admire the boldness with which these persons undertake to speak of God. In addressing their argument to infidels, their first chapter is to prove Divinity from the works of nature. I should not be astonished at their enterprise if they were addressing their argument to the faithful; for it is certain that those who have the living faith in their heart see at once that all existence is none other than the work of the God whom they adore. But for those in whom this light is extinguished, and in whom we purpose to rekindle it, persons destitute of faith and grace, who, seeking with all their light whatever they see in nature that can bring them to this knowledge, find only obscurity and darkness; to tell them that they have to look only at the smallest things which surround them, and they will see God openly, to give them as complete proof of the this great and important matter, the course of the moon and planets, and to claim to have concluded the proof with such an argument, is to give them ground for believing the proofs of our religion are weak.[22]

For Pascal, all the metaphysical arguments for God are themselves weak. In answer to his own question of whether "the heavens and birds prove God," he answers: "No. For although it is true in a sense for some souls to whom God gives this light, yet it is false with respect to the vast majority of men."[23] As Avery Dulles observed, for Pascal, "Even if such proofs were valid, to what would they lead except to an empty deism?"[24]

Chesterton's most provocative understanding of this thought is delivered in perhaps his most confusing and yet fascinating book, *The Man Who Was Thursday: A Nightmare*. The tale of Gabriel Syme, who is recruited for a philosophical police force and sent to infiltrate an anarchist ring, is a wild and dreamlike tale—perhaps even a dream—of pursuit of a mysterious

21. Pascal, *Pensées*, 183 (555).
22. Pascal, *Pensées*, 86 (242).
23. Pascal, *Pensées*, 87 (244).
24. Avery Dulles, *A History of Apologetics* (Ignatius, 2005), 162.

figure who goes by the name of Sunday. Toward the end of the novel, Syme offers to explain the problem with nature—that it is hiding a face, presumably the face of God that is not easily visible: "Shall I tell you the secret of the whole world? It is that we have only known the back of the world. We see everything from behind, and it looks brutal. That is not a tree, but the back of a tree. That is not a cloud, but the back of a cloud. Cannot you see that everything is stooping and hiding a face? If we could only get round in front—."[25]

HOW TO FIND A HIDDEN GOD I (PASCAL)

Pascal believed that our reason is weak and tends to succumb to our weaknesses, both physical and moral. "How ludicrous is reason, blown with a breath by every direction!"[26] Pascal's main theme is that human misery comes from knowledge of our relation to God and the angels—and that our happiness is found in that company alone—yet we are separated from God not merely by virtue of our composition, but by our status as sinners. Thus, his emphasis is on the need to *want* to find God and not merely drown ourselves in diversions from the need.

It is because of this bent in our wills—exacerbated by our continued actions against God—that we cannot merely come to find the truth about God through merely rational methods. We will be blown about by the slings and arrows of our own outrageous pursuit of a fortune that does not include God. No, the search must involve all the aspects of the self and involve the will. God "will only be perceived by those who seek Him with all their heart."[27] Far from thinking reason alone can bring one to true belief, Pascal believed the sources of belief included not only reason but also custom and inspiration.

Christianity, he tells us, "alone has reason" but "does not acknowledge as her true children those who believe without inspiration." It is the interior revelation of the God of truth that demands a response on the part of the human person that is the real and true event of saving faith. Yet, for this to happen, the whole person operates together. Pascal does not advocate a pure interiority, whether of the mind or of the heart. Pascal explains that "the mind must be opened to proofs, must be confirmed by custom, and

25. G. K. Chesterton, *The Man Who Was Thursday: A Nightmare* (Ignatius, 1999), 247.

26. Pascal, *Pensées*, 32 (82).

27. Pascal, *Pensées*, 60 (194).

offer itself in humbleness to inspiration, which alone can produce a true and saving grace."[28]

He understands that the monstrous corporeal and spiritual combination that is man will not simply turn toward truth without a surrender of the whole monster. "The external must be joined to the internal to obtain anything from God," Pascal writes. He explains that this means "we must kneel, pray with the lips, etc., in order that proud man, who would not submit himself to God, may be now subject to the creature." No mere mechanical approach, Pascal's holds that "to expect help from these externals is superstition; to refuse to join them to the internal is pride."[29]

Indeed, the glory of Christianity is that it understands how human beings are constituted, both in general and in their diversity. No doubt following the lead of St. Augustine's case for Christianity in *The City of God*, Pascal focuses on the universal quality of Christianity.[30] "Other religions, as the pagan," Pascal writes,

> are more popular, for they consist in externals. But they are not for educated people. A purely intellectual religion would be more suited to the learned, but it would be of no use to the common people. The Christian religion alone is adapted to all, being composed of externals and internals. It raises the common people to the internal, and humbles the proud to the external; it is not perfect without the two, for the people must understand the spirit of the letter, and the learned must submit their spirit to the letter.[31]

Intellectual demonstration is not what fully convinces people anyway, for many of our beliefs are not themselves objects of demonstration—such as whether "there will be a to-morrow, and that we shall die." What we really believe comes as much from our own behaviors that themselves testify to and reinforce our beliefs as much as to any purely logical arguments. It is "custom" that is "the source of our strongest and most believed proofs." This custom bends what Pascal calls "the automaton," which then "persuades the mind without thinking about the matter."[32] The automaton is that power of habit, which is what we have in common with the brutes that operate on instinct and training, that allows them to act in an almost machinelike

28. Pascal, *Pensées*, 37 (245).

29. Pascal, *Pensées*, 38 (250).

30. For more on Augustine's claims, see Thomas P. Harmon, *The Universal Way of Salvation in the Thought of Augustine* (T. & T. Clark, 2024).

31. Pascal, *Pensées*, 39 (251).

32. Pascal, *Pensées*, 89 (252).

fashion. We may be more than brutes, but we can train ourselves in the same way we train animals. By that training, even in the absence of full intellectual conviction, the person who wants to find the truth will open himself to both intellectual arguments as well as "inspiration" (i.e., the voice of God within the human heart).

Because the mind and the heart are imperfect, weak, and erring, Pascal makes clear that custom is always needed. Humans "must have recourse to it when once the mind has seen where the truth is, in order to quench our thirst, and steep ourselves in that belief, which escapes us at every hour; for always to have proofs ready is too much trouble." It is at these times when the intellect has been blown off course that humans must recur to "an easier belief, which is that of custom, which, without violence, without art, without argument, makes us believe things, and inclines all our powers to this belief, so that our soul falls naturally into it."[33] The wager is thus to dare to live as if God exists. Only thus can one open oneself to the inspirations that allow one to perceive and believe in the hidden God.

HOW TO FIND A HIDDEN GOD II (CHESTERTON)

While Chesterton may have rued the influence of the Jansenists on Pascal, his own approach to the hiddenness of God is complementary. For Chesterton, as for Pascal, God's presence does not lie on the surface of things. Yet if one takes the hints, they can lead in the direction of belief. While Chesterton does not deny the place of custom and daring to live as if God exists when one is uncertain, he emphasizes the role of the imagination—that is, the faculty by which the poet tries to "get his head in the heavens"—can be used to follow the trail of crumbs left by a hidden God.

In his famous chapter of *Orthodoxy* titled "The Ethics of Elfland," Chesterton recounts the process of thought by which he came to believe in the God of orthodox Christianity. And the first step was not by a strictly metaphysical argument but from an intuitive and comprehensive argument that was rational but not rationalistic. He was able to see that nature but had more to do with his sense of the insufficiencies of materialist explanations of the world and the use of a logic that encompassed it. He summarized the five steps of his reasoning that brought him to thinking about God long before theological claims entered his mind.

His beginning was the approach to thinking about that mysterious world that we inhabit. "[First,] it may be a miracle with a supernatural explanation; it may be a conjuring trick, with a natural explanation. But the

33. Pascal, *Pensées*, 89 (252).

explanation of the conjuring trick, if it is to satisfy me, will have to be better than the natural explanations I have heard. The thing is magic, true or false."

All the intellectual limitations placed on the human intellect noted by Pascal are turned on their head by Chesterton, who observes that the attempts to explain the world as simply an outworking of "laws" cannot work, for we do not really know the laws of physical necessity in the same way we know logical necessity. "All the terms used in the science books, 'law,' 'necessity,' 'order,' 'tendency,' and so on, are really unintellectual, because they assume an inner synthesis, which we do not possess."[34] Humans might as well see the world as they always have: as magic, the working of laws that are beyond our ken.

Chesterton saw the regularities in nature not as the outworking of abstract laws, but as gifts and indeed weird gifts. What Chesterton reasonably surmised was that there was more happening in nature than can be expressed in mechanistic terms. In fact, what he sensed was its personal aspect. For him, "the repetition in nature seemed sometimes to be an excited repetition, like that of an angry schoolmaster saying the same thing over and over again. The grass seemed signalling to me with all its fingers at once; the crowded stars seemed bent upon being understood. The sun would make me see him if he rose a thousand times. The recurrences of the universe rose to the maddening rhythm of an incantation."[35]

This led him to a second step: "Second, I came to feel as if magic must have a meaning, and meaning must have some one to mean it. There was something personal in the world, as in a work of art; whatever it meant it meant violently."[36] The miraculous and magical quality of the world led him to think that there might be a magician or miracle worker. He thought that facts might well be "miracles in the stricter sense that they were *wilful*," meaning that "they were, or might be, repeated exercises of some will."[37]

This sensation is what led him to think of his very existence as a gift. "We thank people for birthday presents of cigars and slippers. Can I thank no one for the birthday present of birth?"[38] Following this path led him to think not merely that the very existence of the world is a thing that is willed, but also its continued existence and even activity. He surmised that the recurrences in nature might well be the result not of the sun as an autonomous

34. Chesterton, *Orthodoxy*, 58.

35. Chesterton, *Orthodoxy*, 65.

36. Chesterton, *Orthodoxy*, 70.

37. Chesterton, *Orthodoxy*, 66.

38. Chesterton, *Orthodoxy*, 60.

being but the creature of a God who might say to it every morning, "Do it again," just as he told the moon to do the same in the evenings.[39]

Though the world was magical, it was also dangerous. Yet Chesterton's third point was that he found the purpose lurking behind the world "beautiful in its old design, in spite of its defects, such as dragons."[40] There is a perception of the good will that brought forth this miraculous creation. Rather than rage at the problems in the world, the sane person will realize that thanks for the gift of birth is itself the right answer. What kind of thanks? He discerned, on the basis of the customs passed down to him, "that the proper form of thanks to it is some form of humility and restraint: we should thank God for beer and Burgundy by not drinking too much of them. We owed, also, an obedience to whatever made us." The duty to seek God that Pascal wanted people to feel is a duty that Chesterton thinks, on the basis of his own experience, can be felt by paying attention to the world we live in and the customs stored up by humanity in the form of human religious tradition, which sees the good in the world and knows that it must be paid for in some fashion.

Chesterton's final realization was that even the good he perceived was itself only a taste of what had been lost. He described this as "a vague and vast impression that in some way all good was a remnant to be stored and held sacred out of some primordial ruin.[41] It is the burden of the rest of *Orthodoxy* to show how it is that Christianity makes sense of all these discoveries he had made without even being versed in the theological specifics.

THE SPECIFICITY OF THE HIDDEN GOD

Chesterton would certainly not have argued with Pascal's focus on living out what one suspects to be true about God. But what he brings to the conversation is a means by which the one who has not been exposed to Christianity in depth may look at the world in a new light—one that might allow one to begin to see what Christian faith entails even before knowing about the specifics. It is by seeing the duties humans have to wonder at the truth, give thanks for the gifts of existence, and offer some sort of sacrifice of humility and restraint that they can begin the arduous and exciting journey of not only learning about but interacting with this hidden God coming more clearly into view.

39. Chesterton, *Orthodoxy*, 60.
40. Chesterton, *Orthodoxy*, 70.
41. Chesterton, *Orthodoxy*, 70.

The kinds of arguments that Pascal lays out in other parts of his *Pensées* look to the internal theological claims, particularly coherence of the Old Testament prophecies and the miracles that were done to establish Christian faith. Chesterton's later arguments in *Orthodoxy* and elsewhere take a different tack: they aim at showing how the evidence for Christianity consists in how it fulfills not only Judaism but pagan religion, philosophy, and everything else.

Chesterton thought that Pascal's was a large and far-reaching mind. His own was no less. Both understood the catastrophe of human existence under the fall. Both understood that there is hope of finding conviction about the hidden God—and the ways by which one opens oneself to discerning it rationally by our habits. Chesterton showed how even one who has little sense of this hidden God can find the clues to his being and goodness in a world that, watched closely, displays a hidden, mysterious, and benevolent divine hand waiting to be discovered. He wanted his readers to know that there is a way, provided by God, to get around to the back side of the world and begin to discern the Face that is already looking at us.

BIBLIOGRAPHY

Chesterton, G. K. *The Everlasting Man*. San Francisco: Ignatius, 1995.

———. *The Man Who Was Thursday: A Nightmare*. San Francisco: Ignatius, 1999.

———. *Orthodoxy*. San Francisco: Ignatius, 1995.

———. *St. Thomas Aquinas*. Vol. 2 of *The Collected Works of G. K. Chesterton*. Edited by George Marlin. San Francisco: Ignatius, 1986.

———. *The Thing*. Vol. 3 of *The Collected Works of G. K. Chesterton*. Edited by George Marlin. San Francisco: Ignatius, 1990.

Dulles, Avery. *A History of Apologetics*. San Francisco: Ignatius, 2005.

Harmon, Thomas P. *The Universal Way of Salvation in the Thought of Augustine*. London: T. & T. Clark, 2024.

Pascal, Blaise. *Pensées*. Translated by W. F. Trotter. New York: Random House, 1941.

Ward, Maisie. *Gilbert Keith Chesterton*. New York: Sheed and Ward, 1943.

[W]hat do modern men say when apparently confronted with something that cannot, in the cant phrase, be naturally explained? Well, most modern men immediately talk nonsense. When such a thing is currently mentioned, in novels or newspapers or magazine stories, the first comment is always something like, "But my dear fellow, this is the twentieth century!" It is worth having a little training in philosophy if only to avoid looking so ghastly a fool as that. It has on the whole rather less sense or meaning than saying, "But my dear fellow, this is Tuesday afternoon." If miracles cannot happen, they cannot happen in the twentieth century or in the twelfth. If they can happen, nobody can prove that there is a time when they cannot happen. The best that can be said for the sceptic is that he cannot say what he means, and therefore, whatever else he means, he cannot mean what he says. But if he only means that miracles can be believed in the twelfth century, but cannot be believed in the twentieth, then he is wrong again . . . because an intelligent recognition of possibilities does not depend on a date but on a philosophy.

—"The Revival of Philosophy—Why?" *The Common Man*

In these days we are accused of attacking science because we want it to be scientific. Surely there is not any undue disrespect to our doctor in saying that he is our doctor, not our priest or our wife or ourself. It is not the business of the doctor to say that we must go to a watering-place; it is his affair to say that certain results of health will follow if we do go to a watering-place. After that, obviously, it is for us to judge. . . . To mix science up with philosophy is only to produce a philosophy that has lost all its ideal value and a science that has lost all its practical value. I want my private physician to tell me whether this or that food will kill me. It is for my private philosopher to tell me whether I ought to be killed.

—"Science and Religion," *All Things Considered*

7

Hume's Faith and Chesterton's Doubt

Landon Loftin

There are two kinds of people in the world: the conscious dogmatists and the unconscious dogmatists. I have always found myself that the unconscious dogmatists were by far the most dogmatic.

—"On Europe and Asia," *Generally Speaking*

No one will be surprised to find that the ideas of G. K. Chesterton and David Hume are at odds in many ways. Since Hume died before Chesterton was born, we can only speculate about how he would have responded to anything that Chesterton wrote, but something definite can be said about Chesterton's thoughts on Hume. That he had read Hume is known by several mentions of Hume's name in his published writings, though most are only passing expressions of disdain for Hume's work as a historian and a general dislike of the uniquely Scottish brand of skepticism that he represented.

Though Chesterton never engaged them explicitly, he had likely read not only Hume's *History of England*, but also his philosophical writings. This is probable in part because no one as widely and well-read as Chesterton (especially in "the scientific and sceptical literature of my time") is likely to have neglected works like Hume's *Enquiry Concerning Human Understanding*, or his *Dialogues Concerning Natural Religion*.[1] More to the point, however, it is difficult to read certain passages in Chesterton's writings without imagining that they were written with Hume's arguments in mind.

ON MIRACLES

For example, Chesterton argued that testimony about miracles can and often should be believed. This is contrary to Hume, who is history's most notorious detractor of miracle-claims. As a historian, Hume aimed to provide naturalistic explanations of all historical events; as a philosopher, he attempted to justify this approach to history with arguments against the credibility of all testimony about miraculous occurrences.[2] Indeed, the most famous of these arguments, which is found in book 10 of Hume's *Enquiry Concerning Human Understanding*, was composed, by his admission, because he was frustrated that historians, "sacred and secular," continued to pass on stories of the miraculous based on the testimony of alleged witnesses, instead of seeking naturalistic interpretations thereof.[3] The enormous consequence of this can be seen in the fact that Hume's argument (if sound) undermines belief in the testified miracles upon which the veracity of entire religions, like Christianity, are generally thought to stand. Hume later says that he does not think he is undermining *Christianity* as much as the "dangerous friends or disguised enemies to the Christian religion who have undertaken to defend it by the principles of human reason."[4] He goes on to say that "Our most holy religion is founded on faith, not on reason; and a sure method of making it look bad is to put it to a test that it is in no way fitted to pass."[5] This is widely thought to be a disingenuous admission, however; an addition that was meant to keep Hume in good standing with the academic community.

An important premise of Hume's argument is this: It is always, in any given instance, more probable that a given miracle-claim is false than it is

1. "I read the scientific and sceptical literature of my time—all of it, at least, that I could find written in English and lying about; and I read nothing else; I mean I read nothing else on any other note of philosophy." G. K. Chesterton, *Orthodoxy*, in *The Collected Works of G. K. Chesterton* 1 (Ignatius, 1986), 288.

2. As we shall see, Chesterton considered Hume to be one of the tiresome historians who "discredit supernatural stories that have some foundation, simply by telling natural stories that have no foundation." Chesterton, *Orthodoxy*, 247.

3. David Hume, *Enquiry Concerning Human Understanding* (Early Modern Texts, 2017), 56.

4. Hume, *Enquiry*, 68.

5. Hume, *Enquiry*, 68.

that a miracle has in fact occurred. This, he argued, is because human testimony, while generally reliable, is far from an infallible guide to truth; a person may be mistaken, or may be lying about their experience. On the other hand, since Hume defined miracles as *violations of the laws of nature*, they are not likely at all to happen, for, according to Hume, "firm and unalterable experience has established these laws."[6] Therefore, whether miracles are possible or not, it is never reasonable to believe that a miracle has happened on the basis of testimony. What Hume meant by the "firm and unalterable experience" upon which his judgment about the improbability of a miracle is based, is made clear in the following example: "A dead man's coming to life would be a miracle, because that has *never* been observed *in any age or country*."[7] If this premise is true, and one proportions belief to evidence, as Hume admonishes his readers to do, then Hume's conclusion is likely to be true as well. But how can we know that such an event has never been observed?

If Hume is not here being misrepresented, then it seems he has begged the question, for (as Chesterton pointed out many times) one can only know that human experience is uniform in regard to the laws of nature if one knows that the innumerable testimonies to supernatural events in history are false, but that such testimonies are almost certainly false is what Hume's argument was supposed to establish. And the amount of testimonial evidence against Hume's belief that uniform experience has established the inviolability of nature's laws is immense. Indeed, as Chesterton said, "If it comes to human testimony there is a choking cataract of human testimony in favour of the supernatural."[8] Thus, in a discussion of Hume, C. S. Lewis summed up this objection as follows: "We know the experience against [miracles] to be uniform only if we know that all the reports of them are false. And we can know all the reports to be false only if we know already that miracles have never occurred. In fact, we are arguing in a circle."[9]

6. Hume, *Enquiry*, 58. One Chestertonian critique of this argument that will not be explored here attacks the assumption that because reports of experiences in which the laws of nature did not hold are relatively rare (compared to experiences in which they do), the reports must be inherently unlikely. Chesterton likened this assumption to the man "who when he was told that a witness had seen him commit murder said that he could bring a hundred witnesses who had not seen him commit it." G. K. Chesterton, "Miracles and Modern Civilisation," The Society of G. K. Chesterton, https://www.chesterton.org/miracles-and-modern-civilisation/.

7. Hume, *Enquiry*, 58; emphasis added.

8. Chesterton, *Orthodoxy*, 355.

9. C.S. Lewis, *Miracles: A Preliminary Study* (HarperOne, 1996), 123.

POSSIBLE RESPONSES

One may attempt to rescue Hume's argument from the charge of circularity by pointing out that in the second part of book 10 Hume offers a number of what appear at first to be independent (that is, non-question-begging) reasons for distrusting the actual miracle-claims that have found their place in the annals of history. "I admit," he said, "there may possibly be miracles, or violations of the usual course of nature, of such a kind as to admit of proof from human testimony; though it may be impossible to find any such in all the records of history."[10] From that point forward, he conducts a cursory survey of famous miracle-claims (particularly those that have been hailed as confirmations of religious belief) in an attempt to show that none of them enjoy the support of sufficiently credible witnesses to be worth serious consideration.

Hume's reasons for denying credibility to those who have claimed to witness these miracles would have been, to put it mildly, a great affront to Chesterton's robustly democratic sensibilities. For instance, he denied that any such claims have the support of witnesses who were intelligent and well educated, and that none of the alleged witnesses have had enough "credit and reputation in the eyes of mankind" to have much to lose if their account of a miracle was refuted.[11] Another example of Hume's characteristically modern and aristocratic attitude comes in his claim that most historically attested miracles are discreditable because of their time and place of origin; for instance, he said that most attested miracles come from "ignorant and barbarous nations," or from civilized nations prior to their enlightenment.[12]

Hume is wrong, of course, in asserting that we lack testimonial evidence of miracles from witnesses that meet his criteria of credibility, but Chesterton would not have been impressed even if his claim were historically correct. Indeed, Chesterton would have found Hume's ideal witnesses not less, but more suspect than "the common man."[13] It is easy to imagine that he would have said, for example, that those with much to lose are not less but more likely to be dishonest or self-deceived; or that those with education are much more likely to be able to explain away unusual experiences in accordance with their preferred theory of the universe, etc.[14] And

10. Hume, *Enquiry*, 67.

11. Hume, *Enquiry*, 59.

12. Hume, *Enquiry*, 61.

13. This is a common theme in Chesterton's work. One interesting fictional exploration of this theme is in his novella *The Trees of Pride*.

14. In response, a great number of famous Chestertonian quips could be marshaled (e.g., "Without education we are in a horrible and deadly danger of taking

further, it would not matter if Hume were correct on the point because the accusation of circularity still stands. Though he denigrated their credibility, Hume provided no principled reason why people who are simple, common, vulgar, poor, foreign, or religious should be distrusted on such matters; and though one should be careful drawing inferences from his omission of principled reasons (he may have thought the reasons too obvious to state), the careful reader is left with a strong impression that Hume mistrusts them, at least in part, because they sometimes profess experience of supernatural occurrences.

Chesterton, again, was wary of this further potential for circularity, as is evident from passages like this:

> If I say, "Mediaeval documents attest certain miracles as much as they attest certain battles," they answer, "But mediaevals were superstitious"; if I want to know in what they were superstitious, the only ultimate answer is that they believed in the miracles. If I say "a peasant saw a ghost," I am told, "But peasants are so credulous." If I ask, "Why credulous?" the only answer is—that they see ghosts.[15]
>
> Or, in another place, he says: "If we say miracles are theoretically possible, they say, 'Yes, but there is no evidence for them.' When we take all the records of the human race and say, 'Here is your evidence,' they say, 'But these people were superstitious, they believed in impossible things.'"[16]

To avoid the charge, it seems, Hume, or a defender of Hume's argument, would need to concede that the impossibility of miracles is an assumption brought to the inquiry, not a conclusion derived from it. This may turn out to be a perfectly justifiable move insofar as one has independent justification for metaphysical naturalism, which excludes the possibility of miracles *ex hypothesi*; but this strategy comes at a price that Hume, it seems, was unwilling to pay. For anyone who rejects the considerable historical and contemporary testimonial evidence for miracles on the grounds that miracles are impossible is, at least in this regard, a dogmatist, and even a casual reader of Hume will know that "dogmatist" is a label he would have reviled. Again, Chesterton saw the matter clearly:

> The open, obvious, democratic thing is to believe an old apple-woman when she bears testimony to a miracle, just as you believe an old apple-woman when she bears testimony to a

educated people seriously." G. K. Chesterton, "Education by Fairy Tales").

15. Chesterton, *Orthodoxy*, 355.

16. Chesterton, "Miracles and Modern Civilisation."

> murder. The plain, popular course is to trust the peasant's word about the ghost exactly as far as you trust the peasant's word about the landlord. . . . If you reject it, you can only mean one of two things. You reject the peasant's story about the ghost either because the man is a peasant or because the story is a ghost story. That is, you either deny the main principle of democracy, or you affirm the main principle of materialism—the abstract impossibility of miracle. You have a perfect right to do so; but in that case you are the dogmatist.[17]

Hume, it seems, chose to "deny the main principle of democracy." Whether he or Chesterton was right in regard to the credibility of common people need not be settled here. But defenders of Hume's argument remain unconvincing insofar as they cannot offer a noncircular defense of Hume's criteria for the credibility of witnesses. However, a deeper critique of Hume's position on miracles can be developed from a comparison of his views on causation to those of Chesterton.

ON CAUSATION

Foundational to Hume's radically skeptical philosophy were his doubts about causation: an idea upon which most human knowledge depends.[18] By "causation," Hume referred to the idea of a necessary and comprehensible connection between kinds of events that are, or seem to be, constantly conjoined in human experience. When a billiard ball hits another, so long as the second is not impeded, we expect it to be set in motion. We expect this because such an event as one billiard ball hitting another is, in our

17. Chesterton, *Orthodoxy*, 355.

18. Some scholars argue that Hume was not, in fact, skeptical about causes. They interpret Hume as demonstrating the futility of reason by showing how it leads to conclusions that cannot be accepted by any sane and healthy person. Thus, Hume famously reflected, after considering the conclusions of his philosophical inquiry: "I am confounded with all these questions, and begin to fancy myself in the most deplorable condition imaginable. . . . Most fortunately it happens, that since Reason is incapable of dispelling these clouds, Nature herself suffices to that purpose, and cures me of this philosophical melancholy and delirium, either by relaxing this bent of mind, or by some avocation, and lively impression of my senses, which obliterate all these chimeras. I dine, I play a game of backgammon, I converse, and am merry with my friends. And when, after three or four hours' amusement, I would return to these speculations, they appear so cold, and strained, and ridiculous, that I cannot find in my heart to enter into them any farther." *A Treatise on Human Nature* 1.7. The interpretive question is whether the "real Hume" was the Hume playing backgammon with his friends or the Hume writing philosophical treatises in his study. Either way, the interpretation of Hume as a radical skeptic has been immensely influential and seems more likely.

experience, constantly conjoined with such an event as the second billiard ball being set in motion. But our expectation is not, Hume argued, based on an apprehension of a necessary connection between the two events; we have no such apprehension, only a habit of associating one event with the other, formed by past experience. Thus, in Hume's own words: "When we look about us towards external objects, and consider the operation of causes, we are never able, in a single instance, to discover any power or necessary connexion; any quality, which binds the effect to the cause, and renders the one an infallible consequence of the other. We only find that the one does actually, in fact, follow the other."[19]

Since Hume's time, philosophers have, in various ways, attempted to rebut his argument out of concern that the conclusion would undermine the entire edifice of human knowledge. It is therefore surprising that a similarly radical skepticism about physical causation was defended by none other than G. K. Chesterton himself. In *Orthodoxy*, for instance, Chesterton made this Humean point as follows:

> The man of science says, "Cut the stalk, and the apple will fall"; but he says it calmly, as if the one idea really led up to the other. The witch in the fairy tale says, "Blow the horn, and the ogre's castle will fall"; but she does not say it as if it were something in which the effect obviously arose out of the cause. . . . She does not muddle her head until it imagines a necessary mental connection between a horn and a falling tower. But the scientific men do muddle their heads, until they imagine a necessary mental connection between an apple leaving the tree and an apple reaching the ground.[20]

Thus, Chesterton continued, people "talk as if they had found not only a set of marvelous facts, but a truth connecting those facts. . . . They feel that because one incomprehensible thing constantly follows another incomprehensible thing the two together somehow make up a comprehensible thing."[21]

And the semblance goes deeper. A more detailed summary of Hume's argument would have gone back to his famous bifurcation of all knowledge into the categories of "relations of ideas" and "matters of fact."[22] Roughly, the former consists of the laws of logic, the principles of mathematics, and any other truths that do not depend on the contingencies of nature and history; the latter consists of contingent truths learned through experience.

19. Hume, *Enquiry*, 31.
20. Chesterton, *Orthodoxy*, 255.
21. Chesterton, *Orthodoxy*, 255.
22. Hume, *Enquiry*, 11.

According to Hume, since knowledge of causation is not included in the category of "relations of ideas," it must be included in "matters of fact." But matters of fact are derived from experience, and experience gives no indication of a necessary connection between events, only of constant conjunction.

A similar bifurcation of knowledge is adopted by Chesterton between "the science of mental relations" and "the science of physical facts."[23] The former category, like Hume's "relations of ideas," includes the laws of logic and mathematical truths: "For instance," Chesterton said, "if the Ugly Sisters are older than Cinderella, it is (in an iron and awful sense) *necessary* that Cinderella is younger than the Ugly Sisters."[24] The latter category includes all contingent facts that are learned from experience: for instance, that certain kinds of trees, given the right conditions, have borne apples. Like Hume, Chesterton denied that causation falls into "the science of mental relations," and specifically notes that in "the science of physical facts "there are no laws, but only weird repetitions."[25]

Chesterton's apparent agreement with Hume's skepticism about physical causation (and the reasoning on which it is supported) is surprising for a number of reasons, the most obvious being that both thinkers make this point in the context of larger projects that stand in diametric opposition to each other. For Hume it was, or was intended to be, a building block in a broadly skeptical philosophy; for Chesterton, it was part of the ground that supported a theistic and Christian worldview.

Consider Hume's skepticism first: He believed that unless we have knowledge of necessary connections between associated events—that is, of causes—then we cannot trust in the reliability of inductive inferences that appeal to past experience in order to establish conclusions about the future. One may, at this point, be tempted to object that we need not understand *why* one kind of event always precedes another kind of event in order to know *that* one kind of event always has (and therefore probably will) follow another kind of event; that is, we need not fully comprehend the causal mechanism that makes induction reliable in order to know that induction is, in fact, reliable. Induction has, after all, proven to be reliable in the past. But this would be a mistake. As Hume points out, any attempt to justify induction itself on the grounds that induction has proved reliable in the past is arguing in a circle for, by appealing to past experience to establish the conclusion, we have presupposed the reliability of induction.[26] Hume concluded, then, that our firm

23. Chesterton, *Orthodoxy*, 255.

24. Chesterton, *Orthodoxy*, 254; emphasis original.

25. Chesterton, *Orthodoxy*, 254.

26. For a clear explanation of this, see the chapter on Hume in *A History of Western*

belief that the future will be like the past is merely an irrational prejudice that must nevertheless be adopted (for sanity's sake).

Consider, now, how Chesterton's skepticism about causation (or at least the impersonal kind of causation that Hume had in mind)[27] grounded his acceptance of theism: Unlike Hume, who thought that without knowledge of a causal mechanism that explains the regularity of nature's behavior there could be no valid reason to count on its future regularity, Chesterton believed that there was an alternative explanation. He assumed from the outset that uniformity and repetition in nature signified life and will at the back of the universe that could be known just as one can know the mind of another person. He saw no justification for the common assumption that "if a thing goes on repeating itself it is probably dead," for it contradicts what can easily be observed. For example, he maintained that

> the variation in human affairs is generally brought into them, not by life, but by death; by the dying down or breaking off of their strength or desire. A man varies his movements because of some slight element of failure or fatigue. He gets into an omnibus because he is tired of walking; or he walks because he is tired of sitting still.[28]

Fullness of life and energy has the opposite result. "The sun rises regularly," Chesterton suggested, "because he never gets tired of rising. His routine might be due, not to a lifelessness, but to a rush of life."[29] This principle is also observed in the behavior of children: "Because children have abounding vitality, because they are in spirit fierce and free, therefore they want things repeated and unchanged. They always say, 'Do it again'; and the grown-up person does it again until he is nearly dead."[30] God, possessing that of which the vitality of a child is but a shadow, may never tire of making one kind of event follow another kind of event; as a result it is only we, blinded by the veil of familiarity, that fail to see that the workings of the world do not grow less wonderful because they are repeated; we merely

---

Philosophy: From the Pre-Socratics to Post-Modernism by C. Stephen Evans (IVP Academic, 2018), 343–45.

27. Interestingly, Chesterton's view appears to be that of the greatest of Hume's contemporaries, Thomas Reid. According to Evans, Reid dealt with Hume's arguments about causation by explaining all cases of "event causation" in terms of "agent causation." Reid thought, like Chesterton, that God was the direct cause of all regularities in nature. See Evans, *History of Western Philosophy*, 373.

28. Chesterton, *Orthodoxy*, 263.

29. Chesterton, *Orthodoxy*, 263.

30. Chesterton, *Orthodoxy*, 263.

forget to wonder. What appears to us to be dull, predictable, and repetitive is, to God (who is undoubtedly in possession of a sane mind and vital spirit), an eternal *encore* of his own creative activity. So, while Chesterton, like Hume, found nothing in experience that *necessarily* connects events that are constantly conjoined, he did have a principled reason to expect nature to behave in the future as it has in the past; he believed that God is the direct and eternal cause of nature's regularity.

MIRACLES, AGAIN

It is not hard to see why Chesterton was hesitant to attribute the dependable regularities in nature to "laws" for, in his words, "a law implies that we know the nature of the generalization and enactment; not merely that we have noticed some of the effects."[31] This is important because in Chesterton's view, while the behavior of the physical world is predictable enough for practical purposes, there is no reason to suppose that the regularity of nature is *necessary*. Thus, regarding a prediction about one kind of event following another kind of event, he said that "though we can count on it happening practically, we have no right to say that it must always happen. . . . We do not count on it; we bet on it. We risk the remote possibility of a miracle . . . not because it is a miracle, and therefore an impossibility, but because it is a miracle, and therefore an exception."[32] He concluded, then, that it is wrong to use a term like "law" to explain the workings of nature because it assumes "an inner synthesis, which we do not possess."[33] And this, Chesterton thought, was confirmation of his faith: "What Christianity says is merely this. That this repetition in Nature has its origin not in a thing resembling a law but a thing resembling a will."[34]

Hume's argument against the credibility of miracle-claims appeals to our knowledge not only of the "laws of nature," but of the extreme improbability or impossibility of their violation, which is supposedly established by past experience. But it should now be obvious that this is inconsistent with the skepticism about causation that Hume argues for later in the *Enquiry*. For Hume, causes are necessary connections that are supposed to exist between events that have been constantly conjoined in experience; similarly, a law of nature is, in Owen Barfield's words, "a something, an *x*, which binds or

31. Chesterton, *Orthodoxy*, 255.
32. Chesterton, *Orthodoxy*, 255.
33. Chesterton, *Orthodoxy*, 255.
34. Chesterton, "Miracles and Modern Civilisation."

connects otherwise discrete phenomena."[35] That *x* which represents the supposed connection between associated events (such that an event of one kind serves as sufficient condition for an event of another kind) is precisely that of which Hume is skeptical. Furthermore, the laws of nature, if there are such things, can only be known by induction; past experience with the regularity of nature's behavior implies future regularity of nature's behavior. Hume's skepticism about physical causation (and his failure to consider the alternative of agent causation) as the basis of nature's regularity led to his inability to justify induction; belief in natural laws, on Hume's own premises, is therefore untenable. Hume presents his reader with contrary lines of argument, but he cannot consistently have it both ways: He can either use "the laws of nature" as a premise in his argument against miracles, or he can maintain that skepticism of causes invalidates all inferences about the future from uniformity of past experience. In the latter case, it is important to emphasize that on his own premises, the possibility that the laws of nature will not hold is not only real, but there is no noncircular reason to suspect that they are likely to hold at all. Chesterton, on the other hand, was able to consistently believe both in the regularity and practical predictability of nature without compromising his belief that miracles can and probably do happen, and that a person can be justified in believing that they do happen on the basis of testimony. He is not forced to deny all reports of miracles but he remains free to deny those that, for non-question-begging reasons, are incredible.

BIBLIOGRAPHY

Barfield, Owen. *A Barfield Reader: Selections from the Writings of Owen Barfield*. Edited by G. B. Tennyson. Middletown, CT: Wesleyan University Press, 1999.

Chesterton, G. K. "Education by Fairy Tales." Chesterton Digital Library. https://library.chesterton.org/education-by-fairy-tales-34987/.

———. "Miracles and Modern Civilisation." The Society of G. K. Chesterton. https://www.chesterton.org/miracles-and-modern-civilisation/.

———. *Orthodoxy*. In vol. 1 of *The Collected Works of G. K. Chesterton*. San Francisco: Ignatius, 1986.

Evans, C. Stephen. *A History of Western Philosophy: From the Pre-Socratics to Post-Modernism*. Downers Grove, IL: IVP Academic, 2018.

Hume, David. *An Enquiry Concerning Human Understanding*. N.p.: Early Modern Texts, 2017. https://www.earlymoderntexts.com/assets/pdfs/hume1748.pdf.

———. *A Treatise of Human Nature*. N.p.: Early Modern Texts, 2017. https://www.earlymoderntexts.com/assets/pdfs/hume1739book1.pdf.

Lewis, C. S. *Miracles: A Preliminary Study*. San Francisco: HarperOne, 1996.

35. Owen Barfield, *A Barfield Reader: Selections from the Writings of Owen Barfield*, ed. G.B. Tennyson (Wesleyan University Press, 1999), 140; italics original.

Christianity does appeal to a solid truth outside itself; to something which is in that sense external as well as eternal. It does declare that things are really there; or in other words that things are really things—In this Christianity is at one with common sense; but all religious history shows that this common sense perishes except where there is Christianity to preserve it. It cannot otherwise exist, or at least endure, because mere thought does not remain sane. In a sense it becomes too simple to be sane. The temptation of the philosophers is simplicity rather than subtlety. They are always attracted by insane simplifications, as men poised above abysses are fascinated by death and nothingness and the empty air. It needed another kind of philosopher to stand poised upon the pinnacle of the Temple and keep his balance without casting himself down.

—"The Demons and the Philosophers," *The Everlasting Man*

All this unavoidable theory (for theory is always unavoidable) may be popularly pulled together thus. We are to regard existence as a raid or great adventure; it is to be judged, therefore, not by what calamities it encounters, but by what flag it follows and what high town it assaults. The most dangerous thing in the world is to be alive; one is always in danger of one's life. But anyone who shrinks from this is a traitor to the great scheme and experiment of being. The pessimist of the ordinary type, the pessimist who thinks he would be better dead, is blasted with the crime of Iscariot. Spiritually speaking, we should be justified in punishing him with death. Only, out of polite deference to his own philosophy, we punish him with life.

—"What Is Right with the World,"
The Apostle and the Wild Ducks

8

Transcending Pessimism and Optimism

Edward A. W. Stengel

> No man knows how much he is an optimist, even when he calls himself a pessimist, because he has not really measured the depths of his debt to whatever created him and enabled him to call himself anything. At the back of our brains, so to speak, there was a forgotten blaze or burst of astonishment at our own existence.
>
> —"How to Be a Lunatic," *Autobiography*

It is hard to imagine any two thinkers more opposed than Arthur Schopenhauer and G. K. Chesterton. As William Oddie notes, "Chesterton's distaste for Schopenhauer needs no explanation; two human beings could hardly have been more different in mind and heart."[1] Schopenhauer's famously dour, atheistic pessimism contrasts almost perfectly with Chesterton's cheerful disposition and deeply Christian philosophy, which places humility at the root of virtue and embraces gratitude as its fruit. Chesterton

1. William Oddie, *Chesterton and the Romance of Orthodoxy* (Oxford University Press, 2008), 375.

expressed contempt for Schopenhauer's pessimism on many occasions, and Schopenhauer (were he alive during Chesterton's time) would likely have returned volley with equal passion. It may therefore surprise some readers to find that there was an early period in Chesterton's life when he not only admired Schopenhauer's work, but sympathized with his worldview. In fact, while attending the Slade School of Fine Arts in London, the looming specter of pessimism, which had found its fullest and most articulate philosophical expression in Schopenhauer, played a major role in pushing young Gilbert to the edge of despair. This brief but important phase in Chesterton's development, which was memorably recorded in Chesterton's *Autobiography*, was so dark that he was tempted by what he would later consider to be the worst of all sins: suicide. Fortunately (for his sake and for the sake of the multitudes who would eventually become beneficiaries of his wisdom), Chesterton managed not only to escape the dark abyss of pessimism but also to avoid the pendulum's swing towards the ecstatic and untethered optimism of figures, like Walt Whitman, that Chesterton otherwise admired.

For Schopenhauer, pessimism was more than a negative attitude or disposition: It was a carefully articulated negation of existence itself and a reasoned defense of the thesis that suffering is the most fundamental and ineradicable feature of human life. In the course of his career, he developed and defended this thesis both through technical metaphysical arguments and also concrete, practical reflections on the human condition. The former can be found in *The World as Will and Representation*, where Schopenhauer argues (among other things) that the whole phenomenal world depends upon "will," and that all human striving, however vain it may turn out upon inspection to be, can be explained in terms of an innate, universal, and irrational "will to live," which is both the source of our life and the cause of our misery.[2] More concrete and practical reflections are expressed with great rhetorical force in a set of essays collected under the title *Studies in Pessimism*. There, Schopenhauer argues that pain and suffering are the only positive and permanent aspects of human experience. Turning the traditional Christian view on its head, Schopenhauer asserts not that suffering and evil are mere privations of pleasure and goodness, but that pleasure and goodness are themselves mere privations of suffering and evil: "Evil is just what is positive," he argued. "It makes its own existence felt. It is the good which is negative; in other words, happiness and satisfaction always imply

2. Arthur Schopenhauer, *The World as Will and Presentation*, 2 vols., ed. Jonathan Bennett (Early Modern Texts, 2017).

some desire fulfilled, some state of pain brought to an end."[3] Schopenhauer proceeds to develop this interpretation of human experience by means of reflections on a range of topics such as the contingency and finitude of human life, the transience of positive human experience, the unrelenting character of human needs, and the inevitability of boredom. Reflections on these and other topics all lead Schopenhauer to the same conclusion: "Life," he says, "is . . . a disappointment, nay, a cheat."[4]

Chesterton was at least passingly familiar with Schopenhauer's pessimistic writings by the time of his emotional and spiritual crisis at the Slade School of Art; but Schopenhauer's most pernicious influence was indirect, for he was among the principal architects of the intellectual and cultural edifice in which the London *intelligentsia* dwelt during these difficult years of Chesterton's life. For this reason, though he was an enthusiastic and skilled artist being trained at a prestigious institution, Chesterton remembered his time at the Slade as something of a single, continuous nightmare. In this atmosphere of pessimism and decadence, Chesterton became depressed, and he attempted to cope with the situation by indulging some of his baser instincts and passions: "I had an overpowering impulse," he wrote, "to record or draw horrible ideas and images; plunging in deeper and deeper as in a blind spiritual suicide."[5]

Fortunately, Chesterton's native proclivities would not be long suppressed: His rapid and terrible descent, like Dante's, turned out to be nothing more than the unhappy prelude of an ascent to new and greater heights: "When I had been for some time in these, the darkest depths of the contemporary pessimism, I had a strong inward impulse to revolt; to dislodge this incubus or throw off this nightmare."[6] In doing this, Chesterton conceived a "mystical theory" that was founded upon astonishment at the bare fact of existence. Building on this foundation, Chesterton was able to reach the conclusion that if there were anything on earth that one could be unqualifiedly grateful for, then that thing alone discredited Schopenhauer's pessimistic thesis. And once he had made up his mind, he found it shockingly easy to find occasions for sincere and unadulterated gratitude: sunsets, sunrises, rain on one's window, good cigars, and hot meals (to name a few). In light of these and other blessings, Chesterton felt more justified in rejecting the pessimist's philosophy. And this revelation led Chesterton to

3. Arthur Schopenhauer, *The Essays of Arthur Schopenhauer: Studies in Pessimism*, trans. T. Bailey Saunders (Swan Sonnenschein and Co., 1893), 11.

4. Schopenhauer, *Essays of Arthur Schopenhauer*, 14.

5. G. K. Chesterton, *The Autobiography of G. K. Chesterton* (Sheed and Ward, 1936), 89.

6. Chesterton, *Autobiography*, 89.

begin the task that would occupy much of his long career as a writer: that is, to expound a philosophy founded upon a resounding and unqualified affirmation of existence as such: "Anything," he confidently declared, "was magnificent as compared to nothing."[7]

Though he was right in rejecting pessimism, Chesterton recognized that this period of his intellectual and spiritual journey put him in danger of swinging from one insane extreme to another. While Chesterton's settled position can be accurately labeled as a kind of optimism, it was not predicated on naivety about the suffering and evil that hold pride of place in the pessimist's interpretation of experience. This belief in the ultimate good of all things, espoused in varying degrees by admirable writers like Browning, Stevenson, and Whitman, called to Chesterton as a fire calls to a man who is cold to the point of death. And though his proverbial limbs had been numbed by Schopenhauer's icy breath, he had to avoid the temptation to plunge them into the blazing fires of uncritical positivity, for one can lose their hand to both cold and fire. The naive optimist is ready and willing to love the world, but too easily succumbs to the temptation of wearing blinders that prevent full consciousness of the world they love, which is marred by the festering wounds of sin. Thus, while Chesterton's sympathies would always lay with the optimist, he saw that the truth transcends any simple dichotomy between these simplistic alternatives: "The evil of the pessimist," he argued,

> is . . . not that he chastises gods and men, but that he does not love what he chastises—he has not this primary and supernatural loyalty to things. What is the evil of the man commonly called an optimist? Obviously, it is felt that the optimist, wishing to defend the honour of this world, will defend the indefensible. He is the jingo of the universe; he will say, "My cosmos, right or wrong." He will be less inclined to the reform of things; more inclined to a sort of front-bench official answer to all attacks, soothing every one with assurances. He will not wash the world, but whitewash the world.[8]

For Chesterton, then, the truest and best attitude lay in neither extreme, nor—crucially—in a meager compromise between the two, but in a characteristically Chestertonian conjunction of extremes:

> No one doubts that an ordinary man can get on with this world: but we demand not strength enough to get on with it, but strength enough to get it on. Can he hate it enough to change it, and yet love it enough to think it worth changing? Can he look

7. Chesterton, *Autobiography*, 89.

8. G. K. Chesterton, *Orthodoxy* (Image, 1959), 68.

> up at its colossal good without once feeling acquiescence? Can he look up at its colossal evil without once feeling despair? Can he, in short, be at once not only a pessimist and an optimist, but a fanatical pessimist and a fanatical optimist? Is he enough of a pagan to die for the world, and enough of a Christian to die to it? In this combination, I maintain, it is the rational optimist who fails, the irrational optimist who succeeds. He is ready to smash the whole universe for the sake of itself.[9]

Though it may not have been his direct intention or conscious aspiration, the enormous body of work that Chesterton would produce over the coming decades stands as a magnificent counterpoint to Schopenhauer's pessimistic philosophy. And yet, the conscious aspiration may have arisen. As Chesterton notes in his *Autobiography*: "When I did begin to write, I was full of a new and fiery resolution to write against the Decadents and the Pessimists who ruled the culture of the age."[10] Thus, as Oddie observes, there is, from early on, a "theme which begins to recur in his thinking, the problem (both cultural and personal) of 'pessimism.' This became for him, almost obsessively (and for the rest of his life), one distinguishing mark of the great intellectual enemy of the times, the dragon that had to be slain."[11] It is no surprise, therefore, that one of Chesterton's earliest journalistic publications was a review of a book on Schopenhauer by Bailey Saunders. In this review (which is included as the next chapter of the present volume) Chesterton puts forward his most direct engagement with Schopenhauer's ideas.

BIBLIOGRAPHY

Chesterton, G. K. *The Autobiography of G. K. Chesterton*. New York: Sheed and Ward, 1936.

———. *Orthodoxy*. New York: Image, 1959.

Oddie, William. *Chesterton and the Romance of Orthodoxy*. Oxford: Oxford University Press, 2008.

Schopenhauer, Arthur. *The Essays of Arthur Schopenhauer: Studies in Pessimism*. Translated by T. Bailey Saunders. London: Swan Sonnenschein and Co., 1893.

———. *The World as Will and Representation*. Edited by Jonathan Bennett. N.p.: Early Modern Texts, 2017. https://earlymoderntexts.com/assets/pdfs/schopenhauer1818.pdf.

9. Chesterton, *Orthodoxy*, 71.
10. Chesterton, *Autobiography*, 91.
11. Oddie, *Chesterton and the Romance of Orthodoxy*, 101.

Obviously, it will not do to take our ideal from the principle in nature; for the simple reason that (except for some human or divine theory), there is no principle in nature. For instance, the cheap anti-democrat of to-day will tell you solemnly that there is no equality in nature. He is right, but he does not see the logical addendum. There is no equality in nature; also there is no inequality in nature. Inequality, as much as equality, implies a standard of value. To read aristocracy into the anarchy of animals is just as sentimental as to read democracy into it. Both aristocracy and democracy are human ideals: the one saying that all men are valuable, the other that some men are more valuable. But nature does not say that cats are more valuable than mice; nature makes no remark on the subject. She does not even say that the cat is enviable or the mouse pitiable. We think the cat superior because we have (or most of us have) a particular philosophy to the effect that life is better than death. But if the mouse were a German pessimist mouse, he might not think that the cat had beaten him at all. He might think he had beaten the cat by getting to the grave first. Or he might feel that he had actually inflicted frightful punishment on the cat by keeping him alive. Just as a microbe might feel proud of spreading a pestilence, so the pessimistic mouse might exult to think that he was renewing in the cat the torture of conscious existence. It all depends on the philosophy of the mouse. You cannot even say that there is victory or superiority in nature unless you have some doctrine about what things are superior. You cannot even say that the cat scores unless there is a system of scoring. You cannot even say that the cat gets the best of it unless there is some best to be got.

—"The Eternal Revolution," *Orthodoxy*

9

The Great Pessimist[1]

G. K. Chesterton

Mr. Bailey Saunders has written a very interesting study of the great father of modern pessimism. He is quite right in saying that the popularity of Schopenhauer at the present day far surpasses the popularity of any of his contemporaries in philosophy. It seems strange that the average man should exhibit so profound a desire to believe that his bread and cheese is valueless and his beer an empty show. But there can be no question, I think, that the influence of Schopenhauer over the present age is vast indeed, and I fancy that if our puritan commercialism and our new politics of violence and vanity could really be dissected, it would be found that at the root of them, as at the root of all evil, is loss of hope. A man must have some real joy in him before he can become a martyr. No high enterprise or great national sacrifice will be possible until we understand some great happiness. Even Schopenhauer must have been thoroughly happy once—when he laid down his pen after writing his eloquent essay *The Misery of Life*.

Mr. Bailey Saunders is certainly quite right in insisting on one of the great merits of Schopenhauer: that he put more faith in the artist than in the philosopher. It may be added that he himself was much more of an artist than a philosopher. The great popularity of his pessimistic philosophy with the world chiefly consists in the fact that in reading him the average man has

1. G. K. Chesterton, *The Daily News*, June 7, 1901.

the satisfaction of telling himself that he is plunging into the most portentous depths of philosophy; while he has also the pleasure of reading a most brisk and entertaining author. But Schopenhauer's finest passages are purely rhetorical. At the end of his essay on *The Metaphysics of Love*, he describes how amid all the strife and agony of life two lovers look at each other. "But why so secretly, timidly, and stealthily? Because these lovers are the truest, secretly endeavouring to perpetuate all this distress and drudgery, that otherwise would reach a timely end." A more dramatic touch in the literary sense would be difficult to imagine, it has all the energy of some scripture of the devil. But if Schopenhauer asked any sane man to believe that this really was the reason of the shyness of lovers, he was a man simply devoid of any conception of the meaning of fact or falsehood.

Schopenhauer was a poet, and he had all the advantages of that position. The poet may see only a fraction of the universe, but at least it will be a fraction of the real universe, the universe of passion and experience. A philosopher may live in a mere phantom universe, a universe of symbols and generalisations, as painted as the scenery of a pantomime. His stars and spaces are often more artificial, more the work of his own hands, than the elf-lands of the artist. All this advantage of the realism of poetry Schopenhauer had. But there goes with the mission of the poet one very serious condition. A man may put only a part of himself into piling up millions or building up empires; but he must put the whole of himself into a song. It is the fashion to say that "art is unmoral"; but in truth it is far more moral than anything else, in so far that the colour of the whole character must pass into its creations. A work of art is like a prayer; no sin must be kept back in it, or it becomes false. Thus, in the case of writers like Schopenhauer, Nietzsche, or Carlyle, who write philosophy with the impulse of poetry, we gain a right to speak of them personally and morally which we should not have with mere philosophers. To speak personally of Kant or Herbert Spencer would seem as impertinent as to complain of a street because the builder was a drunkard, or of a soap because the inventor was an atheist. But in the case of Schopenhauer, tingling all the heavens with his own tremendous mood, it is inevitable that we should speak personally. And of all men whose souls have influenced the world, Schopenhauer appears to me the most contemptible.

He never seems to have realised that what he conceived to be an audacious photograph of existence was in truth a mere nightmare induced by lack of nerve. "A thousand pleasures," he quotes, "are not worth a single torment." They are not worth it to cowards; but that they are worth it and more to ordinary men, climbing, fighting, and a hundred other things demonstrate. In his most famous essay, "The Misery of Life," he moans that "every satisfied wish begets a new one," which seems to me the definition of happiness. But Schopenhauer had not the nervous energy to wish properly, far less to pursue his wish. He conceived, with all the ignorance of an anchorite criticising the world, that men's happiness, if it existed, would consist in the attainment of pleasure, and that effort was merely a heavy price that was paid for it. He did not understand that of all earthly things desire is the most desirable. To this truth even pessimism bears witness: it is not the satisfactions of youth, but its hungers, that the Byronic poet regrets. Schopenhauer positively complains of the fact that the heart has "a bottomless abyss," as if to find a bottom to it would not be the end of all human hope. In the same way, men speak of the awfulness of the idea of infinite space, as if the discovery of a place where space ended would not be too horrible for the brain to bear.

The whole of Schopenhauer's accusation against existence comes back, therefore, to a mere matter of artistic taste: he hated the stars as some men hate the smell of hawthorn. Change the mental attitude to a humbler and more alert one, and every one of his philosophical inferences becomes inconclusive. "The present is for ever unsatisfactory, the future uncertain, the past irrevocable." This he urges as a reason for taking refuge in the cloister of philosophy from the horrors of the will to live. But to a man of heart (as the French say) that the present is unsatisfactory is its glory: if we are never satisfied we are never sated: the words are even derivatively the same. That the future is uncertain is its glory: no one could endure to live in a world in which the future was certain. It is not the false prophets who should be stoned, but the true ones. That the past is irrevocable is its glory: no mountain of marble is so strong as the broken loves and hopes that death has made immortal. But this vision of the richness of life is only given to brave and ordinary men. It would be difficult to conceive a more pitiful figure than is cut by the philosopher striving to preach retreat to soldiers who will not listen, and offering to dry the tears of victims who will not weep.

Another defect which arises from the dominantly-aesthetic character of Schopenhauer's philosophy is his extraordinarily illogical method of argument. The reader is at last quite bewildered by the way in which the pessimistic serpent eats its own tail. Take an instance at random. "If life itself were a valuable possession and decidedly preferable to non-existence, the gate need not be occupied by such terrible guards as death and its terrors." Existence must be evil, it seems, because we are kept out of death, which would be our greatest happiness. And why would death be our greatest happiness? Because existence is an evil. In other words, Schopenhauer has to assume that there is a curious kind of diabolical providence in order to prove that there is one. Again, he says: "But who would persevere in life if death were less frightful?" There are scores of quite painless forms of death;

and painless death we have all known for an eternity before our birth. If we shrink from it, it is not because it is frightful, but because it is the end of an experience which we value. It is not a question of who would endure life if death were really tolerable, but of who would fear death if life were really intolerable. Sometimes Schopenhauer makes up for the lack of reasons by sheer bullying. "It is as clear as day," he vociferates, "that if each one of us could have previously inspected the gift, we should have declined it." I wonder how clear day was to Schopenhauer.

When Schopenhauer declares that all good and happiness is an illusion, it is difficult to see what he can mean. Sport or wine or friendship are no more and no less illusions than the toothache. And here, strangely enough, Schopenhauer fails ultimately in imagination. He had not that highest order of imagination which can see the things which surround us on every side with purified and primitive eyes. Had he possessed this he would have felt, as we all dimly feel, that a child unborn offered the chance and risk of so vivid and magical an experience as existence could no more resist taking it than a living child could resist opening a cupboard in which, he was told, were toys of which he could not even dream. He did not realise that the question of whether life contains a preponderance of joy or of sorrow is entirely secondary to the fact that life is an experience of a unique and miraculous character, the idea of missing which would be intolerable if it were for one moment conceivable. He made the old mistake of the sages in conceiving of being as an ancient thing, going on heavily age after age, whereas it and all its ages are one divine and dazzling experiment as dramatic as a display of fireworks.

I had tried to be happy by telling myself that man is an animal, like any other which sought its meat from God. But now I really was happy, for I had learnt that man is a monstrosity. I had been right in feeling all things as odd, for I myself was at once worse and better than all things. The optimist's pleasure was prosaic, for it dwelt on the naturalness of everything; the Christian pleasure was poetic, for it dwelt on the unnaturalness of everything in the light of the supernatural. The modern philosopher had told me again and again that I was in the right place, and I had still felt depressed even in acquiescence. But I had heard that I was in the *wrong* place, and my soul sang for joy, like a bird in spring. The knowledge found out and illuminated forgotten chambers in the dark house of infancy. I knew now why grass had always seemed to me as queer as the green beard of a giant, and why I could feel homesick at home.

—"The Flag of the World," *Orthodoxy*

If people must not be taught religion, they might be taught reason, philosophy. If the State must not teach them to pray it might teach them to think. And when I say that children should be taught to think I do not mean (like many moderns) that they should be taught to doubt; for the two processes are not only not the same, but are in many ways opposite. To doubt is only to destroy; to think is to create.

—*The Daily News*, June 22, 1907

10

Manalive Through a Kierkegaardian Lens

Joe Grabowski

CHESTERTON'S NOVEL *MANALIVE* ELUDES easy summation. Ostensibly, it is a simple, lighthearted story about how the lives of four young people residing in a London lodging house are upended by the arrival of Innocent Smith, one of the most memorable and enigmatic characters in all of literature. When concerns arise about Smith's quixotic antics and mysterious past, he is subjected to an *ad hoc* trial on the premises, eventually being cleared of all charges.

On a deeper level, Chesterton's narrative deliberately mirrors the careers of Socrates, and even of Christ himself: An innocent man is accused by the authorities of corrupting his young followers and stirring up rebellion with his dangerous and unconventional doctrines. On another level, the story's thematic concerns—the maladies afflicting the lives of the young people and Smith's dramatic prescriptive cures—parallel both the spiritual ills and philosophical remedies presented in the works of a man who was himself a kind of modern Socrates: the so-called "gadfly of Denmark," Søren Aabye Kierkegaard.

Though there is no evidence that Chesterton had heard of Kierkegaard, there is a striking resonance between Chesterton's philosophy and that of the man sometimes heralded as the father of existentialism. As merely one demonstration of the potential fruitfulness of reading Chesterton in a Kierkegaardian light, I will offer a comparative thematic interpretation of *Manalive*.

NO ILL WIND—AGENCY, SELFHOOD, AND THE ESCAPE FROM DESPAIR

As is typical in many novels, the opening chapter of *Manalive* deals chiefly with introducing the story's main characters. Less typical is the arrival of Innocent Smith, who is not introduced at all: He is just suddenly *there*.[1] The chapter is entitled, "How the Great Wind Came to Beacon House," and Smith is indeed presented to the reader as a personification of that same "Great Wind."

Chesterton worked hard to ensure that his reader does not miss this Pentecostal symbolism of spiritual revival. The book's final chapter, following the remarkable transformations that Smith has wrought in the lives of four young proteges, is called "How the Great Wind Went from Beacon House." We see here not only an *inclusio* hearkening back to the beginning, but a significance in the phrasing: The Great Wind does not *leave* Beacon House; it simply *goes* from it. The Wind is no longer in and with Smith alone, but shared by those transformed through their encounters with him.

Just prior to Smith's arrival on the scene, the Beacon House residents are puzzling over an enigmatic telegram from Smith, containing a single phrase which is redolent of the book's title: "Man found alive with two legs." At this point in the story, neither the characters—nor, indeed, the reader—can make heads or tails of this cryptic phrase. "The message is clearly insane," says Dr. Warner—and we are inclined to agree. After all, as Warner points out, "Even a baby does not expect to find a man with three legs."[2] Yet the point of Smith's message has nothing to do with the expectedness or unexpectedness of a man being found with two or any other number of legs; rather, it is about how remarkable certain unremarkable facts can be. The most remarkable, the most decidedly unexpected thing, is a man—any man—being found *alive*.

Here we find our first resonance with Kierkegaard. In *Sickness unto Death*, "Anti-Climacus" (Kierkegaard's pseudonym) presents selfhood as a

1. Later in the story, one character is depicted noticing the initials on Smith's luggage: "I.S." No comment is made to suggest significance to these initials other than the obvious—i.e., that they stand for "Innocent Smith"—yet Chesterton deliberately drawing the reader's attention to the coincidence with the fundamental verb of being (and the revealed name of Almighty in the Hebrew Scriptures) is significant indeed. G. K. Chesterton, *Manalive* (Thomas Nelson, 1912), 47.

2. Chesterton, *Manalive*, 23.

jeopardy: not merely a given state, but rather a *task of striving*, to be negotiated amidst the universal condition of "despair."[3] The work of the individual is to locate itself both in relation to itself and as a "synthesis" wherein actuality and potentiality, infinity and finitude, interact.[4] According to the Anti-Climacus, the self comes to be fully actualized when, "in relating itself to itself and in willing to be itself . . . [it] rests transparently in the power that established it."[5] Paradoxically, the best catalyst for this self-realization or self-actualization is the very thing that can stymie it: *despair*. Despair motivates and challenges; it is both "an excellence and a defect."[6] There are many forms this "sickness unto death" can take, but among them is "weakness": the "despair not to will to be oneself. Or even lower: in despair not to will to be a self. Or lowest of all: in despair to will to be someone else, to wish for a new self."[7]

It is significant that in *Manalive* the first "character" introduced with any sense of agency does not appear as a "self" at all, but rather as the "Great Wind," described in notably anthropomorphic terms. Other characters subsequently presented, namely the lodgers and guests at Beacon House, are depicted as passive, literally "wind-swept" people being blown about, listless and despairing in the Kierkegaardian sense: "[Their] despair is only a suffering, a succumbing to the pressure of external factors; in no way does it come from within as an act."[8] Just as they are physically moved by the Wind, the precursor of Smith himself, so even their very conversation is dominated by him, revolving around his enigmatic telegram. Even before he arrives physically on the scene, the book's *dramatis personae* are dominated by *his* agency: he is already the one and only true "self" in the book, the only man truly *alive*.

Chesterton's description of Arthur Inglewood, one of the young tenants, aptly captures this contrast with Smith. Inglewood is a creature of passivity

3. Cf. Søren Kierkegaard, *The Sickness unto Death: A Christian Psychological Exposition for Upbuilding and Awakening*, eds. and trans. Howard Hong and Edna Hong (Princeton University Press, 1983), 13–14; 22. The concepts of "the self," "the individual," "the single individual," etc., are themselves multifaceted and complex ideas within Kierkegaard's works. When these terms are used in this essay, they are used in a standard English sense and not as special categories unless specifically noted. For a deeper understanding of the Kierkegaardian usage of these terms in distinction from one another, see his *Concluding Unscientific Postscript*.

4. Kierkegaard, *Sickness unto Death*, 14–17.

5. Kierkegaard, *Sickness unto Death*, 14.

6. Kierkegaard, *Sickness unto Death*, 14.

7. Kierkegaard, *Sickness unto Death*, 52–53.

8. Kierkegaard, *Sickness unto Death*, 51.

and despair in the form of "weakness," particularly regarding his frustrated and abandoned love for Diana Duke, the young heiress of the house:

> Long since the pulverising rationalism of his friend Dr. Warner had crushed [his] youthful ignorances and disproportionate dreams. Under the Warnerian scepticism and science of hopeless human types, Inglewood had long come to regard himself as *a timid, insufficient, and "weak" type*, who would never marry; to regard Diana Duke as a materialistic maid-servant; and to regard his first fancy for her as the small, dull farce of a collegian kissing his landlady's daughter.[9]

Inglewood cannot actualize his own agency; he needs the spur of Smith's activity after bounding onto the scene. Inglewood needs to be motivated first to recognize his despair, and then to be goaded by that recognition into deeper self-realization. This need to be moved by external force chimes closely with the description of despair-as-weakness in *Sickness unto Death*: "Now something *happens* that impinges . . . upon this immediate self and *makes it despair*. . . . Since the self has no reflection, there must be an external motivation for the despair, and the despair is nothing more than submitting."[10] Recalling that despair is both "excellence and defect," here we see the self presented as moving through stages of despair, from the first weakness of not willing/realizing selfhood to a later (though still, in Kierkegaardian terms, despairing) striving to become a self.[11] This movement happens when a self is "acted upon" from the outside, no longer despairing, in weakness, *not* to be a self, but now rather in defiance "to will to be oneself."[12] Inglewood—indeed all the young residents of Beacon House—are moved precisely thus by Smith, who forces them first to face their lack of agency and then to engage actively in upbuilding self-realization.

The complete curative course is a paradoxical one—fittingly enough, as both Kierkegaard and Chesterton are famous for their love of paradox. Becoming a self in Anti-Climacian terms involves both assertion and abnegation, not accidentally the very same paradoxical combination at the heart of the Christian life: "Whosoever will save his life shall lose it" (Matt 16:25). As Anti-Climacus notes: "The opposite to being in despair is to have faith. Therefore, the formula set forth above . . . is also the formula for faith."[13] Fit-

9. Chesterton, *Manalive*, 49; emphasis added.

10. Kierkegaard, *Sickness unto Death*, 51.

11. See Kierkegaard, *Sickness unto Death*, 49–74.

12. Kierkegaard, *Sickness unto Death*, 67; cf. 70.

13. Kierkegaard, *Sickness unto Death*, 49. The "formula" to which he refers is the very same already quoted: "In relating itself to itself and in willing to be itself, the self

tingly, then, the four youths of Beacon House chart their paths to authentic selfhood not *individually*, but only in *relation*. The four solitary individuals become two couples by the end of the book. Such other-relatedness is vitally necessary because a self ultimately only fully actualizes resting in relation to one particular "Other" who is "the power that established [the self]." By the end of the book, Inglewood and Diana have not only found one another in romance—they have also under Smith's tutelage taken the first steps toward truly finding themselves.

MANY WEDDINGS, ONE WIFE—THE EXPERIMENTAL REPETITIONS OF INNOCENCE

The crisis that forms the main plot of *Manalive* occurs toward the end of the first part of the book. Innocent Smith attempts (seemingly) to shoot the psychologist, Dr. Warner. Though shaken, he is not altogether surprised. It turns out that Warner had brought another man of science with him, the criminologist Dr. Pym, to try to apprehend Smith, whom they have discovered by research into his past to be "one of the most cruel and terrible of the enemies of humanity."[14]

The whole second part of the book is the trial at Beacon House, inquiring into the many alleged crimes of Innocent Smith. The first set of these involves several charges of attempted murder, recalling the crime allegedly witnessed in the house involving Dr. Warner. Smith's first "attempted murder" had seen him brandishing the very same revolver at yet another academic, a morose and nihilistic philosopher. Yet, as the cross-examination of evidence reveals, Smith's intention then, as in the latest instance, was not murderous, but life-giving. Indeed, the nihilistic professor had received it as such: he had been shocked from his obsession with death by being confronted with its real prospect. Smith had furthermore avowed to the professor after that earlier affair his motive for all such future "crimes": "I am going to hold a pistol to the head of the Modern Man. But I shall not use it to kill him—only to bring him to life."[15] Smith is again presented as the "external motivation for the despair" spurring self-discovery.[16] However, the remainder of his crimes involve another Kierkegaardian concept: *repetition*.

In *Repetition*, pseudonymous author Constantin Constantius calls the title concept a "new category," which he offers as a building upon the

rests transparently in the power that established it" (14).

14. Chesterton, *Manalive*, 117.

15. Chesterton, *Manalive*, 226.

16. Kierkegaard, *Sickness unto Death*, 51.

work of the ancient Greek philosophers and as an alternative fundamental dialectic to the one proffered by Hegel.[17] Constantius fails to give a concise definition, but the general idea is that repetition explains and gives meaning to a universe in which there is motion/change and yet substantial being/identity, not by mediating between the two but joining them in the experience of the single individual. He writes: "The dialectic of repetition is easy, for that which is repeated has been—otherwise it could not be repeated—but the very fact that it has been makes the repetition into something new. When the Greeks said that all knowing is recollecting, they said that all existence, which is, has been; when one says that life is a repetition, one says: actuality, which has been, now comes into existence."[18] As another way of distinguishing between the Greeks' recollection (*anamnesis*) and the new category of repetition, Constantius explains: "Repetition and recollection are *the same movement*, except in opposite directions, for what is recollected has been, is repeated backward, whereas genuine *repetition is recollected forward*. Repetition, therefore, if it is possible, makes a person happy, whereas recollection makes him unhappy."[19] As with most of the chief concepts in Kierkegaard's writings, repetition is about the tension and interplay in the composite human experience (or the "synthesis" of the self) between forces finite and infinite, temporal and eternal.[20] Thus, while there are vast metaphysical and religious implications, these are primarily explored and investigated through questions of the ethical and the practical, a main question being whether there can be true repetition outside of eternity. The book offers two perspectives on this question, Constantius' own and those of an anonymous young friend reporting on his experiments with repetition through a series of letters.[21]

17. Søren Kierkegaard, *Fear and Trembling / Repetition*, eds. and trans. Howard Hong and Edna Hong (Princeton University Press, 1992), 148–49.

18. Kierkegaard, *Repetition*, 149.

19. Kierkegaard, *Repetition*, 131; emphasis added. Regarding "if it is possible," see 331n below.

20. See Kierkegaard, *Sickness unto Death*, 13.

21. Paradoxically, Constantius himself seems to conclude that actual repetition is impossible in practice, based on his own investigations (see Kierkegaard, *Repetition*, 172–76; 186); yet, he is primarily concerned with reporting the positive experiments of the young man, his friend, and in Constantius' own final letter to the reader, he commends the young man's experience as the real content of his book (see 225–31). As for Kierkegaard himself, in his journals and papers he reports that he finds repetition "everywhere," but explains that Constantius could not get further because he was unreligious, whereas "'Repetition' is and remains a religious category. . . . Eternity is indeed the true repetition." (326–27).

Innocent Smith is Chesterton's version of that same young man, vigorously carrying out a program of experiments in repetition. Even in the case of attempted murder (which we might actually call attempted "*un*-murder") it is noteworthy that he has made *repeated* forays of his peculiar praxis. But in the remaining alleged crimes—burglary, desertion, and polygamy—the concept of repetition is even more concretely evidenced. In the first case, the trial at Beacon House reveals that the house into which Smith had led an accomplice via the chimney in a break-in was, in fact, Smith's own. When his accomplice (comically, a clergyman) protested at Smith's drinking the wine in the house, Smith, with a deep but unregistered irony, replied that it would do the owner of the house good. The clergyman then asked whether Smith knew the owner and whether he somehow approved of Smith's actions. Smith's cryptic reply is deeply meaningful, seen through the lens of *repetition*: "I am always trying to find him—to catch him unawares. I come in through skylights and trapdoors to find him; but whenever I find him—he is doing what I am doing."[22] Smith gives a remarkably similar explanation when, finally, the clergyman and he are interrupted by the lady of the house whom Smith introduces as his wife: "'I know there's a fellow called Smith,' [Smith] said in his rather weird way, 'living in one of the tall houses in this terrace. I know he is really happy, and yet I can never catch him at it.'"[23]

Smith here is clearly operating in the tension between recollection and repetition. He finds a contrast between his current relation to his home and possessions and the early joy and wonder of them (recollection); so, he endeavors to rediscover them anew by treating them as another man's possessions so that he can have the joy again of coming into ownership (repetition). In other words, he brings the content of the past into the present via "the same movement" so that he might not merely fondly remember but *recapitulate* the earlier experience.[24]

Smith's other alleged crimes essentially follow the same pattern. His "desertion" of his wife was undertaken to circumnavigate the globe, to see as much as possible of the world outside his home so that he might see his own home from a fresh perspective.[25] As Smith paradoxically explains, "It was not the house that grew dull, but *I that grew dull in it.* My wife was better than all women, and yet *I could not feel it*. . . . I am a man who left his own house because he could no longer bear to be away from it. . . . I

22. Chesterton, *Manalive*, 276–77.

23. Chesterton, *Manalive*, 285.

24. Cf. Kierkegaard, *Repetition*, 131.

25. Chesterton, *Manalive*, 291–338.

have become a pilgrim to cure myself of being an exile."[26] And the charge of polygamy, it turns out, resulted from him placing his wife into various strange lodgings (including Beacon House) under false names, in order that he could seek her out and woo her again as though she were a stranger.[27] As Michael Moon summarizes for the defense: "Innocent Smith has had many wooings, and many weddings for all I know; but he has had only one wife. . . . It is just because he does not want to commit adultery that he achieves the romance of sex; it is just because he loves one wife that he has a hundred honeymoons."[28] Many weddings, one wife: whatever Constantine Constantius might say, Smith discovered, like Constantius' young friend, that repetition is really possible.

INMATES IN THE ASYLUM—THE ANXIOUS AND THE BORED

I have already observed that the condition of the young people at Beacon House, before the irruption of Innocent Smith, is deeply redolent of what Kierkegaard meant by "despair." However, there are definite indications of the prevalence of two other spiritual diseases that Kierkegaard diagnosed, namely *anxiety* and *ennui*.[29]

Anxiety

In *The Concept of Anxiety* by the pseudonymous author "Vigilius Haufniensis," the title condition (sometimes alternatively known as *dread* or *angst*) is the "*discrimen* [ambiguity] of subjectivity."[30] It is a condition brought about in the tension between human freedom and the indeterminacy of the future, when an individual actualizes potential through their choices,

26. Chesterton, *Manalive*, 309; 327–28; emphasis added.

27. Chesterton, *Manalive*, 339–75.

28. Chesterton, *Manalive*, 367; 372–73.

29. Both concepts have been translated from Kierkegaard's original in various ways. For the former, "anxiety" has sometimes been rendered "angst" or "dread," and all are equally familiar. In the case of the latter, "boredom" seems more standard; yet, owing to the popular resonance of "*ennui*," especially for those familiar with later, especially French, existentialist writers, I have preferred here the less common translation.

30. Søren Kierkegaard, *The Concept of Anxiety: A Simple Psychologically Orienting Deliberation on the Dogmatic Issue of Hereditary Sin*, eds. and trans. Reidar Thomte and Albert B. Anderson (Princeton University Press, 1980), 197.

and thus faces the possibility of making the wrong choice (i.e., sinning).[31] Again, we can see the pattern of the subjective experience of a self who is a "synthesis" grappling here at the "border" of being and nonbeing.[32] The book discusses this notion in several different aspects, but the one particularly relevant to the present discussion is that of "inclosing reserve."[33] This, for Haufniensis, is a form of "unfreedom" that anxiety can bring about when an individual adopts certain routines that provide an illusion of "continuity" (or a "pseudocontinuity"), but really succumbs to a life of "suddenness" and *dis*continuity because the individual refuses to relate to that which is outside itself.[34] This kind of unfreedom, Haufniensis observes, "manifests itself in hypochondria, *in capriciousness*."[35]

At Beacon House, this is exemplified in the household manager, Diana Duke. Her introduction is significant: She is described as "one of the most *prosaic and practical* creatures alive."[36] Later, the narrator again notes that "nothing . . . could be more prosaic and *impenetrable* than the domestic energies of Miss Diana Duke."[37] The strenuousness with which Duke maintains domestic order and routine is a perfect example of the paradoxical anxiety-born "continuity" that is really "capriciousness":

> The whole house revolved on her as on a rod of steel. It would be wrong to say that she commanded; for her own efficiency was so impatient that she obeyed herself before anyone else obeyed her. Before electricians could mend a bell or locksmiths open a door, before dentists could pluck a loose tooth or butlers draw a tight cork, it was done already with the silent violence of her slim hands. She was light; but there was nothing leaping about her lightness. She spurned the ground, and she meant to spurn

31. Kierkegaard, *Concept of Anxiety*, 41–44. For Haufniensis, anxiety is the condition prior to the determination set in motion by a choice, which comes from the fact that the actual self ("something") is forced into relation to that which is not yet (i.e., "nothing"): The paradox is that "something" *cannot* relate to "nothing" and, hence, an experience of anxiety or existential dread.

32. Cf. Kierkegaard, *Concept of Anxiety*, 90–91; see also 196–97. "Border" is another translation of *discrimens* which captures a different shade of the rich meaning here.

33. See Kierkegaard, *Concept of Anxiety*, 123.

34. Kierkegaard, *Concept of Anxiety*, 129–30.

35. Kierkegaard, *Concept of Anxiety*, 124; emphasis added. The connection of these two states may not be obvious at first, but both conditions involve a willfulness of a state of affairs cut off from external forces. The individual asserts a reality rather than confront and choose between real possibilities.

36. Chesterton, *Manalive*, 13; emphasis added.

37. Chesterton, *Manalive*, 66; emphasis added.

> it. People talk of the pathos and failure of plain women; but it is a more terrible thing that a beautiful woman may succeed in everything but womanhood.[38]

Equally significant and resonant here is the clear connection to Duke's femininity. According to Haufniensis, "Woman is more anxious than man." In illustration of this, he invites a thought experiment remarkably ahead of its time, invoking what later scholars would come to term the "male gaze": "Picture an innocent young girl; let a man fasten his desirous glance upon her, and she becomes anxious."[39] In *Manalive*, the crisis point for Diana Duke's anxiety is precisely bound up with the mysterious and complex relation of the sexes and the fact that she "succeed[s] in everything but womanhood." When Innocent Smith proposes to a maid in the house (not yet revealed to be his wife) and Michael Moon then proposes to Rosamund Hunt, the circumstances drive Duke to tears, which is as unexpected as "seeing a motorcar shedding tears of petrol."[40] The narrative subtly conveys the complex psychology behind this breakdown. Duke's tears are not due to sadness at being left out, but rather from a fear of being included, from being drawn out from her "inclosing reserve." She is also upset to see her well-managed household descending into a kind of Dionysian madness of romances.

Chesterton's resolution to the crisis might be found unbelievable, even offensive, to some modern readers. For the present discussion, however, this is beside the point: what is noteworthy here is how closely the resolution tracks against the Kierkegaardian category of the "unfreedom" of "inclosing reserve." Inglewood first seeks to console Diana about the domestic problems Smith is creating, all in vain. The curative comes only when he first forces Duke to accept her immediate weakness, abandoning her self-assertion and determined "continuity"; and then proposes marriage to her, drawing her out of routine and making her reckon a choice between real possibilities.[41] What else may be said about the scene, justly or otherwise, about its realism and appropriateness or the lack thereof—these things can be left for other commentators. However, it works (or doesn't work) as an account of the sensitive matter of the relation between the sexes, it functions very well as an illustration of the Kierkegaardian notion of anxiety.

38. Chesterton, *Manalive*, 14–15.

39. Kierkegaard, *Concept of Anxiety*, 66–67.

40. Chesterton, *Manalive*, 99.

41. Chesterton, *Manalive*, 99–100.

Ennui

Ennui, or boredom, is perhaps the most widespread existential malaise, frequently subject to memes and parodies; yet it never was a central point for Kierkegaard nor for most other major philosophers considered existentialists. Perhaps its pop culture prominence comes rather from the remembered experience of undergraduates reading Sartre than from the actual content of that reading. The notion is thus more inchoate than other major themes, and even difficult to distinguish as a *per se* condition instead of a mild form of "despair." Even so, it is important in the Kierkegaardian presentation of the aesthetic mode or stage of life, particularly in the writings of the young "*A*" in *Either/Or*.

A characterizes *ennui* as "the root of all evil,"[42] as well as being practically a universal condition: "All human beings . . . are boring."[43] Yet, he distinguishes between the "person who bores others" and "someone who bores himself," the former being "the plebians, the crowd, the endless train of humanity" and the minority being "the chosen ones, the nobility" who "bore themselves [but] entertain others."[44] *A*, not without a hint of presumption, places himself among the latter group.

Ensconced in the aesthetical life, *A* combats *ennui* by a method he analogously calls "the rotation of crops," which, he explains, "does not consist in changing the soil but, like proper crop rotation, consists in changing the method of cultivation and the kinds of crops."[45] Crucial to *A*'s approach is a *willful forgetfulness*: one avoids becoming bored really by approaching everything with a light and carefree detachment. *A* even counsels against friendship and marriage as attachments preventing such forgetful ambivalence.[46] It is easy to see how this approach to life could be mistaken with despair; it recalls the cynical maxim attributed to Alexander Pope: "Blessed is he who expects nothing, for he shall never be disappointed." Indeed, there is in the background of *A*'s philosophy a listless sourness of experience reminiscent of some popular forms of nihilism in the nineteenth century.

42. Søren Kierkegaard, *Either/Or: Part I*, eds. and trans. Howard Hong and Edna Hong (Princeton University Press, 1987), 291.

43. Kierkegaard, *Either/Or*, 288.

44. Kierkegaard, *Either/Or*, 288.

45. Kierkegaard, *Either/Or*, 292.

46. Kierkegaard, *Either/Or*, 294–99. Notably, *A*'s philosophy is a sort of precursor to the more mature experimentations of the young man in *Repetition* and the far more advanced exercises of resignation advanced by Johannes de Silentio in *Fear and Trembling*. The "moves" involved in each of the Kierkegaardian "stages"—the aesthetical, the ethical, and the religious—are in fact very similar to one another, like fractal patterns seen from a synoptic level of resolution.

Consider *A*'s "ecstatic discourse" from whence the book gets its name: "Marry, and you will regret it. Do not marry, and you will also regret it. Marry or do not marry, *you will regret it either way*. . . . Hang yourself, and you will regret it. Do not hang yourself, and you will also regret it. . . . Whether you hang yourself or do not hang yourself, *you will regret it either way*. This, gentlemen, is the quintessence of all the wisdom of life."[47]

A's counterpart in Beacon House is Michael Moon: "An obscure and flippant journalist" who "had once been hazily supposed to be reading for the Bar," though "it was mostly at another kind of bar that his friends found him. . . . He shared that strange trick of all men of his type, intellectual and without ambition—the trick of going about with his mental inferiors."[48] Moon particularly favors one such companion whose "vitality and vulgarity amused Michael so much that he went round with him from bar to bar, like the owner of a performing monkey."[49] In other words, Moon is very much of *A*'s "nobility," boring himself but entertaining others. This exchange between Moon and Inglewood captures this paradoxical condition well:

> "Inglewood," said Michael Moon, "have you ever heard that I am a blackguard?"
>
> "I haven't heard it, and I don't believe it," answered Inglewood, after an odd pause. "But I have heard that you were—what they call rather wild."
>
> "If you have heard that I am wild, you can contradict the rumour," said Moon, with an extraordinary calm; "I am tame. I am quite tame; I am about the tamest beast that crawls. I drink too much of the same kind of whisky at the same time every night. I even drink about the same amount too much. I go to the same number of public-houses. I meet the same damned women with mauve faces. I hear the same number of dirty stories—generally the same dirty stories. You may assure my friends, Inglewood, that you see before you a person whom civilization has thoroughly tamed."[50]

Later in the story, during a conversation with his beloved Rosamund Hunt, the intensity of Moon's *ennui* and "tameness" comes powerfully to the surface. Again, Moon mirrors *A* in his depth of perception and elite intelligence; he seems not only to grasp his own condition, but that of everyone in the household. Hunt, amused by Innocent Smith's antics, provokes Moon by

47. Kierkegaard, *Either/Or*, 38–39; emphasis added.

48. Chesterton, *Manalive*, 19–20.

49. Chesterton, *Manalive*, 20.

50. Chesterton, *Manalive*, 55–56.

suggesting that Smith should be locked up in an asylum. "I don't think it's at all necessary," Moon replies. "He is in one now. . . . Why, didn't you know?"[51]

When Rosamund protests in shock, Moon goes on:

> "I'm sorry," he continued, with a sort of harsh humility. "Of course we don't talk about it much . . . but I thought we all really knew . . . Beacon House is a certain rather singular sort of house—a house with the tiles loose, shall we say? Innocent Smith is only the doctor that visits us." . . .
>
> "You daren't say such a thing!" cried Rosamund in a rage. "You daren't suggest that I—"
>
> "Not more than I am," said Michael soothingly; "not more than the rest of us. Haven't you ever noticed that Miss Duke never sits still—a notorious sign? Haven't you ever observed that Inglewood is always washing his hands—a known mark of mental disease? I, of course, am a dipsomaniac."
>
> "I don't believe you," broke out his companion, not without agitation. "I've heard you had some bad habits—"
>
> "All habits are bad habits," said Michael, with deadly calm. "Madness does not come by breaking out, but by giving in; by settling down in some dirty, little, self-repeating circle of ideas; by being tamed."[52]

Confronted with the realization of his "madness" of unamused amusement, Moon does finally decide to "break out." Almost immediately following this exchange, during which he called her a lunatic, he proposes marriage to Rosamund.

In an early journalistic essay, when Chesterton was still very much a new, up-and-coming figure in Fleet Street, he wrote: "Of one thing l am certain, that the age needs, first and foremost, to be startled; to be taught the nature of wonder. It is the extraordinary peculiarity of cities that they produce things more astonishing than the world has ever known before, and yet are not astonished; that they work marvels and do not marvel at them."[53] This certainty and the preoccupation to which it gave rise remained throughout Chesterton's entire writing career. Whether it is in his own voice through his

51. Chesterton, *Manalive*, 82.

52. Chesterton, *Manalive*, 82–84.

53. G. K. Chesterton, "That Black Is White," *Black & White* (London), February 14, 1903, The British Newspaper Archive, https://www.britishnewspaperarchive.co.uk/viewer/bl/0004617/19030214/024/0008.

many nonfiction works, or through fictional mouthpieces from Innocent Smith to Father Brown, he is continually calling contemporary man to turn about, to stand up astonished at the profound gift of existence, even if that standing up means, paradoxically, standing on one's head.

This philosophical project, along with the mechanisms of paradox and humor with which he engaged it, cannot help but resonate with any reader familiar with the work and legacy of Søren Kierkegaard. The latter notes, through Anti-Climacus in *The Sickness unto Death*, that "the greatest hazard of all, losing the *self*, can occur very quietly in the world, as if it were nothing at all. No other loss can occur so quietly; any other loss—an arm, a leg, five dollars, a wife, etc.—is sure to be noticed."[54] It is indeed easy to take notice, even to be astonished, at a man who has lost a leg. For Kierkegaard and Chesterton alike, the more difficult and important task is rather to be astounded each and every day at finding, in one's neighbor or even in one's self, the man with two legs, and that man *alive*.

BIBLIOGRAPHY

Chesterton, G. K. *Manalive*. London: Thomas Nelson and Sons, 1912.

———. "That Black Is White."

Kierkegaard, Søren. *The Concept of Anxiety: A Simple Psychologically Orienting Deliberation on the Dogmatic Issue of Hereditary Sin*. Edited and translated by Reidar Thomte and Albert B. Anderson. Princeton: Princeton University Press, 1980.

———. *Concluding Unscientific Postscript to Philosophical Fragments*. Edited and translated by Howard V. Hong and Edna H. Hong. Princeton: Princeton University Press, 1992.

———. *Either/Or: Part I*. Edited and translated by Howard V. Hong and Edna H. Hong. Princeton: Princeton University Press, 1987.

———. *Fear and Trembling* and *Repetition*. Edited and translated by Howard V. Hong and Edna H. Hong. Princeton: Princeton University Press, 1992.

———. *The Sickness unto Death: A Christian Psychological Exposition for Upbuilding and Awakening*. Edited and translated by Howard V. Hong and Edna H. Hong. Princeton: Princeton University Press, 1983.

54. Kierkegaard, *Sickness unto Death*, 32–33; emphasis added.

Nietzsche, as every one knows, preached a doctrine which he and his followers regard apparently as very revolutionary; he held that ordinary altruistic morality had been the invention of a slave class to prevent the emergence of superior types to fight and rule them. Now, modern people, whether they agree with this or not, always talk of it as a new and unheard-of idea. It is calmly and persistently supposed that the great writers of the past, say Shakespeare for instance, did not hold this view, because they had never imagined it; because it had never come into their heads. Turn up the last act of Shakespeare's *Richard III* and you will find not only all that Nietzsche had to say put into two lines, but you will find it put in the very words of Nietzsche. Richard Crookback says to his nobles:

Conscience is but a word that cowards use,
Devised at first to keep the strong in awe.

As I have said, the fact is plain. Shakespeare had thought of Nietzsche and the Master Morality; but he weighed it at its proper value and put it in its proper place. Its proper place is the mouth of a half-insane hunchback on the eve of defeat. This rage against the weak is only possible in a man morbidly brave but fundamentally sick; a man like Richard, a man like Nietzsche. This case alone ought to destroy the absurd fancy that these modern philosophies are modern in the sense that the great men of the past did not think of them. They thought of them; only they did not think much of them. It was not that Shakespeare did not see the Nietzsche idea; he saw it, and he saw through it.

—"On Reading," *The Common Man*

11

Thus Spake Chesterton

Ted Janiszewski

What I don't at all care for in that Jesus of Nazareth or his apostle Paul is that they *put so much into the heads of little people*, as if their modest virtues were worth anything.

—Friedrich Nietzsche, *The Will to Power*[1]

G. K. Chesterton and Friedrich Nietzsche are about as opposed in their thinking as two thinkers can be. As stated in the epigraph, Nietzsche regarded "little people" with open scorn—his was an aristocratic philosophy, concerned only with great men and their affairs.[2] Chesterton, on the other

1. Pg. 205; translation mine. Henceforward, quotations from Nietzsche are taken, often with adaptations, from Oscar Levy's edition of *The Complete Works of Friedrich Nietzsche* (T. N. Foulis, 1909–13), abbreviated CWFN; quotations of Chesterton are, where possible, taken from *The Collected Works of G. K. Chesterton* (Ignatius, 1986–2012), abbreviated CWGKC.

2. As Nietzsche writes in *The Will to Power*, 120: "Our esteem for *great men and things* is more natural. . . . We find nothing great which does not involve a great crime; we conceive of all greatness as placing oneself outside of morality" (CWFN 14.99, modified; emphasis original).

hand, relished his role as champion of the little people against those "snobs and aristocrats who had no love of common things or of the common man."[3]

Nietzsche died in 1900, when a twenty-six-year-old Chesterton was just making his debut as a writer. The literary scene onto which he emerged was obsessed with Nietzsche, whose writings, newly available in English, had mesmerized the Edwardian chattering classes with talk of the Death of God, the will to power, and above all, the Superman.[4] Chesterton found the German philosopher both personally odious and intellectually intolerable, and so threw himself into combatting Nietzscheanism with vigor and unusual seriousness.[5] In the judgment of historians of the period, Chesterton distinguishes himself as one of Nietzsche's principal antagonists, with Patrick Bridgwater going so far as to call him the "foremost" British anti-Nietzschean at a time when "most contemporary *literati* fell for Nietzsche hook, line and sinker."[6]

At the same time, there is a strange kinship between the two—in form, if not in content. Nicholas Boyle quips that Chesterton "is the nearest thing to an English Nietzsche."[7] Garry Wills draws out the comparison:

> Chesterton's method of teaching was not unlike Nietzsche's—parable, story, aphorism, pugnacious attack and challenge; all dramatic and rhetorical in structure, based on great knowledge and insight but never on the painstaking methods of the scholar. Both men were incisive, not exhaustive. . . . *Zarathustra* resembles, in one sense, *The Wild Knight*, while on another level it works with the strategy of *The Everlasting Man*; and nothing

3. Dale Ahlquist, *Common Sense 101: Lessons from G. K. Chesterton* (Ignatius, 2006), 90. Humorously, the Distributist League (est. 1926) of which Chesterton was founding president was nearly called "The League of Little People" (Joseph Pearce, *Wisdom and Innocence: A Life of G. K. Chesterton* [London: Hodder & Stoughton, 1996], 321).

4. Nietzsche's reception is amply documented in David S. Thatcher, *Nietzsche in England, 1890–914: The Growth of a Reputation* (University of Toronto Press, 1970) and Patrick Bridgwater, *Nietzsche in Anglosaxony: A Study of Nietzsche's Impact on English and American Literature* (Leicester University Press, 1972). Chesterton himself wryly recalls the days preceding World War I "when this theme was the topic of the hour . . . when the evolutionary fancy of Nietzsche was the new cry among the intellectuals" (*Eugenics and Other Evils* [CWGKC 4.293]).

5. Chesterton's critique of Nietzscheism has been given extensive treatment in three contemporary studies: John D. Coates, *Chesterton and the Edwardian Cultural Crisis* (Hull University Press, 1984); Mark Knight, *Chesterton and Evil* (Fordham University Press, 2004); Ralph C. Wood, *Chesterton: The Nightmare Goodness of God*, "The Making of the Christian Imagination" (Baylor University Press, 2011).

6. Bridgwater, *Nietzsche in Anglosaxony*, 18–19.

7. Nicholas Boyle, *Sacred and Secular Scriptures: A Catholic Approach to Literature* (University of Notre Dame Press, 2005), 131.

> more resembles Chesterton writing on Browning or Shakespeare than Nietzsche discussing Wagner or Sophocles.[8]

The combination of his diametrically opposed principles, his great similarity of method, and his profound warmth of feeling on the issues makes Chesterton's critique of Nietzsche a fascinating topic of study, and, in light of the contemporary revival of interest in Nietzscheanism, a timely one.

Although Chesterton's engagements with Nietzsche run from his very earliest published works to the end of his literary career, the following pages approach them thematically rather than chronologically, so as better to show the breadth and scope of Chesterton's acquaintance with Nietzsche's thought and the success of his refutation. This however raises a question which first must be addressed.

HOW WELL DID CHESTERTON KNOW NIETZSCHE?

Chesterton has long been dismissed by critics as a journalist rather than a serious thinker.[9] In the case of his feud with Nietzsche, complaints from the Nietzschean side have long centered on the charge that he was unfamiliar with his subject, and so only capable of critiquing a straw man. For instance, Bridgwater writes that "Chesterton's criticism . . . has every appearance of being prompted . . . by a distaste for contemporary Nietzscheanism rather than by any profound knowledge of Nietzsche's own writings."[10] Gertrud von Petzold is even more dismissive:

> His discussion of the philosopher suggests a very fleeting acquaintance with his writings. . . . We see that Chesterton in reality has no idea of the seriousness of Nietzschean philosophy. He has come into contact with English translators in journalistic circles here and there, and has even broken an occasional lance with Dr. Oscar Levy, the editor of Nietzsche's works, but as a man of the moment and *bon vivant*, an overgrown child and free spirit, he lacks receptivity to Nietzsche's revolutionary thinking, and understands neither the deadly import and titanic struggle of the philosopher, nor the creative power of the artist.[11]

8. Garry Wills, *Chesterton: Man and Mask* (Sheed and Ward, 1961), 48.

9. Nietzsche himself, although he did not live to answer Chesterton in person, nevertheless derides him proleptically in *The Will to Power*, 132: "We stand in contempt of every culture that tolerates the reading of newspapers—let alone writing for them" (CWFN 14.107, modified).

10. Bridgwater, *Nietzsche in Anglosaxony*, 19.

11. Gertrud von Petzold, "Nietzsche in englisch-americanischer Beurteilung bis

This chapter is directed in no small part to answering such charges. On the one hand, Chesterton, to my knowledge, kept no private collection of Nietzsche's works.[12] On the other hand, if he always kept copies of the books he had read, he would have needed to lease a warehouse.[13] There are several explicit citations of Nietzsche: *Thus Spake Zarathustra* is quoted thrice,[14] *Twilight of the Gods* once.[15] Chesterton was also friends with Oscar Levy, whose translations of the Nietzschean corpus are well known.[16]

Whatever gaps there may have been in his textual knowledge of Nietzsche (which, I stress, have been alleged rather than demonstrated—*et quod gratis asseritur, gratis negatur*), there is undeniable evidence that Chesterton grappled verbally with Nietzsche's English epigones in lecture halls and learned conversation, moving as he did in literary circles where the German philosopher's ideas were the talk of the day. For instance, Chesterton recounts in his *Autobiography* the day he met Rev. Conrad Noel—the Anglican priest who would later preside over his wedding with Frances—at

zum Ausgang des Weltkrieges," *Anglia* 53 (1929) 134–218 at 215–17, translation mine. Although she published this study during Chesterton's lifetime, it seems doubtful he knew about it.

12. Chesterton's personal library is divided between Wheaton College, the G. K. Chesterton Collection of Notre Dame, London, and the British Library, none of which retains any books by Nietzsche.

13. As Maisie Ward relates, "His memory was prodigious. All his friends testify to his knowing by heart pages of his favourite authors (and these were not few). Ten years after his time with Fisher Unwin, Frances told Father O'Connor that he remembered all the plots and most of the characters of the 'thousands' of novels he had read for the firm" (Maisie Ward, *Gilbert Keith Chesterton* [Sheed and Ward, 1943], 166).

14. In *Heretics*, "Man is a thing which has to be surpassed" (CWGKC 1.80; cf. CWFN 11.16); in *The Appetite of Tyranny*, "Thou goest with women; forget not thy whip" (CWGKC 5.258; cf. CWFN 11.77); also in *The Appetite of Tyranny*, "We must have chaos within, that we may give birth to a dancing star" (CWGKC 5.272; cf. CWFN 11.12). *In George Bernard Shaw*, Chesterton makes an allusion to the prologue of *Zarathustra*: "Nietzsche had said that just as the ape ultimately produced the man, so should we ultimately produce something higher than the man" (CWGKC 11.461; cf. CWFN 11.6). When Chesterton writes in *Heretics* that "Nietzsche . . . has a description somewhere—a very powerful description in the purely literary sense—of the disgust and disdain which consume him at the sight of the common people with their common faces, their common voices, and their common minds" (CWGKC 1.139), he is likely referring to the chapter in *Zarathustra* entitled "The Rabble" (CWFN 113–16).

15. In *Orthodoxy*, "A new commandment I give to you, 'be hard'" (CWGKC 1.82; cf. CWFN 16.121). In *The Flying Inn* (CWGKC 7.652), when Lord Ivywood asks, "Doesn't Nietzsche say somewhere that the delight in destiny is the mark of the hero?" it is an invocation of Nietzsche's doctrine of *amor fati*, not an exact quotation.

16. Chesterton carried on an open correspondence with Levy in *G. K.'s Weekly* and *The New Age*, and called him in *Orthodoxy* "the only intelligent Nietzscheite" (CWGKC 1.327).

a session of the Christo-Theosophic Society in 1900. Chesterton tells us that "somebody was lecturing on Nietzsche"[17]—neglecting to mention that that "somebody" was Chesterton himself![18]

Nor was this the only time Chesterton spoke publicly on Nietzsche. In 1904, A. R. Orage invited Chesterton to speak to the Leeds Arts Club, which he had founded in 1903 "with the object of 'reducing Leeds to Nietzscheism.'"[19] Expecting a larger crowd than would fit in the Arts Club rooms, Orage rented the Philosophical Hall of the Leeds Museum. The event was packed; and as Tom Steele writes, "Chesterton did not disappoint his audience for his talk was no less than a subtle debunking of the Nietzschean Superman theories so forcefully presented by the Club's founders."[20] Orage was of course one of the leading popularizers of Nietzsche's thought in England, whose principal virtue lay in his willingness to engage in dialogue with anyone, even of an opposing viewpoint, who would raise the level of discourse.[21] And Orage thought highly enough of Chesterton to showcase him several times as a speaker, then later as a regular contributor to his weekly magazine, *The New Age*.[22]

In 1911, Chesterton was chosen by the Cambridge Heretics to answer a previous address by George Bernard Shaw. Chesterton spoke for an hour to an audience of a thousand students on Shaw's Nietzscheism, and then for another hour fielded questions from all corners of the room.[23] This very fact—that in an age obsessed with Nietzscheism, Chesterton was recognized as an authority on Nietzsche to the point of repeatedly being sought after to speak about him to large audiences—alone should suffice to silence the snide condescension of modern critics. His contemporaries, who met him in the lists of England's periodicals and crossed wits with him on the debate stage, had not the faintest doubt that he was a worthy adversary who knew whereof he spoke.

17. CWGKC 16.152.

18. Rev. Noel's recollection of the event is recorded in Sidney Dark, ed., *Conrad Noel: An Autobiography* (J. M. Dent & Sons, 1945), 66.

19. Tom Steele, *Alfred Orage and the Leeds Arts Club, 1893–1923* (Scolar, 1990), 1.

20. Steele, *Alfred Orage*, 82. There is an account of Chesterton's talk in *Leeds Mercury* (October 3, 1904), 3.

21. Thatcher, for instance, devotes an entire chapter to him (*Nietzsche in England*, 219–68).

22. In fact, as Coates relates, Orage would go on to repudiate Nietzsche's views on the Superman thanks in no small part to the influence of Chesterton (*Chesterton and the Edwardian Cultural Crisis*, 240–42).

23. A full account of Chesterton's speech was printed in *Cambridge Daily News* (November 18, 1911), 4.

CHESTERTON'S CRITIQUE OF NIETZSCHE

Before turning to Chesterton's critique of Nietzsche, it is worth pausing to note that Chesterton recognized and freely acknowledged his opponent's genius. For instance he concedes in *Orthodoxy* that "no one will deny that he was a poetical and suggestive thinker."[24] Elsewhere, he says that Nietzsche "had a wonderful poetic wit; and is one of the best rhetoricians of the modern world."[25] In "Sentimental Literature," Chesterton goes so far as to say that "one of the most brilliant men of the nineteenth century was the philosopher of force and supremacy, Nietzsche."[26]

The Hypocrisy of Nietzsche

It is this last point that prompted the most scathing of Chesterton's critiques: that "the philosopher of force" was in his person anything but forceful. Not that Nietzsche had any opposition to the *idea* of force. He wrote, for instance, that "the man who has renounced war has renounced a grand life,"[27] and that "man shall be trained for war, and woman for the recreation of the warrior: all else is folly."[28] But when it came to waging war himself, Nietzsche's record was rather undistinguished.[29] Chesterton calls him in one essay "a very fragile aristocrat"[30] and elsewhere writes:

> By descent Nietzsche was a Pole, and probably a Polish noble; and to say that he was a Polish noble is to say that he was a frail, fastidious, and entirely useless anarchist. . . . His whole work is shot through with the pangs and fevers of his physical life,

24. CWGKC 1.309.

25. Chesterton, *George Bernard Shaw* (CWGKC 11.460).

26. "Sentimental Literature" in Dorothy Collins, ed., *The Spice of Life and Other Essays* (Dufour, 1966), 12. Chesterton ends the sentence, "And he died in a madhouse."

27. Friedrich Nietzsche, *Twilight of the Idols* (CWFN 16.29).

28. Friedrich Nietzsche, *Thus Spake Zarathustra* (CWFN 11.75).

29. Chesterton alludes to Nietzsche's military career in *Manalive*: "Why, Nietzsche stood in a row of ramrods in the silly old Prussian army" (CWGKC 7.391). Nietzsche lasted a year into his mandatory service before he was medically discharged for a riding injury. Later (and to his credit), Nietzsche volunteered to serve as a medical orderly in the Franco-Prussian War—which as a Swiss citizen he was under no compulsion to do. This time, after only a month in, he fell ill on a particularly taxing train ride and was again medically discharged. Nietzsche's health never fully recovered. See Curtis Cate, *Friedrich Nietzsche* (Overlook, 2002), 77–78, 115–16.

30. Chesterton, "Thomas Carlyle," in *Twelve Types* (Arthur L. Humphreys, 1902), 138.

> which was one of extreme bad health; and in early middle age his brilliant brain broke down into impotence and darkness.[31]

Chesterton's personal attack on Nietzsche exposes a cruel irony: the man seeking to propound a philosophy of contempt against weakness was himself a weak man. As Chesterton writes elsewhere, "The false and feeble doctrine that might is right . . . is invariably preached by physical weaklings like Nietzsche."[32] In *Heretics*, he diagnoses Nietzsche's disgust at the common man not as rarefied nobility, but mere nervous pathology:

> Nietzsche's aristocracy has about it all the sacredness that belongs to the weak. When he makes us feel that he cannot endure the innumerable faces, the incessant voices, the overpowering omnipresence which belongs to the mob, he will have the sympathy of anybody who has ever been sick on a steamer or tired in a crowded omnibus. Every man has hated mankind when he was less than a man. Every man has had humanity in his eyes like a blinding fog, humanity in his nostrils like a suffocating smell. But when Nietzsche has the incredible lack of humour and lack of imagination to ask us to believe that his aristocracy is an aristocracy of strong muscles or an aristocracy of strong wills, it is necessary to point out the truth. It is an aristocracy of weak nerves.[33]

But perhaps the most devastating passage in Chesterton on the hypocrisy of Nietzsche is his unfavorable comparison of the German philosopher to *Bow Bells Novelettes*—a weekly magazine purveying melodramas to Cockney Londoners:

> Nietzsche and the *Bow Bells Novelettes* have both obviously the same fundamental character; they both worship the tall man with curling moustaches and herculean bodily power, and they both worship him in a manner which is somewhat feminine and hysterical. Even here, however, the *Novelette* easily maintains its philosophical superiority, because it does attribute to the strong man those virtues which do commonly belong to him, such virtues as laziness and kindliness and a rather reckless benevolence, and a great dislike of hurting the weak. Nietzsche, on

31. Chesterton, *George Bernard Shaw* (CWGKC 11.460).

32. Chesterton, "Thoughts About Koepenick," in *All Things Considered* (Methuen, 1908), 139–40.

33. CWGKC 1.139.

> the other hand, attributes to the strong man that scorn against weakness which only exists among invalids.[34]

This aspect of Chesterton's critique may, of course, raise cries of *ad hominem*. Certainly, if Nietzsche had supported his ideas with his person—or if another thinker of physical courage and valor were to preach Nietzscheism without hypocrisy—this entire line of attack would fall flat. But Chesterton's aim in these personal attacks on Nietzsche is strategic, not philosophical: He was trying to diminish the popularity of Nietzscheism in England by laying bare the hypocrisy of its inceptor.[35]

"The Death of God"

One of the most memorable passages in Nietzsche is the episode of the Madman who runs into the marketplace one morning and declares, "God is dead! God remains dead! And we have killed him!"[36] Nietzsche's system is atheistic at the level of presupposition: He advances no arguments—he simply assumes that there is no God, recognizes (unlike many atheists) that the absence of God is terrible, bearing with it the ineluctable implication of nihilism, and proceeds to try to fill the void left by the Death of God with an attempt at summoning out of the void some new meaning of his own.

This nihilism of Nietzsche affected Chesterton deeply as a young man. Although he does not dwell on the point, it would seem that Chesterton encountered, and was profoundly shaken by, this doctrine during his unhappy years at Slade School of Art.[37] Mark Knight has pieced together the evidence,[38] especially Chesterton's encounter with Nietzschean amorality

34. CWGKC 1.139, 1.146–47. Chesterton makes a similar point in *George Bernard Shaw*: "There are indeed doctrines of Nietzsche that are not Christian, but then, by an entertaining coincidence, they are also not true. His hatred of pity is not Christian, but that was not his doctrine but his disease. Invalids are often hard on invalids" (CWGKC 11.461).

35. Chesterton's many references to the madness of Nietzsche should be taken in the same vein—and not as a cheap shot at Nietzsche's illness, but a considered judgment on his philosophy. For instance, in *Orthodoxy*, "If Nietzsche had not ended in imbecility, Nietzscheism would end in imbecility" (CWGKC 1.246).

36. Friedrich Nietzsche, *The Gay Science* (CWFN 10.168). Mark Knight argues that "the prophetic figure who dominates Nietzsche's parable 'The Madman' appears to be part of the inspiration behind the character of Lucian Gregory, the one true anarchist in *The Man Who Was Thursday: A Nightmare*, who declares to anyone who will listen his intention 'to abolish God'" (*Chesterton on Evil*, 31).

37. As he writes in his *Autobiography*, "A very negative and even nihilistic philosophy . . . threw a shadow over my mind" (CWGKC 16.94).

38. Knight, *Chesterton and Evil*, 33–35.

in one of his fellow students, which he describes in his essay, "The Diabolist," as being "by far the most terrible thing that has ever happened to me in my life."[39]

William Oddie, who describes Chesterton's time at the Slade at length, shares the important detail that the Irish novelist George Moore was "an influence over the Slade's teaching staff."[40] Moore was one of the earliest carriers of Nietzsche's nihilism and its ethics across the language barrier into English. He wrote, for instance:

> Pity, that most vile of all vile virtues, has never been known to me. . . . Now the world proposes to interrupt the terrible austere laws of nature which ordain that the weak shall be trampled upon, shall be ground into death and dust, that the strong shall be really strong,—that the strong shall be glorious, sublime. . . . Hither the world has been drifting since the coming of the pale socialist of Galilee; and this is why I hate Him, and deny His divinity.[41]

Hence, as Oddie remarks, "It is not surprising that in *Heretics*, Chesterton was, uncharacteristically, to write of George Moore with such absolute personal contempt."[42]

Although Chesterton's entire *oeuvre* can be seen as a polemic against nihilism, his sharpest engagement with its specifically Nietzschean form, the doctrine of the Death of God, is without a doubt his epic, *The Ballad of the White Horse*.[43] His *pithiest* answer, of course, is in *The Everlasting Man*:

39. G. K. Chesterton, *Tremendous Trifles* (Dodd, Mead & Co., 1909), 268.

40. William Oddie, *Chesterton and the Romance of Orthodoxy: The Making of GKC, 1874–1908* (Oxford University Press, 2008), 120, 84–125. The chapter is entitled "Nightmare at the Slade."

41. George Moore, *Confessions of a Young Man* (Swan Sonnenschein, 1888), 187–88.

42. Oddie, *Chesterton and the Romance of Orthodoxy*, 120. Later on, in *The New Jerusalem*, Chesterton writes: "Mr. George Moore was anticipating Nietzsche, sailing near, as he said, 'the sunken rocks about the cave of Zarathustra.' He said, if I remember right, that Cromwell should be admired for his injustice. He implied that Christ should be condemned, not because he destroyed the swine, but because he delivered the sick" (CWGKC 20.325).

43. As Ralph C. Wood writes, it is in this poem that Chesterton "offers his most convincing response . . . to Nietzsche and the nihilists" (*Chesterton: The Nightmare Goodness of God*, 161). Wood goes on to present a deep analysis of how the Danes, whom he aptly styles "Nietzscheans *avant la lettre*" (164), are confronted and confuted over the course of the poem.

"Christianity has died many times and risen again; for it had a God who knew the way out of the grave."[44]

"The Transvaluation of Values"

One of Nietzsche's great philosophical projects was his "transvaluation of values," which rests upon a distinction that he draws between "*master-morality*" and "*slave-morality*."[45] Nietzsche develops a narrative of "the slave revolt in morality,"[46] according to which the master morality of the heroic past was overthrown by the slave morality of Judaism and Christianity. The slaves replaced the heroic moral axis of "noble" and "base" with the diseased values of "good" and "evil," according to which the strong are bound to serve and protect the weak. Nietzsche proposes a return to the ethical system of the proud Vikings and noble Greeks,[47] in which the strong are once more free—"superior to humanity in power, in loftiness of soul,—in contempt."[48]

Some of Chesterton's passing barbs at Nietzsche may strike the superficial reader as hyperbolic to a comical extent. For instance, in *The Man Who Was Thursday*, when Lucian Gregory, in an effort "to understand the position of those who, like Nietzsche, admire violence" impersonated a major, waved a sword around, and "often said, 'Let the weak perish; it is the Law.'"[49] Chesterton also parodies the pedagogy of Shaw: "When you tell Tommy not to hit his sick sister on the temple, you must make sure of the

44. CWGKC 2.382.

45. Friedrich Nietzsche, *Beyond Good and Evil* (CWFN 5.227, emphasis original).

46. Friedrich Nietzsche, *Genealogy of Morals* (CWFN 15.34, modified).

47. As Chesterton writes, "Nietzsche took the next step by throwing over Christian ethics as well as theology, and invoking the old gods of violence and war" ("The Reaction of the Intellectuals," in *The Well and the Shallows* [Sheed and Ward, 1935], 85).

48. Friedrich Nietzsche, *Antichrist* (CWFN 16.126). Chesterton attacks this attitude in his essay "A Defence of Humility": "The most brilliant exponent of the egoistic school, Nietzsche, with deadly and honourable logic, admitted that the philosophy of self-satisfaction led to looking down upon the weak, the cowardly, and the ignorant. Looking down on things may be a delightful experience, only there is nothing, from a mountain to a cabbage, that is really seen when it is seen from a balloon. The philosopher of the ego sees everything, no doubt, from a high and rarified heaven; only he sees everything foreshortened or deformed" ("A Defence of Humility," in *The Defendant* [R. Brimley Johnson, 1901], 101).

49. CWGKC 6.491. Wood further discusses how Dr. Bull (*Chesterton: The Nightmare Goodness of God*, 199–200) and, to a lesser degree, Prof. De Worms (203–4) are ciphers for Nietzsche.

presence of some Nietzscheite professor, who will explain to him that such a course might possibly serve to eliminate the unfit."[50]

Chesterton was in fact well acquainted with Nietzsche's ethics, and first of all exposes it as nothing novel in the history of ideas:

> Nietzsche, as every one knows, preached a doctrine which he and his followers regard apparently as very revolutionary; he held that ordinary altruistic morality had been the invention of a slave class to prevent the emergence of superior types to fight and rule them. Now, modern people, whether they agree with this or not, always talk of it as a new and unheard-of idea. It is calmly and persistently supposed that the great writers of the past, say Shakespeare for instance, did not hold this view, because they had never imagined it; because it had never come into their heads.[51]

Chesterton goes on cooly to observe that the idea was in fact known to Shakespeare, who showed its absurdity by putting it into the mouth of the deranged villain, Richard III:

> Conscience is but a word that cowards use,
> Devised at first to keep the strong in awe.[52]

In *Orthodoxy*, Chesterton further attacks the imprecision of Nietzsche's language, which he shows to be nothing more than a smokescreen to conceal the incoherence of his thought:

> He never put his own meaning before himself in bald abstract words: as did Aristotle and Calvin, and even Karl Marx, the hard, fearless men of thought. Nietzsche always escaped a question by a physical metaphor, like a cheery minor poet. He said, "beyond good and evil," because he had not the courage to say, "more good than good and evil," or, "more evil than good and evil." Had he faced his thought without metaphors, he would have seen that it was nonsense.[53]

50. Chesterton, *George Bernard Shaw* (CWGKC 11.448–49). Although extreme, these statements are not actually hyperbolic. Chesterton was merely taking Nietzsche at his word. For example, in *Antichrist*: "The weak and the failures shall perish: the first principle of our humanitarianism. And they ought even to be helped to perish" (CWFN 16.128, modified).

51. Chesterton, "On Reading," in *The Common Man* (Sheed and Ward, 1950) 23.

52. William Shakespeare, *Richard III*, act 5, scene 3.

53. CWGKC 1.309.

Earlier in the same work, Chesterton exposes the fundamental arbitrariness of Nietzsche's theories on the evolution of morality. If there is no objective good, then there are no grounds for passing judgment on changing mores:

> Akin to these is the false theory of progress, which maintains that we alter the test instead of trying to pass the test. We often hear it said, for instance, "What is right in one age is wrong in another." This is quite reasonable, if it means that there is a fixed aim, and that certain methods attain at certain times and not at other times. If women, say, desire to be elegant, it may be that they are improved at one time by growing fatter and at another time by growing thinner. But you cannot say that they are improved by ceasing to wish to be elegant and beginning to wish to be oblong. If the standard changes, how can there be improvement, which implies a standard? Nietzsche started a nonsensical idea that men had once sought as good what we now call evil; if it were so, we could not talk of surpassing or even falling short of them. How can you overtake Jones if you walk in the other direction? You cannot discuss whether one people has succeeded more in being miserable than another succeeded in being happy. It would be like discussing whether Milton was more puritanical than a pig is fat.[54]

Nietzsche famously critiqued Christian morality as slavish, defining Christianity as "the revolt of all things that crawl on their bellies against everything that is lofty."[55] Chesterton argues that this critique addresses only a distorted caricature of Christianity:

> Nietzsche imagined he was rebelling against ancient morality; as a matter of fact he was only rebelling against recent morality, against the half-baked impudence of the utilitarians and the materialists. He thought he was rebelling against Christianity; curiously enough he was rebelling solely against the special enemies of Christianity. . . . Historic Christianity has always believed in the valour of St. Michael riding in front of the Church Militant; and in an ultimate and absolute pleasure, not indirect or utilitarian, the intoxication of the spirit, the wine of the blood of God.[56]

54. CWGKC 1.238–39.
55. Nietzsche, *Antichrist* (CWFN 16.187).
56. Chesterton, *George Bernard Shaw* (CWGKC 11.461).

At the same time that he upholds Christianity's commitment to valor, Chesterton refuses to renounce its commitment to pity:

> Christianity . . . is not indeed so narrow as Nietzsche; it does not deny the truths of Nietzsche. It does not exclude pugnacity as he excludes pity. . . . We think St. Michael glorious when he strikes down the titanic traitor; but we think St. Gabriel more glorious when he stoops in salutation to the peasant girl; and the supreme and mystical moment for us is in the moment of the softening of strength by chivalry and charity; when the devouring thing gives food and out of the strong comes forth sweetness. The heart of Christendom is a heart; and we are serious when we call it a sacred heart.[57]

"The Will to Power"

Having discarded good and evil as slavish, Nietzsche takes as the driving force of his new ethics his idea of a "will to power." As Nietzsche describes it, "My idea is that every specific body strives to become master of all space, and to extend its power (its will to power), and to thrust back everything that resists it."[58] He writes further, "A living thing seeks above all to discharge its strength—life itself is *Will to Power*."[59]

Chesterton understands Nietzsche's concept as being akin to Dante's "*primum mobile* of which all the mystics have spoken: energy, the power to create," and engages with it at some length in *Orthodoxy*.[60] After an opening salvo in which he points out the self-defeating nature of any such doctrine,[61] Chesterton turns to the task of answering it, which he principally accomplishes through the person of John Davidson:

57. G. K. Chesterton, "A Word with Dr. Oscar Levy," in *G. K.'s Weekly* (October 16, 1926), 72.

58. Friedrich Nietzsche, *The Will to Power* 636 (*Nachlaß* 1888, 14 [186]; CWFN 15.121).

59. Friedrich Nietzsche, *Beyond Good and Evil* (CWFN 5.20, emphasis original).

60. G. K. Chesterton, *Appreciations and Criticisms of the Works of Charles Dickens* (CWGKC 15.241). He goes on immediately afterwards, "I will not call it 'the will to live,' for that is a priggish phrase of German professors."

61. "Nietzsche denied egoism simply by preaching it. To preach anything is to give it away. First, the egoist calls life a war without mercy, and then he takes the greatest possible trouble to drill his enemies in war. To preach egoism is to practise altruism" (CWGKC 1.241).

> I have no space to trace or expound this philosophy of Will. It came, I suppose, through Nietzsche, who preached something that is called egoism. . . . Mr. John Davidson, a remarkable poet, is so passionately excited about it that he is obliged to write prose. He publishes a short play with several long prefaces. This is natural enough in Mr. Shaw, for all his plays are prefaces: Mr. Shaw is (I suspect) the only man on earth who has never written any poetry. But that Mr. Davidson (who can write excellent poetry) should write instead laborious metaphysics in defence of this doctrine of will, does show that the doctrine of will has taken hold of men. . . . They are all excited; and well they may be. For by this doctrine of the divine authority of will, they think they can break out of the doomed fortress of rationalism. They think they can escape.
>
> But they cannot escape. . . . All the will-worshippers, from Nietzsche to Mr. Davidson, are really quite empty of volition. They cannot will, they can hardly wish. And if any one wants a proof of this, it can be found quite easily. It can be found in this fact: that they always talk of will as something that expands and breaks out. But it is quite the opposite. Every act of will is an act of self-limitation. To desire action is to desire limitation. In that sense every act is an act of self-sacrifice. When you choose anything, you reject everything else. That objection, which men of this school used to make to the act of marriage, is really an objection to every act. Every act is an irrevocable selection exclusion. Just as when you marry one woman you give up all the others, so when you take one course of action you give up all the other courses. If you become King of England, you give up the post of Beadle in Brompton. If you go to Rome, you sacrifice a rich suggestive life in Wimbledon. It is the existence of this negative or limiting side of will that makes most of the talk of the anarchic will-worshippers little better than nonsense. For instance, Mr. John Davidson tells us to have nothing to do with "Thou shalt not"; but it is surely obvious that "Thou shalt not" is only one of the necessary corollaries of "I will."[62]

With a stroke, Chesterton deflates the whole distended edifice of thought: Nietzsche's idea of the will as extending endlessly through space is a fundamental misunderstanding of the nature of the will. Will is the faculty of choice, and choice implies limitation, not expansion.

62. CWGKC 1.241–43.

"The Superman"

Perhaps the Nietzschean idea which Chesterton contended with the most—in no small part because it was the most popular idea in England before World War I—was that of the Superman.[63] According to Nietzsche, the Superman represented the next stage of human evolution, achieved by transcending conventional morality and the limitations it imposes: "What is the ape to man? A laughing-stock, a thing of shame. And just the same shall man be to the Superman: a laughing-stock, a thing of shame."[64]

Chesterton levels the same critique against Nietzsche's Superman that he did against his transvaluation of values: that first of all, his poetic language serves not to ornament his thought, but to obscure its lack of sense.[65] Second, Chesterton demonstrates the logical fatuity of the doctrine of Superman—simply put, there can be no "progress" without some objective standard against which to measure it:

> We cannot be expected to have any regard for a great creature if he does not in any manner conform to our standards. For unless he passes our standard of greatness we cannot even call him great. Nietzsche summed up all that is interesting in the Superman idea when he said, "Man is a thing which has to be surpassed." But the very word "surpass" implies the existence of a standard common to us and the thing surpassing us.[66]

Much of Chesterton's critique on this matter is carried out by proxy. Although the fountainhead of the error is Nietzsche, Chesterton met with it in his friends and contemporaries. George Bernard Shaw was particularly affected by Nietzsche's Superman, even writing a play with the title *Man and Superman* in 1903. Chesterton answers as follows:

> This was the one doctrine which caught the eye of Shaw and captured him. He was not influenced at all by the morbid attack

63. In *Eugenics and Other Evils*, Chesterton recalls how the outbreak of war led to the downfall of Nietzsche's doctrine of the Superman in England: "The very name of Nietzsche, who had held up this hope of something superhuman to humanity, was laughed at for all the world as if he had been touched with lunacy" (CWGKC 4.417).

64. Nietzsche, *Thus Spake Zarathustra* 3 (CWFN 11.6).

65. For instance, Chesterton writes in *Orthodoxy*, "When he describes his hero, he does not dare to say, 'the purer man,' or 'the happier man,' or 'the sadder man,' for all these are ideas; and ideas are alarming. He says 'the upper man,' or 'over man,' a physical metaphor from acrobats or alpine climbers. Nietzsche is truly a very timid thinker. He does not really know in the least what sort of man he wants evolution to produce" (CWGKC 1.309).

66. G. K. Chesterton, *Heretics* (CWGKC 1.80).

> on mercy. It would require more than ten thousand mad Polish professors to make Bernard Shaw anything but a generous and compassionate man. But it is certainly a nuisance that the one Nietzsche doctrine which attracted him was not the one Nietzsche doctrine that is human and rectifying. Nietzsche might really have done some good if he had taught Bernard Shaw to draw the sword, to drink wine, or even to dance. But he only succeeded in putting into his head a new superstition, which bids fair to be the chief superstition of the dark ages which are possibly in front of us—I mean the superstition of what is called the Superman.
>
> In one of his least convincing phrases, Nietzsche had said that just as the ape ultimately produced the man, so should we ultimately produce something higher than the man. The immediate answer, of course, is sufficiently obvious: the ape did not worry about the man, so why should we worry about the Superman? If the Superman will come by natural selection, may we leave it to natural selection? If the Superman will come by human selection, what sort of Superman are we to select? If he is simply to be more just, more brave, or more merciful, then Zarathustra sinks into a Sunday-school teacher; the only way we can work for it is to be more just, more brave, and more merciful; sensible advice, but hardly startling. If he is to be anything else than this, why should we desire him, or what else are we to desire? These questions have been many times asked of the Nietzscheites, and none of the Nietzscheites have even attempted to answer them.[67]

Chesterton also contends with Nietzsche's concept of the Superman as he encountered it in the fiction of H. G. Wells, whose 1904 novel *The Food of the Gods* is shot through with Nietzschean ideas, especially that of the Superman. In reply, Chesterton addresses both the actual cause behind the Nietzschean

67. Chesterton, *George Bernard Shaw* (CWGKC 11.461–62). Chesterton also addresses Shaw's Nietzscheism in *Heretics*: "He has even been infected to some extent with the primary intellectual weakness of his new master, Nietzsche, the strange notion that the greater and stronger a man was the more he would despise other things. The greater and stronger a man is the more he would be inclined to prostrate himself before a periwinkle" (CWGKC 1.68). See also his satirical essay "How I Found the Superman" (CWGKC 11.359–62). Even a staunch Nietzschean like Thatcher cannot help but hold Chesterton's critique of Shaw in grudging admiration: "Chesterton's distorted view of Nietzsche has all the mischievous wickedness of wilful caricature, but some of the barbs he launched in Shaw's direction struck firmly home" (*Nietzsche in England*, 210).

Superman—a very ordinary yearning for the strong man[68]—and addresses his fundamental misunderstanding of what it means to be strong:

> But that is at bottom the meaning of all modern hero-worship and celebration of the Strong Man, the Caesar, the Superman. That he may be something more than man, *we* must be something less.
>
> Doubtless there is an older and better hero-worship than this. But the old hero was a being who, like Achilles, was more human than humanity itself. Nietzsche's Superman is cold and friendless. Achilles is so foolishly fond of his friend that he slaughters armies in the agony of his bereavement. Mr. Shaw's sad Caesar says in his desolate pride, "He who has never hoped can never despair." The Man-God of old answers from his awful hill, "Was ever sorrow like unto my sorrow?" A great man is not a man so strong that he feels less than other men; he is a man so strong that he feels more.[69]

In his essay "Is Humanism a Religion?" Chesterton reveals the emptiness of such an attitude of the soul—it is not more than human, but far less:

> Not only Nietzsche, but many Neo-Pagans working on his lines, have suggested such hardness as a higher intellectual purity. And having read many modern poems about the Man of the Future, made of steel and illumined with nothing warmer than green fire, I have no difficulty in imagining a literature that should pride itself on a merciless and metallic detachment.[70]

Chesterton also explores the idea of the Superman in his own fiction. John D. Coates examines this with great depth and insight in connection with *The Flying Inn*, which he calls "Chesterton's most satisfactory examination of Nietzscheanism."[71] And Ralph C. Wood writes that "though Nietzsche is never named, Lord Philip Ivywood—a member of Parliament converted to Ammon's Islamist philosophy—has a decidedly Nietzschean cast of mind. . . . Hence his self-declared ascent to the solitary self-sufficiency

68. As Chesterton writes elsewhere, "There have been many things, friendly and hostile, said about Nietzsche's philosophy, but few so far have pointed out the basic fact that it is sentimental. It yields utterly to one of the oldest, most generous, and most excusable of the weaknesses of humanity, the hunger for the strong man" ("Sentimental Literature," in *The Spice of Life*, 12).

69. Chesterton, *Heretics* (CWGKC 1.82, emphasis original). The contrasting quotations are from Shaw's play *Caesar and Cleopatra*, act 4, and Lam 1:12.

70. G. K. Chesterton, *The Thing* (CWGKC 3.154).

71. Coates, *Chesterton and the Edwardian Cultural Crisis*, 85.

of the Nietzschean Superman."[72] The text Wood quotes is a perfect illustration of Nietzsche's misunderstanding of greatness:

> I would walk where no man has walked; and find something beyond tears and laughter. My road shall be my road indeed. . . . And my adventures shall not be in the hedges and the gutters, but in the borders of the ever advancing human brain. I will think what was unthinkable until I thought it; I will love what was never loved until I loved it—I will be as lonely as the First Man.[73]

In *The Blatchford Controversies*, Chesterton delivers with finality what must be any sane man's response to Nietzsche's invitation to evolve:

> But if a man came up to us (as many will soon come up to us) to say, "I am a new kind of man. I am the super-man. I have abandoned mercy and justice"; we should answer, "Doubtless you are new, but you are not nearer to the perfect man, for he has been already in the mind of God. We have fallen with Adam and we shall rise with Christ; but we would rather fall with Satan than rise with you."[74]

"Eternal Return"

There is a famous passage in which Nietzsche imagines a demon disclosing that men are fated to relive the same life endlessly, without the slightest change.[75] Nietzsche's doctrine of "eternal return" describes an inevitable consequence of his atheism: that the world as it exists is all there is. The third part of *Thus Spake Zarathustra* is in large part taken up in reconciling with this reality, ending in the hymn of the seven seals, in which the prophet affirms his love for eternity rather than cursing it.[76]

In *St. Thomas Aquinas*, Chesterton measures this doctrine of Nietzsche against the similar teaching of Buddha:

> He who will not climb the mountain of Christ does indeed fall into the abyss of Buddha.

72. Wood, *Chesterton: The Nightmare Goodness of God*, 112. Ivywood does in fact quote Nietzsche explicitly, as noted above.

73. G. K. Chesterton, *The Flying Inn* (CWGKC 7.612).

74. Chesterton, CWGKC 1.385.

75. Nietzsche, *Gay Science* (CWFN 10.270–71).

76. Nietzsche, CWFN 11.280–84.

> The same is true, in a less lucid and dignified fashion, of most other alternatives of heathen humanity; nearly all are sucked back into that whirlpool of recurrence which all the ancients knew. Nearly all return to the one idea of returning. That is what Buddha described so darkly as the Sorrowful Wheel. It is true that the sort of recurrence which Buddha described as the Sorrowful Wheel, poor Nietzsche actually managed to describe as the Joyful Wisdom. I can only say that if bare repetition was his idea of Joyful Wisdom, I should be curious to know what was his idea of Sorrowful Wisdom. But as a fact, in the case of Nietzsche, this did not belong to the moment of his breaking out, but to the moment of his breaking down. It came at the end of his life, when he was near to mental collapse; and it is really quite contrary to his earlier and finer inspirations of wild freedom or fresh and creative innovation. Once at least he had tried to break out; but he also was only broken on the wheel.[77]

In Chesterton's estimation, the systems of Nietzsche and Buddha are really identical—except that Nietzsche's attempted affirmation of the wheel of recurrence is ultimately futile. To call it "joyful" is to paint a smile on the cadaver. Chesterton elsewhere refers to "the pessimism of the German professor; and if we accept such oblivion, then doubtless our 'cycle' will really curl up like a worm on the floor and lie still for ever."[78]

The systems of both Nietzsche and Buddha represent forms of the wheel—the endless recurrence of history with no hope of escape. Christianity, on the other hand, is in the form of a mountain—an ascent to divine intimacy and eternal bliss.

Polarity with Tolstoy

Chesterton's engagement with Nietzsche was not purely negative[79]—he also makes positive use of Nietzsche's thought by considering his ideas in tension

77. Chesterton, CWGKC 2.491.

78. G. K. Chesterton, "On the Contiguous Past," in *All I Survey* (Methuen, 1934), 139.

79. As Chesterton writes in *George Bernard Shaw*, "All that was true in his teaching was this: that if a man looks fine on a horse it is so far irrelevant to tell him that he would be more economical on a donkey or more humane on a tricycle. In other words, the mere achievement of dignity, beauty, or triumph is strictly to be called a good thing. I do not know if Nietzsche ever used the illustration; but it seems to me that all that is creditable or sound in Nietzsche could be stated in the derivation of one word, the word 'valour.' Valour means *valeur*; it means a value; courage is itself a solid good; it is an ultimate virtue; valour is in itself *valid*" (CWGKC 11.460; emphasis original).

with Tolstoy's. In fact, Chesterton's first mention of the German philosopher in print is an uncredited article in the *Daily News*—"Ages and Their Ideals"—in which he contrasts the antithetical philosophies of Nietzsche and Tolstoy. Nietzsche's is identified as "the ideal of unscrupulous power: the Beyond-man, who has overstepped the limitations of good and evil. . . . Nietzsche would have the strong override all obstacles to the full development of self—would weaken the restrictions imposed by law upon the strong; Tolstoi will not sanction the invoking of law, even to protect society against the violent criminal."[80]

This dialectic between Nietzsche and Tolstoy recurs with regularity in Chesterton's subsequent works. For instance, in *Heretics* he asks "whether we should love everybody with Tolstoy, or spare nobody with Nietzsche,"[81] and in *Appreciations and Criticisms of the Works of Charles Dickens*, writes:

> But of all the signs of modern feebleness, of lack of grasp on morals as they actually must be, there has been none quite so silly or so dangerous as this: that the philosophers of to-day have started to divide loving from fighting and to put them into opposite camps. There could be no worse sign than that a man, even Nietzsche, can be found to say that we should go in for fighting instead of loving.[82] There can be no worse sign than that a man, even Tolstoi, can be found to tell us that we should go in for loving instead of fighting. The two things imply each other; they implied each other in the old romance and in the old religion, which were the two permanent things of humanity. You cannot love a thing without wanting to fight for it. You cannot fight without something to fight for.[82]

Nietzsche and Tolstoy are somewhat irreverently lampooned in chapters 5 and 6 of *The Ball and the Cross*, in which the duelists meet first a Tolstoian pacifist who calls the police on them, and then a violence-worshiping professor named Morrice Wimpey who flees when challenged to a fight.[83]

In his most memorable mention of the pair, the contrast between Nietzsche and Tolstoy rises to the level of classic Chestertonian paradox as the seemingly irreconcilable values of peace and war coalesce in the person of St. Joan of Arc:

80. Julia Stapleton, ed., *G. K. Chesterton at the* Daily News: *Literature, Liberalism and Revolution, 1901–1913* (Routledge, 2016), 1:65.

81. Chesterton, CWGKC 1.53.

82. Chesterton, CWGKC 15.255.

83. Chesterton, CWGKC 7.87–106. Tolstoy and Nietzsche are explicitly contrasted at the end of the book (7.246). See analysis in Ralph C. Wood, *Chesterton: The Nightmare Goodness of God*, 143–44.

> Joan, when I came to think of her, had in her all that was true either in Tolstoy or Nietzsche, all that was even tolerable in either of them. I thought of all that is noble in Tolstoy, the pleasure in plain things, especially in plain pity, the actualities of the earth, the reverence for the poor, the dignity of the bowed back. Joan of Arc had all that and with this great addition, that she endured poverty as well as admiring it; whereas Tolstoy is only a typical aristocrat trying to find out its secret. And then I thought of all that was brave and proud and pathetic in poor Nietzsche, and his mutiny against the emptiness and timidity of our time. I thought of his cry for the ecstatic equilibrium of danger, his hunger for the rush of great horses, his cry to arms. Well, Joan of Arc had all that, and again with this difference, that she did not praise fighting, but fought. We know that she was not afraid of an army, while Nietzsche, for all we know, was afraid of a cow. Tolstoy only praised the peasant; she was the peasant. Nietzsche only praised the warrior; she was the warrior. She beat them both at their own antagonistic ideals; she was more gentle than the one, more violent than the other. Yet she was a perfectly practical person who did something, while they are wild speculators who do nothing.[84]

Chesterton's duel with Nietzsche lay near the heart of his literary efforts. It was a battle against an abyss that had tried to swallow England. It had swallowed a number of men whom Chesterton cared about: George Bernard Shaw, H. G. Wells, and John Davidson. And it was an abyss into which Chesterton himself had gazed as a young man—and which had nearly broken him. Chesterton understood Nietzsche viscerally, and pursued his combat against him with determination and resolve—as is apparent both in his having engaged with every major facet of Nietzsche's thought and in the extent to which his arguments have succeeded in refuting them.

BIBLIOGRAPHY

Ahlquist, Dale. *Common Sense 101: Lessons from G. K. Chesterton*. San Francisco: Ignatius, 2006.

Bridgewater, Patrick. *Nietzsche in Anglosaxony: A Study of Nietzsche's Impact on English and American Literature*. Leicester: Leicester University Press, 1972.

84. G. K. Chesterton, *Orthodoxy* (CWGKC 1.247–48).

Boyle, Nicholas. *Sacred and Secular Scriptures: A Catholic Approach to Literature*. South Bend, IN: University of Notre Dame Press, 2005.

Cate, Curtis. *Friedrich Nietzsche*. Woodstock, NY: Overlook, 2002.

Chesterton, G. K. *All I Survey*. London: Methuen, 1934.

———. *All Things Considered*. London: Methuen, 1908.

———. *Appreciations and Criticisms of the Works of Charles Dickens*. In vol. 15 of *The Collected Works of G. K. Chesterton*. San Francisco: Ignatius, 1989.

———. *Autobiography*. In vol. 16 of *The Collected Works of G. K. Chesterton*. San Francisco: Ignatius, 1989.

———. *The Common Man*. London: Sheed and Ward, 1950.

———. *Eugenics and Other Evils*. In vol. 4 of *The Collected Works of G. K. Chesterton*. San Francisco: Ignatius, 1986.

———. *The Flying Inn*. In vol. 7 of *The Collected Works of G. K. Chesterton*. San Francisco: Ignatius, 2004.

———. *George Bernard Shaw*. In vol. 11 of *The Collected Works of G. K. Chesterton*. San Francisco: Ignatius, 1989.

———. *Heretics*. In vol. 1 of *The Collected Works of G. K. Chesterton*. San Francisco: Ignatius, 1986.

———. *Manalive*. In vol. 7 of *The Collected Works of G. K. Chesterton*. San Francisco: Ignatius, 2004.

———. *The New Jerusalem*. London: Hodder and Stoughton, 1920.

———. *Orthodoxy*. In vol. 1 of *The Collected Works of G. K. Chesterton*. San Francisco: Ignatius, 1986.

———. "Sentimental Literature." In *The Spice of Life and Other Essays*, edited by Dorothy Collins. Dublin: Dufour Editions, 1966.

———. *The Thing*. In vol. 3 of *The Collected Works of G. K. Chesterton*. San Francisco: Ignatius, 1986.

———. *The Well and the Shallows*. London: Sheed and Ward, 1935.

———. "A Word with Dr. Oscar Levy." *G. K.'s Weekly*, October 16, 1926, 72.

———. *Twelve Types*. London: Arthur L. Humphreys, 1902.

Coates, John D. *Chesterton and the Edwardian Cultural Crisis*. Hull: Hull University Press, 1984.

Dark, Sidney, ed. *Conrad Noel: An Autobiography*. London: J. M. Dent and Sons, 1945.

Knight, Mark. *Chesterton and Evil*. New York: Fordham University Press, 2004.

Mencken, H. L. "Some Novels—and a Good One." *The Smart Set*, May 1909.

Moore, George. *Confessions of a Young Man*. London: Swan Sonnenschein, 1888.

Nietzsche, Friedrich. *The Antichrist*. In vol. 16 of *The Complete Works of Friedrich Nietzsche*, edited by Oscar Levy. London: T. N. Foulis, 1911.

———. *Beyond Good and Evil*. In vol. 5 of *The Complete Works of Friedrich Nietzsche*, edited by Oscar Levy. London: T. N. Foulis, 1909.

———. *The Birth of Tragedy*. In vol. 1 of *The Complete Works of Friedrich Nietzsche*, edited by Oscar Levy. London: T. N. Foulis, 1909.

———. *The Gay Science*. In vol. 10 of *The Complete Works of Friedrich Nietzsche*, edited by Oscar Levy. London: T. N. Foulis, 1910.

———. *Genealogy of Morals*. In vol. 15 of *The Complete Works of Friedrich Nietzsche*, edited by Oscar Levy. London: T. N. Foulis, 1913.

———. *The Twilight of the Idols*. In vol. 16 of *The Complete Works of Friedrich Nietzsche*, edited by Oscar Levy. London: T. N. Foulis, 1911.

———. *Thus Spake Zarathustra*. In vol. 11 of *The Complete Works of Friedrich Nietzsche*, edited by Oscar Levy. London: T. N. Foulis, 1909.

———. *The Will to Power*. In vol. 15 of *The Complete Works of Friedrich Nietzsche*, edited by Oscar Levy. London: T.N. Foulis, 1913.

Oddie, William. *Chesterton and the Romance of Orthodoxy: The Making of GKC, 1874–1908*. Oxford: Oxford University Press, 2008.

Pearce, Joseph. *Wisdom and Innocence: A Life of G. K. Chesterton*. London: Hodder and Stoughton, 1996.

Petzold, Gertrud von. "Nietzsche in englisch-americanischer Beurteilung bis zum Ausgang des Weltkrieges." *Anglia* 53 (1929) 134–218.

Stapleton, Julia, ed. *G. K. Chesterton at the Daily News: Literature, Liberalism and Revolution, 1901–1913* 1. London: Routledge, 2016.

Steele, Tom. *Alfred Orage and the Leeds Arts Club, 1893–1923*. Aldershot: Scolar, 1990.

Thatcher, David S. *Nietzsche in England, 1890–914: The Growth of a Reputation*. Toronto: University of Toronto Press, 1970.

Ward, Maisie. *Gilbert Keith Chesterton*. London: Sheed and Ward, 1943.

Wills, Garry. *Chesterton: Man and Mask*. London: Sheed and Ward, 1961.

Wood, Ralph C. *Chesterton: The Nightmare Goodness of God*. Waco, TX: Baylor University Press, 2011.

The great human dogma . . . is that the wind moves the trees. The great human heresy is that the trees move the wind. When people begin to say that the material circumstances have alone created the moral circumstances, then they have prevented all possibility of serious change. For if my circumstances have made me wholly stupid, how can I be certain even that I am right in altering those circumstances?

The man who represents all thought as an accident of environment is simply smashing and discrediting all his own thoughts—including that one. To treat the human mind as having an ultimate authority is necessary to any kind of thinking, even free thinking. And nothing will ever be reformed in this age or country unless we realise that the moral fact comes first. . . .

We have people who represent that all great historic motives were economic, and then have to howl at the top of their voices in order to induce the modern democracy to act on economic motives. The extreme Marxian politicians in England exhibit themselves as a small, heroic minority, trying vainly to induce the world to do what, according to their theory, the world always does. The truth is, of course, that there will be a social revolution the moment the thing has ceased to be purely economic. You can never have a revolution in order to establish a democracy. You must have a democracy in order to have a revolution.

—"The Wind and the Trees," *Tremendous Trifles*

12

First as Tragedy, Then as Marx

Duncan Reyburn

The work of Karl Marx displays a fervent and pervasive desire for revolution. He wanted to break with the given way of things and fashion a new world order: "We have nothing to lose but our chains," he and Engels declare[1]—though we certainly won't keep our possessions[2] or our sanity if Marx gets his way.

Marx famously suggested a break from the philosophical tradition by claiming that, while philosophers have thus far only "interpreted the world," a better aim would be "to change it."[3] These words (which are etched onto Marx's tombstone under the text "WORKERS OF ALL LANDS UNITE") emphasize his commitment to setting action against contemplation by focusing on economic and material realities alone. But implied in this is the Marxian insistence that "ideas and notions" are really only "the ideological superstructure of the material process of production which overdetermines

1. Karl Marx and Friedrich Engels, *The Communist Manifesto*, ed. Gareth Stedman Jones (Penguin, 2002), 258. The *Manifesto* in question, translated by Samuel Moore with Engels' oversight, was first published in England in 1888 and was widely circulated in the late nineteenth and early twentieth centuries. While the *Manifesto* is somewhat lacking in nuance it would have been the main way Marx's thinking became known in Chesterton's time, just as it remains the bestselling work of Marx today.

2. Marx and Engels, *Communist Manifesto*, 235.

3. Karl Marx, *Theses on Feuerbach*, trans. Tim Newcomb (Newcomb Libraria, 2023), 6.

all social life."[4] However, even with Marx's revolutionary intentions in mind, we should not overlook his insistence upon historical continuity. In fact, one prominent journalist—G. K. Chesterton—came to believe that Marx was hardly the revolutionary he claimed to be. His supposed break from the established order, Chesterton argued, was far less radical than he imagined. In the end, Marx appeared less a prophet of change than a hypocrite cloaked in revolutionary garb: "Communism is merely the child and heir of Capitalism, and nobody knew it better than Karl Marx."[5]

In saying this, Chesterton delicately skewered Marx's supposedly revolutionary vision by stressing its dependence upon the very order he claimed to oppose. In Chesterton's view, Marxism was a mirror image of industrial capitalism. Both systems demand the same production and power, even if communism replaces private tycoons with state bureaucrats.[6] Marxism, he thought, was a parasite, very much dependent upon capitalism for its existence: Without capitalism, there could be no Marxism; without capitalism, we would not have Marx. Marx therefore exemplifies what Chesterton calls the "negative spirit"—he knew what he did not want but he was less sure about why his alternative was any better.[7]

Marxian Communism, wrote Chesterton, "is not really an adventure apart from Capitalism; it is not really an attack on Capitalism. . . . It continues the mood and mind of the modern industrial system as it already exists in all the industrial countries. It has quite as much of the materialism; and even more of the militarism."[8] Chesterton contrasted Marx's adherence to the nineteenth century's mechanical delusions with William Morris' far more sensible refusal to submit to them.[9] Marxism's reliance on industrial progress, he argued, made it less a radical departure from capitalism than a consolidation of its logic under state control.

Historically speaking, Marxism fueled many fires in the early twentieth century, from the Bolshevik upheaval in Russia to socialist agitations across Europe. Chesterton knew a great deal about these things. He perceived how Marxism intensified the excessive and dehumanizing effects of industrial capitalism. Indeed, wherever Marxism has been implemented, albeit with interpretive variations, the best elements of capitalism have been eradicated

4. Slavoj Žižek, *Absolute Recoil* (Verso, 2014), 181.

5. G. K. Chesterton, *Illustrated London News*, August 3, 1935.

6. G. K. Chesterton, *Daily News*, November 20, 1909.

7. G. K. Chesterton, *The Collected Works of G. K. Chesterton* (Ignatius, 1986), 1:47–53.

8. Chesterton, *Illustrated London News*, August 3, 1935.

9. G. K. Chesterton, *As I Was Saying* (London, 1936), 127–32.

and the worst elements have been retained. It is no historical secret that the political stagings of Marx have left misery in their wake; and as Lesek Kołjakowski points out, these political stagings are not really inconsistent with Marxian thinking, even if Marx's apologists object.[10]

In what follows, I focus on Chesterton's interpretation of Marx as a fashionable but perilously flawed thinker. It should be clear by now that Chesterton saw his system being undermined by assumptions that are reductive, deterministic, unwisely optimistic, and riddled with blind spots. While granting that Marx was capable of intellectual coherence, Chesterton rejected his philosophy as a stifling denial of both human freedom and spiritual reality. His own outlook was and remains truer to history and human nature, and so offers a better defense of human dignity. He even offered a more virtuous alternative, including distributist economic propositions in service of choice, wonder, and the dignity of the human person. Below, I begin by noting Chesterton's restrained concession to Marx's intellectual contribution, then present his critique of materialism and determinism, and conclude with a hint of what he offers in contrast to Marx's vision.

ON MARX'S CONTRIBUTION

It will come as no surprise to those familiar with Chesterton that his perfunctory engagements with Marx were far from generous. For him, Marx was typically modern in his tendency to look at the whole world through the lens of a single idea. Like Freud and Nietzsche, Marx took a "hundredth part of the truth, and then offered it not merely as something but as everything."[11]

In a 1935 column, Chesterton described Marx as being "consistent" and "lucid," much in the way that John Calvin was "consistent" and "lucid."[12] But this was a backhanded compliment—an example of damning Marx with faint praise. Indeed, the comparison served chiefly to emphasize what he saw as their shared rigidity of thought. It was also done to note the similarity, despite certain differences, between Calvin's determinism and the determinism of Marx. Elsewhere, Chesterton noted the same comparison while making it clear that determinism was the "worst part of Calvinism" accepted by Marx.[13]

10. Lesek Kołakowski, *Is God Happy? Selected Essays* (Basic, 2013), 92–114.
11. Quoted by Dale Ahlquist in *Common Sense 101* (Ignatius, 2006), 109–10.
12. G. K. Chesterton, *Illustrated London News*, October 5, 1935.
13. G. K. Chesterton, *Daily News*, July 6, 1910.

When Chesterton said that Marx "had an answer for everything," he was not thereby celebrating Marx's genius.[14] In fact, there are echoes in this of his assessment of the archetypal "maniac," who has an "explanation" that is "always complete, and often in a purely rational sense satisfactory."[15] The maniac's mind moves in a "perfect but narrow circle."[16] While a "small circle is quite as infinite as a large circle," it is "not as large."[17] This assessment follows a paragraph in which Chesterton criticizes the "Marxian Socialist" for being imprisoned in a theoretical framework, more concerned with what he is thinking than what is actually going on beyond him. He noted that the "insane explanation" is, in essence, "unanswerable," but this is not at all the same as saying that it is correct.[18] What Chesterton said of Shaw can also be applied to Marx: "I am concerned with him as a Heretic—that is to say, a man whose philosophy is quite solid, quite coherent, and quite wrong."[19] Even if it "covers the facts" as much as the sane explanation does, it is wrong.[20] Thus, Marx's clarity was, and remains, double-edged: Whatever he gains, in terms of neatness and consistency, he loses by excluding—*ex hypothesi*—every aspect of reality that does not fit neatly within his reductionistic view of the world. In fact, his aim to "win [the] whole world" is a recipe for losing his soul.[21]

The obvious question to ask, then, is this: Why did Chesterton bother engaging Marx at all? Chesterton's restrained—or, perhaps, strained—nod to Marx's contribution may have been a tactical move. He had no choice but to acknowledge Marx as a figure of some importance. Marx was one of the big names of his time, and remains a big name today. Given that Marx was taken seriously by many of Chesterton's contemporaries, he could not dismiss him entirely.[22] However, Chesterton uses Marx largely as a foil—a thinker whose intellectual rigidity contrasts with the richer, freer reality that he wanted to welcome his reader into.

14. Chesterton, *Illustrated London News*, October 5, 1935.
15. Chesterton, *Collected Works* 1:222.
16. Chesterton, *Collected Works* 1:222.
17. Chesterton, *Collected Works* 1:222.
18. Chesterton, *Collected* 1:222.
19. Chesterton, *Collected Works* 1:46.
20. Chesterton, *Collected Works* 1:222.
21. Marx and Engels, *Communist Manifesto*, 258.
22. G. K. Chesterton, *Illustrated London News*, November 23, 1925.

AGAINST ECONOMIC REDUCTIONISM

Chesterton was well aware of Marx's fixation on economics. Marx's belief that "all the important things in history are rooted in an economic motive" struck Chesterton as a piece of imbecility—a philosophical dead end.[23] Of course, Marx's view on this "economic motive" needs some nuance. His idea is not that people simply chase money out of greed but that the material conditions of society shape people's consciousness, relationships, and actions. This may be part of the truth, but it cannot be the whole truth. What is significant for Marx is not individual choice, but the broader systems in which individuals live.[24] Indeed, Marx seems intent on obscuring the part played by individuals in economic matters, which is perhaps why he could not see the evil of his own desire to abolish private property.

In all this—echoed in Marx's idea of the "fetishism of commodities"—there is more than a hint that real human motivations are masked by market exchanges and labor conditions. Marx was trying, perhaps rightly, to disturb the common assumption that the world that confronts us is a collection of objects instead of a system of relationships. But he failed to rightly understand that system of relationships. The consequences of this can be (and, indeed, have proven to be) unnerving. All who aim for a utopia built upon a false conception of human nature ensure the creation of dystopia. Like Marx, we might be able to see that something is horribly wrong; that we have ordered the world in troubling ways. But unlike Marx, we should be careful about diagnosing the true nature of the problem. Our caution may save us from the potentially terrible consequences of poorly considered intentions.

Granted, a few wretched souls may be driven solely by material concerns, but this can hardly be true of everyone—and is likely true of no more than a handful of people. Chesterton mocked this materialistic fixation for stripping history of its human essence: "Man would not have any history if he were only economic."[25] To illustrate his meaning, Chesterton brings to mind the image of cows, which appear to be driven solely by appetite—that is, by material needs. This is a not-too-subtle way of drawing our attention to the Marxian reduction of humans to subhuman status: "The need for

23. G. K. Chesterton, *Daily News*, July 31, 1909; October 21, 1911.

24. In *The German Ideology* (1846), Marx and Engels suggest that life "is not determined by consciousness, but consciousness by life." Karl Marx and Frierich Engels, *The German Ideology*, in *Marx/Engels Collected Works* (Moscow: Progress, 1964), 5:36. By "life," he means the material conditions of existence, especially how people secure their survival through work.

25. G. K. Chesterton, *Daily News*, July 31, 1909.

food is certainly universal, so universal that it is not even human."[26] But this poses a problem for Marx's emphasis on an economic motive. Unlike people, merely materialistically minded cows have no history. "A History of Cows," says Chesterton, "would be one of the simplest and briefest of standard works."[27] One cannot imagine a bovine discourse on the dialectics of culinary vicissitudes and continuities. Cows lack history because they lack a rational soul, with its many hermeneutical transformations, moral choices, and conflicts.[28]

For Chesterton, Marx's materialism lacks sufficient depth to account for the richness of history, which stems from the various "twists and turns" of human agency. Marx consistently subordinated the individual to collective action and class struggle, and thus often, perhaps inadvertently, talked about people as if they were mere cogs in a dialectical machine. He implied something like personal responsibility in his work, but even saying this feels like an exaggeration. We can learn a great deal from economics in general, of course, but what is significant about economics is that it is made by man and for man, according to various complex desires and philosophical assumptions. If anything, economics itself points to the irreducibility of the human being to any merely economic motive.

Economics, as Marx thought of it, had already drifted very far from its origin in the idea of *oikonomikos* or *oikonomos*—the running of the home: Indeed, Marx and Engels believed the home itself must be abolished, and their stress on economics was the way to do this.[29] In this way, they gave precedence to the abstract idea—in this case the communist ideal—instead of the concrete reality; they overlooked the way people, especially families, naturally relate. Chesterton might have said to this that the trouble with Marxists was that they were not materialistic enough. They were too idealistic and too trusting of their abstractions. Another Marx, Groucho Marx (no relation!), once joked: "Who do you want to believe, me or your eyes?"[30] Karl Marx used his theory to constrict our capacity to perceive things rightly. He wanted us to believe him, not our eyes.

26. Chesterton, *Daily News*, July 31, 1909.

27. Chesterton, *Daily News*, July 31, 1909.

28. Chesterton, *Daily News*, July 31, 1909.

29. Marx and Engels, *The Communist Manifesto*, 239.

30. *Duck Soup*, directed by Leo McCarey (1933; Hollywood, CA: Paramount Pictures), film.

AGAINST MARX'S HISTORICAL DETERMINISM

As the earlier allusion to John Calvin suggests—in line with his critique of economic reductionism and its emphasis on material conditions—Chesterton's principal objection to Marx lies not in Marxian economics *per se*, but in the "materialist theory of history," which Chesterton saw as a reductive and soulless distortion of human nature and experience.[31] Chesterton was a lifelong opponent of determinism because it misunderstands the relationships between causes and effects. Marx reduces causality to a straightforward theory about how change is brought about by agents without taking sufficient account of final and formal causality. For Chesterton, determinism represented a "disastrous lapse in . . . logic," because it assumed that it knows everything with such magnificent sufficiency that it can be sure of how causes will produce certain effects, and fails easily and obviously if it can be shown that a certain action, "even a lunatic's, can be causeless."[32] "If the chain of causation can be broken for a madman, it can be broken for a man."[33]

Of particular interest to Chesterton, on Marx's historical-dialectical reductionism, is Marx's claim that history follows inevitable economic stages: nomadic, feudal, capitalist, and finally socialist. But for all its supposed dialectical subtlety, this scheme fails to do justice to the unpredictability of human will, and amounts to little more than a mechanistic fantasy. In a 1923 article, Chesterton seized on an irony evident in the Russian Revolution: Socialism, he said, triumphed "in the wrong place"—a preindustrial Russia—and this defied Marx's predictions.[34] "The Bolshevists were victorious," he wrote, "and were puzzled by their victory."[35] What happened, Chesterton contended, was not something their Marxian philosophy accounted for or predicted, but this mattered little to the Bolsheviks. Chesterton wryly noted the scramble of Marxists like Goldenweiser to salvage Marxism by discarding its evolutionary logic.[36] Of course, someone might say that Marx's point is still worth attending to—there was a revolution, after all. And yet, even this suggests that the supposedly organic movement from capitalism to socialism applauded by Marxists was not entirely trustworthy. Why must we make something happen when it is destined to happen anyway? Why must we prove inevitability to be inevitable?

31. Chesterton, *Daily News*, July 31, 1909.
32. Chesterton, *Collected Works* 1:221.
33. Chesterton, *Collected Works* 1:221.
34. G. K. Chesterton, *Illustrated London News*, March 3, 1923.
35. Chesterton, *Illustrated London News*, March 3, 1923.
36. Chesterton, *Illustrated London News*, March 3, 1923.

This is a significant problem in Marx's dialectical system, noted well by Czeslaw Milosz. Dialectics insists on a "must"—a supposedly inescapable ought—that *must* be submitted to by anyone who accepts the Marxian frame. Indeed, even the creative writer can feel that he *must* "surrender to this 'must' merely because he fears for his own skin."[37] The determinist surrenders to a whole set of biases and cognitive distortions in an attempt to defend the integrity of the system. The system is not accurate because it is right but because it is enforced. It is not reflective of materialist processes at all but, rather, reflects many unnatural impositions rooted in warped philosophical convictions. Milosz describes this briefly as follows:

> Paradoxical as it may seem, it is this subjective impotence that convinces the intellectual that the one Method is right. Everything proves it is right. Dialectics: I predict the house will burn; then I pour gasoline over the stove. The house burns; my prediction is fulfilled. Dialectics: I predict that a work of art incompatible with socialist realism will be worthless. Then I place the artist in conditions in which such a work is worthless. My prediction is fulfilled.[38]

A contemporary Marxist, Slavoj Žižek, takes aim at those "critics of Marxism who point out that there are never just two classes opposed in social life" by claiming that "it is precisely because there are never just two opposed classes that there is a class struggle."[39] He then goes on to claim that this is why "class struggle should be 'absolutized': What makes it absolute is that it is never the direct conflict of the two classes but the very excess which displaces such pure confrontation."[40] Here is yet another example of how Marx's thinking, taken up by Žižek, encourages a preference for theory over reality. Žižek uses the sort of paradox that Chesterton would despise: The theory doesn't fit the reality but we must therefore make it fit, even if that means rendering it more absolute. This reeks of insistence on making reality fit the lie so that we are not found out for evading the truth.

Against such fatalism, which mistakes what one makes happen for what would have happened anyway, Chesterton asserts the primacy of freedom: "I believe that, again and again, man was at the cross-roads and might have taken another road."[41] While contesting the views of Middleton Murray, Chesterton dismissed the notion that the past's events were

37. Czesław Miłosz, *The Captive Mind*, trans. Jane Zielonko (Knopf, 1953), 12.

38. Miłosz, *Captive Mind*, 12.

39. Žižek, *Absolute Recoil*, 378.

40. Žižek, *Absolute Recoil*, 378.

41. G. K. Chesterton, *All I Survey* (Methuen, 1934), 104.

"necessary" merely because they happened. Such a notion suggests a hindsight bias. We didn't know what was going to happen but, now that we know what happened, we therefore also know that it must have happened the way it happened. In reality, things are not so predictable.

Chesterton insisted that choice, not destiny, has shaped history.[42] But this was not merely a dispassionate rejection of Marx's ideas. His rejection of Marxism was not just intellectual but visceral. By reducing life to economic conditions, Marx's materialism negated any trace of the "divinity of man."[43] It denied our capacity for wonder, rebellion, and moral striving. For Chesterton, Marxism's determinism would always be a straitjacket on the human spirit, a theory that pretends to explain things while understanding nothing of what truly animates history—and the human heart.

ON HUMAN DIGNITY

Chesterton was aware that human dignity itself was very much under threat in his time, as it still is today. One way to understand his criticisms of Marx's work is to see them as extensions of this concern for human dignity. "This is an age in which we must defend human dignity," he once wrote, and he has been proven right many times over since his death in 1936.[44] The defense of human dignity, rooted in a deeply Christian theology and ethos, is foundational to Chesterton's philosophical outlook.[45] The chief danger embedded in Marx's outlook, already evident in what I noted above about his reductive understanding of human motives, was that he did not understand anything about personhood. He had an impersonal view of persons, who were, to him, like chaff in an economic whirlwind. Linked to this was his faulty view of causation. Like many moderns, Marx saw materiality as the mother of ethics. He thought, therefore, that people would be improved by an improved environment. And while people are, without a doubt, affected by their environment, the assumption that better material conditions will make better people is insupportable. Thus, even while Marx aimed at seemingly ethical ends, his philosophy was destined to fail. It was destined to become unethical.

42. Chesterton, *All I Survey*, 104.

43. G. K. Chesterton, *Daily News*, March 26, 1904.

44. Quoted by A. L. Maycock in the introduction to *The Man Who Was Orthodox* (Denis Dobson, 1963), 74.

45. G. K. Chesterton, *Autobiography* (Ignatius, 2006), 239; *Collected Works* 1:94, 298; *The Everlasting Man* (Ignatius, 1993), 52–53; *Saint Thomas Aquinas, Saint Francis of Assisi* (Ignatius 2002), 36, 177; Duncan Reyburn, *Seeing Things as They Are* (Cascade, 2016), 125; Donald Williams, *Mere Humanity* (B&H Academic, 2006), 15–24.

In contrast, Chesterton's philosophy has proven to be profoundly robust. One reason for this is simply that he refused to reduce the human creature to his image of the human creature. He recognized that man "has to go outside himself for everything that he wants."[46] To be human is to be almost hilariously insufficient and perpetually dependent. In *The Everlasting Man*, Chesterton described the human being as a "very strange being" with remarkable capacities and remarkable incapacities. Man "has an unfair advantage and an unfair disadvantage. He cannot sleep in his own skin; he cannot trust his own instincts. He is at once a creator moving miraculous hands and fingers and a kind of cripple."[47]

But, in saying all of this, Chesterton was more than cognizant of the fact that human needs are not reducible to material needs, just as our decisions are not enslaved to material conditions. Materiality forms only one part of the cosmic order. We are also motivated by spiritual and psychological needs. These spiritual and psychological needs are paradoxical, reflecting both our capacities and our deficits. What remains clear, however, is that our desire for a right relationship with what is material and immaterial—that is, with what is transcendent—means that "it is not seeing straight to see [the human being only] as an animal. It is not sane."[48]

What is particularly indicative of our human state, which includes meandering and zigzagging through history and not just conforming to a dialectical machine, is our capacity for joy. "I never saw an economic determinist smile," says Chesterton in what is possibly his most damning critique of Marxist thought.[49] If an economic determinist were to smile, Chesterton says, it would have to be a particular "dreadful" smile in the face of the fact "that everybody (including himself) is a victim of the environment, poisoned by prejudice about everything."[50] To prove determinism right, the Marxist must constantly eradicate any sense in himself of the surplus of meaning and being that is so blatant in daily life. For Chesterton, this seems to be a raw deal. To trade heaven for a Marxian utopia seems, and has often proven to be, equal to trading heaven for hell. And so, in contrast to a Marxian revolution, Chesterton might propose an "eternal revolution," which does not intend to overthrow the existing order in the name of something worse: It aims to recover what has been forgotten. Marx was like the

46. G. K. Chesterton, *A Miscellany of Men* (Methuen, 1912), 15.
47. Chesterton, *Everlasting Man*, 36.
48. Chesterton, *Everlasting Man*, 36.
49. Chesterton, *Illustrated London News*, March 3, 1923.
50. Chesterton, *Illustrated London News*, March 3, 1923.

man who had forgotten who he was, and Chesterton might have suggested to him, as he would suggest to us, that it is our urgent task to remember.[51]

BIBLIOGRAPHY

Ahlquist, Dale. *Common Sense 101: Lessons from G. K. Chesterton*. San Francisco: Ignatius, 2006.

Chesterton, G. K. *All I Survey*. London: Methuen, 1934.

———. *As I Was Saying*. London: Methuen, 1936.

———. *The Autobiography of G. K. Chesterton*. San Francisco: Ignatius, 2006.

———. *Heretics*. In vol. 1 of *The Collected Works of G. K. Chesterton*, 37–208. San Francisco: Ignatius, 1986.

———. *The Daily News, 1901–1907*. In vol. 27 of *The Collected Works of G. K. Chesterton*. San Francisco: Ignatius, 1986.

———. *The Daily News, 1908–1910*. In vol. 28 of *The Collected Works of G. K. Chesterton*. San Francisco: Ignatius, 1987.

———. *The Daily News, 1911–1913*. In vol. 29 of *The Collected Works of G. K. Chesterton*. San Francisco: Ignatius, 1988.

———. *The Everlasting Man*. San Francisco: Ignatius, 1993.

———. *A Miscellany of Men*. London: Methuen, 1912.

———. *Saint Thomas Aquinas* and *Saint Francis of Assisi*. San Francisco: Ignatius, 2002.

Kołakowski, Leszek. *Is God Happy? Selected Essays*. New York: Basic, 2013.

Marx, Karl. *Theses on Feuerbach*. Translated by Tim Newcomb. N.p.: Newcomb Libraria, 2023.

Marx, Karl, and Friedrich Engels. *The Communist Manifesto*. Edited by Gareth Stedman Jones. London: Penguin, 2002.

———. *The German Ideology*. In vol. 5 of *Marx/Engels Collected Works*. Moscow: Progress, 1964.

Maycock, A. L. Introduction to *The Man Who Was Orthodox*, by G. K. Chesterton. London: Denis Dobson, 1963.

McCarey, Leo, dir. *Duck Soup*. 1933; Hollywood, CA: Paramount Pictures film.

Miłosz, Czesław. *The Captive Mind*. Translated by Jane Zielonko. New York: Alfred A. Knopf, 1953.

Reyburn, Duncan. *Seeing Things as They Are: G. K. Chesterton and the Drama of Meaning*. Eugene, OR: Cascade, 2016.

Williams, Donald T. *Mere Humanity: G. K. Chesterton, C. S. Lewis, and J. R. R. Tolkien on the Human Condition*. Nashville, TN: B&H Academic, 2006.

Žižek, Slavoj. *Absolute Recoil: Towards a New Foundation of Dialectical Materialism*. London: Verso, 2014.

51. Chesterton, *Collected Works* 1:257.

A new philosophy generally means in practice the praise of some old vice. We have had the sophist who defends cruelty, and calls it masculinity. We have had the sophist who defends profligacy, and calls it the liberty of the emotions. We have had the sophist who defends idleness, and calls it art. It will almost certainly happen—it can almost certainly be prophesied—that in this saturnalia of sophistry there will at some time or other arise a sophist who desires to idealize cowardice. And when we are once in this unhealthy world of mere wild words, what a vast deal there would be to say for cowardice! "Is not life a lovely thing and worth saving?" the soldier would say as he ran away. "Should I not prolong the exquisite miracle of consciousness?" the housekeeper would say as he hid under the table. "As long as there are roses and lilies on the earth shall I not remain there?" would come the voice of the citizen from under the bed. It would be quite as easy to defend the coward as a kind of poet and mystic as it has been, in many recent books, to defend the emotionalist as a kind of poet and mystic, or the tyrant as a kind of poet and mystic.

—"THE MESUTHELAHITE," *ALL THINGS CONSIDERED*

The riddle of life is simply this. For some mad reason in this mad world of ours, the things which men differ about most are exactly the things about which they must be got to agree. Men can agree on the fact that the earth goes round the sun. But then it does not matter a dump whether the earth goes around the sun or the Pleiades. . . . Men cannot agree about morals: sex, property, individual rights, fixity and contracts, patriotism, suicide, public habits of health—these are exactly the things that men tend to fight about. And these are exactly the things that must be settled somehow on strict principles. Study each of them, and you will find each of them works back certainly to a philosophy, probably to a religion.

—*ILLUSTRATED LONDON NEWS*, MARCH 16, 1907

13

Chesterton Analyzes Freud

Dale Ahlquist

On Professor Freud—
The ignorant pronounce it Frood,
To cavil or applaud.
The well-informed pronounce it Froyd,
But I pronounce it Fraud.[1]

THEY BOTH SMOKED CIGARS. That might be the only thing they had in common.

Though Sigmund Freud apparently never mentions his contemporary G. K. Chesterton, Chesterton has quite a few things to say about Freud. He also has a lot to say about fashion. Put the two together, add some more alliteration, and you have one of Chesterton's many prophetic pronouncements: "There will be a fashionable fatalism founded on Freud."[2] And though impermanence is part of fashion's nature, it can still leave a lasting

1. G. K. Chesteron, "On Professor Freud," *G. K.'s Weekly*, March 28, 1925, https://library.chesterton.org/on-professor-freud-8593/.

2. G. K. Chesterton, *Illustrated London News*, May 29, 1920.

mark. Though it always flees, it often flees slowly and breaks things while making its long exit.

Freud, known as the father of psychology (though it predates his fatherhood), has had a huge and pervasive influence on modern culture. It is proper to include him among the philosophers because his ideas are far more theoretical than they are scientific. But his theory has nonetheless been embraced by scientists, doctors of medicine, academics, media personalities, entertainers, and advertisers. As Chesterton observes: "The wild and credulous worship of Psychology seems to be especially common in America. As we have seen a new republic of Russia founded entirely upon Marx, perhaps we may eventually see a new republic of America founded entirely upon Freud."[3] As is so often the case, Chesterton accurately describes things before they happen.

Freud's philosophy can be boiled down to one word, and Chesterton says that the student of Freud is forbidden to forget it: sex. Everything we do is based on seeking pleasure, and primarily sexual pleasure. The libido, the sex drive, runs our engine. (If I appear to be oversimplifying anything, try to repress your anger at me.)

Freud says that the psyche is composed of three parts: id, ego, superego. The id is completely unconscious; it desires instant gratification, and represents the largest and most powerful part of our psyche. The ego is the most conscious part, and has the power to delay gratification. The superego is largely unconscious and forbids gratification of certain desires. Thus, the superego is one's "conscience."

The ego tries to balance the id and the superego. The id is not necessarily evil, and the superego is not necessarily good—and is even the source of mental disorders, as it has trouble coping with the id. The most common (and famous) defense mechanism used to deal with the anxiety created by the conflict between the id and the superego is repression. And repression is the primary problem treated by psychotherapy.

Freud claims that sexual desire—and unfulfilled sexual desire—starts early. In infancy and on through youth. A boy's affection for his mother is sexual, and vice versa. The son is jealous of his father and wants to kill him. This is the basis of one of Freud's most infamous concepts: the Oedipus complex.

But the child comes to realize that the father is more powerful than himself. God is simply a projection of the father figure that the child has dreamed up. And the child fears God even more than his earthly father, unless, like Freud, he manages to become an atheist. According to Freud,

3. G. K. Chesterton, Introduction to *Fancies vs. Fads* (Methuen, 1923).

religion is a neurosis. There is no God. Neither is there free will. Everything we do can be blamed on something else.

We are going to consider Chesterton's commentary on Freud's views in regard to four main topics: sex, the unconscious, psychoanalysis, and religion. But it is important to note that Chesterton is not merely a reactionary; he has a cohesive philosophy and it directly collides with Freud's philosophy, which Chesterton argues does not hold together. Chesterton starts with the premise that "it is the only true object of existence to mean something."[4] Nature, he says, is looking for the supernatural. "Take away the supernatural, and what remains is the unnatural."[5] Chesterton starts with God and ends with God. Light from light. Freud passes from the darkness of dreams to the deeds done in the dark. And any contemporary intellectual considering the two is faced with the choice between the clarity of Christianity and the confusion of Freud. "Men have always one of two things: either a complete and conscious philosophy or the unconscious acceptance of the broken bits of some incomplete and shattered and often discredited philosophy."[6]

As for Freud's pet mythological theme, Chesterton responds: "It was the whole point of Oedipus that he did not have the Oedipus-Complex. It was the whole point of him that he only knew certain things too late which our bright and breezy psychoanalysts would introduce us to much too early."[7] Much too early. "The way in which some psychoanalysts talk about the mother-complex would certainly indicate that a mother is rather too complex a thing for their intellects to analyze."[8] For them there is only the sex-instinct rather than the maternal instinct, and they suggest "that holy motherhood or the love of little children has in it something of the unearthly darkness of Oedipus."[9]

Any theory that dismisses or demeans the innocence of children is, to Chesterton, absurd. And a violation. But it is part of the modern tendency to separate everything from everything else, leading to a broken world with

4. Chesterton, *Illustrated London News*, October 28, 1905.

5. G. K. Chesterton, "Christmas and the Aesthetes," in *Heretics* (John Lane, The Bodley Head, 1905).

6. G. K. Chesterton, "The Revival of Philosophy—Why?," in *The Common Man* (Sheed and Ward, 1950).

7. Chesterton, *Illustrated London News*, October 26, 1929.

8. G. K. Chesterton, "The Game of Psychoanalysis," *Century Magazine*, May 1923.

9. Chesterton, *Century Magazine*, May 1923.

broken thinking. The world, he says, has become "one wild divorce court."[10] The separation of sex from love has resulted in the separation of birth from sex. The isolation of sex has transformed it into an idol.

Chesterton likens the Freudian fad of trying to prove that everything is sexual to the Marxian fad of trying to prove that everything is economic. "As the one fad conceives everything about the bird to be connected with mating, so the other conceives everything connected with it to consist of catching worms."[11] These manias do not convince the mind, but cloud it. They are degrading and depressing and disconnected from true conclusions about the world. And they can cause "deep and disastrous wounds and dislocations in the mentality of the individual man."[12]

As for Freud's imposing theory of the unconscious, Chesterton meekly suggests: "Before men analyze the uses of the unconscious mind, it may, perhaps, be well for them to discover the use of the mind."[13] And just as Chesterton compares the fad of Marx with the fad of Freud, he does the same thing with the fad of Darwin: "Fashionable Darwinism seemed to remember everything about the Missing Link except that he was missing. Fashionable Freudism will remember everything about the unconscious mind except that it is unconscious."[14]

> The science of Freud would make it essentially impossible to say how far our reason or unreason does go, or where it stops. For if a man is ignorant of his other self, how can he possibly know that the other self is ignorant? He can no longer say with pride that at least he knows that he knows nothing. That is exactly what he does not know. The floor has fallen out of his mind and the abyss below may contain subconscious certainties as well as subconscious doubts. He is too ignorant even to ignore; and he must confess himself an agnostic about whether he is an agnostic.[15]

For Chesterton, the conscience is not unconscious. "God has given all men a conscience and conscience can give all men a kind of peace."[16] It is also the basis of justice and of the concept of equal rights. If his conscience is

10. G. K. Chesterton, "The Universal Stick," in *What's Wrong With the World* (Cassell, 1910).

11. Chesterton, *Century Magazine*, May 1923.

12. Chesterton, *Century Magazine*, May 1923.

13. Chesterton, *Century Magazine*, May 1923.

14. Chesterton, *Illustrated London News*, May 29, 1920.

15. G. K. Chesterton, "The Battle with the Dragon," in *The New Jerusalem* (Hodder and Stoughton, 1920).

16. G. K. Chesterton, "The Escape from Paganism."

not God-given (that is, if it's not the voice of God), if it's not even the voice of the people (that is, common sense), and if it is not what we call morality, "then his conscience is no more necessarily sacred than his nightmares."[17] But Chesterton maintains that man always has a conscience, even if it be a bad conscience.

It is with our conscience that we exercise our freedom. That means both the power to do good and the power to do evil. To choose to obey God, to follow him, or to disobey God, to defy him. Virtue is a choice. Self-control is self-government, which is the very definition of freedom. It is the cardinal virtue of temperance. "Temperance," says Chesterton, "is the object of morality in all matters—in wine, in war, in sex, in patriotism."[18] Temperance is what makes it possible "to have wine without drunkenness, war without massacre, love without profligacy."[19]

The loss of self-control—that is, giving into temptation—is sin. Sin is separation from God. The conscience calls us to reconcile with God. But to maintain the separation, to live in a state of sin and sinning, dulls the conscience. But it is unsatisfying.

As Plato points out, there is a connection between virtue and happiness. Or, as Chesterton affirms: If you are good, you will be happy. We recognize that the attack on virtue is a threat to ultimate joy. "The measure of the moral shock immediately given to the normal conscience, by certain things, is itself one of the arguments for intellectually condemning them."[20]

As for Freud's famous method of therapy, Chesterton says, "I think these people will go wrong about psychoanalysis, simply because they always go wrong about analysis. They never do really analyse. That is, they never do really resolve a thing into all its parts. They pick out some particular part that happens to take their fancy. They have got hold of only one truth, and they state it entirely out of proportion to a thousand other truths." As mentioned earlier, he says this is true both in the hypothesis of Freud and that of Darwin. For whatever its scientific merits, the "actual effect of Darwinism" was "a vague fashionable feeling that everything was evolution and that evolution was everything"[21]—the idea of endless and inevitable progress. "The same thing will probably happen in the case of the conjectures of Freud, and there will be the same tendency to let a

17. Chesterton, *Illustrated London News*, June 2, 1917.

18. G. K. Chesterton, "The Patriotic Idea," in *England: A Nation* (Cecil Palmer, 1933).

19. Chesterton, "Patriotic Idea."

20. G. K. Chesterton, "The Distributist Difficulties—III," *G. K.'s Weekly*, October 5, 1929.

21. Chesterton, *Illustrated London News*, May 29, 1920.

hypothesis harden into a dogma."[22] Rigid conclusions made about the unconscious and our behavior will be blamed on dark motives beyond our mental grasp. Yet, the one who should be an agnostic about the things of which he is really ignorant "is ready to assert his absolute knowledge of everything to the verge of a contradiction in terms. Just as he will always try to write a history of prehistoric man, so he will always struggle to be conscious of his own unconsciousness."[23] Chesterton succinctly puts the Darwinian and Freudian fads together: "Progress tells us we are better than our fathers, even where conscience tells us we are worse than ourselves."[24] Just as Darwinism pervaded everything, so did Freudianism. Psychoanalysis even found its way into literary criticism. But Chesterton, himself an outstanding literary critic, was not impressed, much less convinced. "The psychoanalysts know nothing at all about the Greek tragedies. I gather this from the astounding fact that they talk about the Oedipus-Complex, obviously without knowing who Oedipus was."[25] As noted earlier, the whole point of Oedipus is that he did not have the Oedipus complex. His tragedy is in the great conflict of fate versus free will, not in the conscious versus the unconscious.

The Freudian literary critics also attempted to make Shakespeare a pupil of Freud. "The psychoanalysts continue to buzz in a mysterious manner round the problem of Hamlet. They are especially interested in the things of which Hamlet was unconscious, not to mention the things of which Shakespeare was unconscious."[26] He says that this sort of criticism "has lost the last rags of common sense. Hamlet requires no such subconscious explanation, for he explains himself, and was perhaps rather too fond of doing so. . . . There was a conflict, but he was conscious of it from beginning to end. He was not an unconscious person; but a far too conscious one."[27] The critics avoid the morality which Shakespeare accepts as a given: "Shakespeare certainly did believe in the struggle between duty and inclination. The critic instinctively avoids the admission that Hamlet's was a struggle between duty and inclination; and tries to substitute a struggle between

22. Chesterton, *Illustrated London News*, May 29, 1920.

23. Chesterton, *Century Magazine*, May 1923.

24. G. K. Chesterton, *New Witness*, July 19, 1918, https://library.chesterton.org/on-professor-freud-8593/.

25. Chesterton, *Illustrated London News*, Oct. 26, 1929.

26. G. K. Chesterton, "Hamlet and the Psycho-Analyst," in *Fancies vs. Fads* (Methuen, 1923).

27. Chesterton, "Hamlet and the Psycho-Analyst."

consciousness and subconsciousness. He gives Hamlet a complex to avoid giving him a conscience."[28]

Chesterton also noticed a trend in the modern novelist to become a psychoanalyst of the fictional characters he has created. He will

> think nothing of tracing the most contradictory motives under the most common actions. He will represent hoary and horrible pagan perversions as disguising themselves under fresh and innocent infantile impulses. He will represent every image that can occur to the mind sleeping or waking as a symbol of something totally different. But it never seems to occur to him that historical dangers can disguise themselves, that old foes can appear with new masks, or that the ghost of the twelfth century can easily put on the hat and trousers of the twentieth. He professes to know what Freud meant when he said that dreams are sexual hieroglyphics written darkly and illegibly.[29]

Interestingly, whatever splash such novelists may have made, they all sank and are not remembered. The particular novelist to which Chesterton is referring is a typical example. How many people still read J. D. Beresford?

One of Chesterton's greatest insights into the phenomenon of Freud and its impact is that psychoanalysis is "confession without absolution."[30] It is without absolution not only because the doctor has no authority or means to provide the needed sacrament, but because there is no repentance. The priest can get rid of the sin. But neither the doctor nor the patient will even admit the sin. And so it remains. Freud won't come to terms with God because he won't come to terms with evil.

Freud takes his place in modern philosophy, which has done its best to rid itself and the world of God. Left to itself it is a ring of madness, for there is nothing other than itself. The most self-contradictory of all the schools of philosophy is psychology, which purports to be a science on par with biology. Its name literally means "the study of the soul." But in practice it denies the very thing it purports to study. Ideally at least, it is the study of sanity, but all it studies is the abnormal mind and divergent behavior, and gives us theories and explanations that tend to defy common sense.

28. Chesterton, "Hamlet and the Psycho-Analyst."

29. Chesterton, *Illustrated London News*, August 6, 1927.

30. G. K. Chesterton, "Fads and Public Opinion," in *What I Saw in America* (Cecil Palmer, 1922).

One of the principal themes in Chesterton's books is sanity. *Orthodoxy* is about what is the most sane philosophy. *The Outline of Sanity* is about what is the most sane economy. *What's Wrong with the World* is about what are the main enemies of a sane culture. The collision of sanity and insanity figures in such fictional works as *The Ball and the Cross*, *The Tales of the Long Bow*, *The Return of Don Quixote*, and of course, *The Poet and the Lunatics*. Sanity is a balance and even a paradox. The sane man, says Chesterton, is one who keeps tragedy in his heart and comedy in his head. But ultimately, the comedy of man outlasts the tragedy of man. Man is an adventurer, and the virtue of the adventurer is "a certain happy temper; an instantaneous instinct for seeking relief in laughter rather than lamentation; a readiness, when the world is overturned, to enjoy it if possible as a topsy-turvydom."[31]

The other key to sanity is humility, to not be obsessed with oneself, to not take oneself so seriously that one collapses into oneself, becoming useless to the world. Insanity is chains; sanity is freedom: "Angels can fly because they can take themselves lightly."[32] Freud was incapable of this; Chesterton soared. Freud had a very dark and despairing view of humanity, and Chesterton had a very bright and hopeful one. Freud hated man and saw him as a disease of the dust. Chesterton loved him and saw him as the image of God.

Yet Chesterton says generously, "I have no right to suggest that Dr. Freud is really anything like so absurd as his admirers have represented him."[33] Certainly Freud's admirers have used Freudian psychology to justify atheism, but also to explain and even exploit both commercial manipulation and political propaganda. And also the sexual revolution. This is especially due to two of Freud's most famous and influential disciples.

The first was his nephew, Edward Bernays. In addition to popularizing Freud in America, Bernays is considered the inventor of public relations. Using his uncle's theory that human behavior was driven by unconscious impulses based on sex and aggression, Bernays showed major corporations how to sell more products by linking them to symbols that appealed to their customers' unconscious desires.

Neither Freud nor Bernays believed in democracy. Just as Freud believed that the id in the individual had to be properly controlled by the superego, so, too, he and Bernays believed that the masses were not driven by rational thought and had to be controlled by the elite few. It was an idea

31. Chesterton, *New Witness*, April 5, 1917.

32. G. K. Chesterton, "The Eternal Revolution," in *Orthodoxy* (John Lane, The Bodley Head, 1908).

33. Chesterton, *Illustrated London News*, October 26, 1929.

that Bernays literally capitalized on, being one of the most profitable business consultants of the twentieth century. People were no longer people but consumers. They were passive and malleable. They bought what they were told to buy by suggestive advertising that appealed to their unconscious desires. They no longer thought for themselves. But this had farther reaching implications. It was the wide acceptance of Freud's philosophy that convinced people, whether consciously or unconsciously, that they were not responsible for their own actions. But as much as his nephew's influence on business had a direct impact on consumerism and culture and general behavior, even more pernicious was the direct application of his techniques in politics, namely in the effective use of propaganda. Ironically, the Nazis whom Freud fled were imitators of his nephew's marketing ploys.

One could argue that Bernays demonstrates the validity of Freud's theories since he so successfully implemented them on a wide scale. But the argument against that is quite simple: Appealing to lust and greed in order to sell clothes and cars does not demand a theory to explain it—only a theory to justify it. And appealing to pride in order to push political agendas simply cannot be justified. There is a reason why propaganda became a dirty word—not for the mud on its hands, but for the blood. "All the evil loves," Chesterton says, are largely responsible for "the making of the conflicts of mankind."[34]

Probably Freud's most influential student was Wilhelm Reich. But Reich took Freud's ideas and applied them in a completely contrary manner. While Freud maintained that we should not give in to the undesirable desires that churn in our unconscious, Reich argued just the opposite: Our psychological problems are based on *not* giving into our sexual urges. Thus he promoted unrestrained and unrestricted sex, not only among adults but among preadults. He also promoted and provided contraception. And not surprisingly, he had multiple affairs, mostly with his patients and his research assistants, resulting in some of them, and even one of his wives, being compelled by him to have abortions.

Reich claimed that sexual energy could cure cancer and make rain. He sold "Orgone" boxes the size of small phone booths that you could sit in and get infused with Orgone energy. The FDA ruled that it was a massive fraud and told him to stop, but he didn't. So he was arrested and sent to prison. That's where he died, insane. But he was already insane when he went in.

His sex box and his subsequent demise make him a textbook example of Chesterton's description of the modern philosopher who traps himself in the clean, well-lit prison of a single idea. Not only do his ideas lead to

34. Chesterton, *Illustrated London News*, January 14, 1911.

madness, but the madness is self-destructive. Yet, unbelievably, the world embraced this madman's single idea. It was Wilhelm Reich who gave us the sexual revolution, a term he coined. He is largely the one to thank for the wide and banal acceptance of premarital and extramarital sex, as well as the consequences connected to it: divorce, contraception, abortion, and perversion. He was a miserable, paranoid, and prideful man who left miserable people in his wake.

Chesterton says, "The minute that sex ceases to be a servant, it becomes a tyrant."[35] What the sexual revolution led to was people who became slaves to their desires. Chesterton, looking at the past, predicted the future.

But perhaps we should not refer to Chesterton's foresight as mere predictions, which have a sort of sideshow effect. They are better understood as prophesies, which have a soul-shaking effect. In 1926, bearing Freud in mind, Chesterton says, "The next great heresy is going to be an attack on morality, especially sexual morality. The madness of tomorrow is not in Moscow, but much more in Manhattan."[36] He would not have known the names of Freud's disciples, Edward Bernays and Wilhelm Reich, who carried out the attack just as Chesterton prophesied, not from outside our borders but from within.

If Bernays brought Freud's psychology into a cul-de-sac, an endless turnaround of manipulation and madness, Reich brought it to a dead end. There is no place else to go. In the end, says Chesterton, again prophetically, "sex becomes sexlessness."[37] But Chesterton, like any true prophet, does not preach despair, but hope. He tells us where the wrong road leads, but he also points the way back to the right road. He offers direction for those who have engaged in the soulless study of the soul: "There will be no future for modern psychology until it again studies the old moral theology."[38]

BIBLIOGRAPHY

Chesterton, G. K. *All Things Considered*. In vol. 3 of *The Collected Works of G. K. Chesterton*. Edited by Lawrence J. Clancy. San Francisco: Ignatius, 1990.

———. *The Common Man*. London: Sheed and Ward, 1950.

———. "The Distributist Difficulties—III." Chesterton Digital Library. https://library.chesterton.org/the-distributist-difficultiesiii-34196/.

———. *England: A Nation*. London: Cecil Palmer, 1933.

35. G. K. Chesterton, "The World St. Francis Found," in *St. Francis of Assisi* (Hodder and Stoughton, 1923).

36. G. K. Chesterton, *G. K.'s Weekly*, June 19, 1926.

37. Chesterton, *Illustrated London News*, March 30, 1929.

38. Chesterton, *Illustrated London News*, March 30, 1929.

———. "The Escape from Paganism." Chesterton Digital Library. https://library.chesterton.org/the-everlasting-man-86494/.

———. *Fancies vs. Fads*. London: Methuen, 1923.

———. "The Game of Psychoanalysis." In *The Century Illustrated Monthly Magazine* (May 1923).

———. *Heretics*. London: John Lane, The Bodley Head, 1905.

———. *The Illustrated London News, 1905–1907*. In vol. 27 of *The Collected Works of G. K. Chesterton*. Edited by Lawrence J. Clancy. San Francisco: Ignatius, 1986.

———. *The New Jerusalem*. London: Hodder and Stoughton, 1920.

———. *Orthodoxy*. London: John Lane, The Bodley Head, 1908.

———. "The Respectable Adventurer." Chesterton Digital Library. https://library.chesterton.org/the-respectable-adventurer-52706/.

———. *St. Francis of Assisi*. London: Hodder and Stoughton, 1923.

———. *The Uses of Diversity*. In vol. 4 of *The Collected Works of G. K. Chesterton*. Edited by Lawrence J. Clancy. San Francisco: Ignatius, 1991.

———. *What I Saw in America*. London: Cecil Palmer, 1922.

———. *What's Wrong with the World*. London: Cassell, 1910.

It is incomprehensible to me that any thinker can calmly call himself a modernist; he might as well call himself a Thursdayite. . . . The real objection to modernism is simply that it is a form of snobbishness. It is an attempt to crush a rational opponent not by reason, but by some mystery of superiority, by hinting that one is specially up to date or particularly "in the know." To flaunt the fact that we have had all the last books from Germany is simply vulgar; like flaunting the fact that we have had all the last bonnets from Paris. To introduce into philosophical discussions a sneer at a creed's antiquity is like introducing a sneer at a lady's age. It is caddish because it is irrelevant. The pure modernist is merely a snob; he cannot bear to be a month behind the fashion.

—"The Case for the Ephemeral," *All Things Considered*

In numberless novels and newspaper articles, we have all read about a process which is still apparently regarded as novel or new; though it has been described in almost exactly the same terms for nearly a hundred years; and in slightly different terms for hundreds of years before that. I mean what is called the growth of doubt or the disturbance of faith; and the only point about it which is pertinent here is this; that it is always described as a revolt of the deeper parts of the mind against something that is comparatively superficial. We need not deny that modern doubt, like ancient doubt, does ask deep questions; we only deny that, as compared with our own philosophy, it gives any deeper answers. And it is a general rule, touching what is called modern thought, that while the questions are often really deep, the answers are often decidedly shallow. And it is perhaps even more important to remark that, while the questions are in a sense eternal, the answers are in every sense ephemeral.

—"My Six Conversions," *The Well and the Shadows*

14

The Paradoxes of Pragmatism

Landon Loftin

There are some people, nevertheless—and I am one of them—who think that the most practical and important thing about a man is still his view of the universe. We think that for a landlady considering a lodger, it is important to know his income, but still more important to know his philosophy. We think that for a general about to fight an enemy, it is important to know the enemy's numbers, but still more important to know the enemy's philosophy. We think the question is not whether the theory of the cosmos affects matters, but whether in the long run, anything else affects them.

—"Introductory Remarks on the Importance of Orthodoxy," *Heretics* (quoted by William James in *Pragmatism: A New Name for Some Old Ways of Thinking*)

Men have always one of two things: either a complete and conscious philosophy or the unconscious acceptance of the broken bits of some incomplete and shattered and often discredited philosophy. Such broken bits are the phrases I have quoted: efficiency and evolution and the rest. The idea of being "practical," standing all by itself, is all that remains of a Pragmatism that cannot stand at all. It is impossible to be practical without a Pragma. And what would happen if you went up to the next practical man you met and said to the poor dear old duffer, "Where is your Pragma?"

—"The Revival of Philosophy—Why?" *The Common Man*

Despite obvious differences, there are some surprising commonalities and connections between G. K. Chesterton and William James. Today, Chesterton is remembered as a journalist, literary critic, and defender of orthodox Christianity. James, on the other hand, is remembered as a forerunner of modern empirical psychology and one of the first Americans to earn a permanent place in the annals of Western philosophy. Among philosophers, his legacy is primarily founded upon a lively defense of two philosophical doctrines: pragmatism and radical empiricism. Though these two doctrines are naturally akin, James insists that there is no strict logical connection between them.[1] I will therefore focus on the former in order to consider Chesterton's surprisingly complex relationship with the pragmatist movement.

James' Pragmatism

According to James, pragmatists can be distinguished from other philosophers by their use of a particular method and, in many cases, by their adherence to a particular theory of truth.[2] He notes that many philosophers have, consciously or not, made use of the pragmatic method without accepting a pragmatic theory of truth; these, in James' view, are pragmatists of a sort, but only in what we may here call "the weak sense" of the term. Philosophers who are pragmatists in the strong sense of the term accept the pragmatic theory of truth as both a justification and consequence of a stringent application of their method.

James once described the pragmatic method as "a method of settling metaphysical disputes that otherwise might be interminable."[3] It is important to note, though, that practitioners of the method do not "settle" these disputes by siding with one or the other party, but by helping disputants on both sides attend to the practical implications (or lack thereof) between alternative views. They then apply the so-called "pragmatic criterion of meaning," which states, in James' words, that there can be "no difference in

1. William James, *Pragmatism: A New Name for Some Old Ways of Thinking* (independently published, 2003), vi.

2. James, *Pragmatism*, 23.

3. James, *Pragmatism*, 16.

abstract truth that doesn't express itself in a difference in concrete fact and in conduct consequent upon that fact."[4] Thus, the first step in applying the pragmatic method to long-debated philosophical questions (e.g., "Is the world one or many?—fated or free?—material or spiritual?") is to ask: "What difference would it practically make to anyone if this notion rather than that notion were true?"[5] According to James, "If no practical difference whatever can be traced, then the alternatives mean practically the same thing, and all dispute is idle."[6] James believed that many of the disputes that loom large in the history of philosophy "collapse into insignificance the moment you subject them to this simple test of tracing a concrete consequence."[7] This is, again, because "there can *be* no difference anywhere that doesn't *make* a difference elsewhere—no difference in abstract truth that doesn't express itself in a difference in concrete fact and in conduct consequent upon that fact."[8]

But, whereas the criterion of meaning justifies a philosopher's use of the pragmatic method, most self-identified pragmatists have believed that the internal logic of their view demands an additional pragmatic criterion, this time of *truth*. According to this criterion, "truth is one species of the good, and not, as is usually supposed, a category distinct from good, and co-ordinate with it. The true," James says, "is the name of whatever proves itself to be good in the way of belief, and good, too, for definite, assignable reasons."[9]

JAMES AND CHESTERTON

It is surprising in one way and unsurprising in another to find that James was an ardent admirer of Chesterton. Some evidence for this can be found in his letters, which contain several references to Chesterton and recommendations of his work. In one letter, for instance, James asks his correspondent whether he has read *Heretics*, then declares Chesterton to be "a tremendously strong writer and true thinker, despite his mannerism of paradox."[10] Other references are similar in form, containing high praise

4. James, *Pragmatism*, 17.
5. James, *Pragmatism*, 17.
6. James, *Pragmatism*, 17.
7. James, *Pragmatism*, 17.
8. James, *Pragmatism*, 17; emphasis original.
9. James, *Pragmatism*, 27.
10. William James, *Collected Letters of William James*, ed. Henry James (Atlantic Monthly, 1920), 2:257.

that is occasionally tempered by reservations about Chesterton's characteristically paradoxical mode of expression. For present purposes, however, the most interesting reference is found in a letter by which James encourages his correspondent "to join the band of 'pragmatistic' or 'humanistic' philosophers," and tentatively claims Chesterton as one of its representatives.[11] Indeed, though James leaves room for the possibility that he is mistaken about Chesterton's views, he ventures to suggest that Chesterton should be considered on a level with himself as part of the second tier of the movement's leading lights.[12]

This letter, though remarkable, is also puzzling. Why did James associate Chesterton with the pragmatist movement? To answer this question, we must first note that James' understanding of Chesterton's philosophical views had, at that time, been formed primarily on his reading of *Heretics* (and possibly, to a lesser extent, on early essays, such as those collected in *The Defendant*); *Orthodoxy*, which contains Chesterton's first explicit statement on pragmatism, had not yet been published. This statement, as we shall see, demonstrates that James was wrong to think of Chesterton as a pragmatist, at least in the strong sense of the term; but, as we shall also see, it contains an admission that may shed some light on James' reasons for suspecting Chesterton of pragmatist leanings.

CHESTERTON'S CRITIQUE

Chesterton wrote *Orthodoxy* as a follow-up to *Heretics* because the latter had been criticized for failing to offer a viable alternative to the worldviews that he pillories therein: "I will begin to worry about my philosophy," said one of his critics, "when Mr. Chesterton has given us his."[13] According to the introduction, *Orthodoxy* is Chesterton's answer to this challenge. But before giving a positive statement of his beliefs, he spends some time surveying some of the then-popular philosophies that were inimical to his project on the grounds that they were "merely destructive," by which he meant that

11. James goes on: "I hope you know and love [Chesterton], who seems to me a great teller of the truth. His systematic preference for contradictions and paradoxical forms of statement seems to me a mannerism somewhat to be regretted in so wealthy a mind; but that is a blemish from which some of our very greatest intellects are not altogether free—the philosopher of Barrytown himself being not wholly exempt." James, *Collected Letters of William James* 2:257.

12. James was being modest, of course. When this letter was written, he was universally recognized as the leading exponent of pragmatism in the English-speaking world.

13. G. K. Chesterton, *Orthodoxy* (Hendrickson Christian Classics, 2006), 3.

they attack not just one thought or another but the very foundations of thinking. This survey ends with a brief though highly suggestive passage on pragmatism, which is worth quoting at length and examining in detail:

> This bald summary of the thought-destroying forces of our time would not be complete without some reference to pragmatism; for though I have here used and should everywhere defend the pragmatist method as a preliminary guide to truth, there is an extreme application of it which involves the absence of all truth whatever. My meaning can be put shortly thus. I agree with the pragmatists that apparent objective truth is not the whole matter; that there is an authoritative need to believe the things that are necessary to the human mind. But I say that one of those necessities precisely is a belief in objective truth. The pragmatist tells a man to think what he must think and never mind the Absolute. But precisely one of the things that he must think is the Absolute. This philosophy, indeed, is a kind of verbal paradox. Pragmatism is a matter of human needs; and one of the first of human needs is to be something more than a pragmatist. Extreme pragmatism is just as inhuman as the determinism it so powerfully attacks. The determinist (who, to do him justice, does not pretend to be a human being) makes nonsense of the human sense of actual choice. The pragmatist, who professes to be specially human, makes nonsense of the human sense of actual fact.[14]

Chesterton's characterization of pragmatism raises some questions that will need to be addressed; before addressing them, though, we should note what this passage tells us about how he understood his own relation to the pragmatist movement. Chesterton here appeals to a distinction that James himself made between the pragmatic method and the pragmatic theory of truth: Chesterton saw value in the method (as he understood it) and claims to have used it himself, but only as "a preliminary guide to truth." He did not, however, accept the "extreme application," which assumes "the absence of all truth whatever." We may therefore characterize Chesterton as pragmatic in the weak sense, but not in the strong. Hence, it is not at every element of pragmatism, or at every pragmatist, but at what he considered an extreme application of the pragmatic method that his critique is principally aimed.

14. Chesterton, *Orthodoxy*, 31.

All the same, a critic may accuse Chesterton of misrepresentation: "Even extreme pragmatists," the critic might say, "do not dispense with the concept of truth altogether, but with certain assumptions about the nature of truth which they regard as unwarranted and problematic." But the context of Chesterton's remark shows that, by "truth," he meant "absolute" or "objective truth": that is, truth that holds independently of all human values and opinions. The real question, then, is whether pragmatism "involves the absence of all [*objective*] truth whatever," and the answer, on a plausible interpretation of William James (especially his later writings), is a qualified "yes."

The qualifications are important, though, and two should be mentioned here. The first is that James believed in the existence of an objective (i.e., mind-independent) world, but this did not translate into an objective view of truth because, in his words, "realities are not *true*, they *are*; and beliefs are true *of* them."[15] Moreover, for James, beliefs are true *of* realities in the pragmatic sense of being useful to the believer in view of their prior commitments, present circumstances, and future aims (which is a slightly more elaborate way of saying that they are "good in the way of belief"). In a similar vein, we should note that though James' theory of truth is ultimately subjective, he does not defend a naive, "anything goes" kind of subjectivism, according to which a person's desires or sincere convictions are sufficient to make their belief true. Indeed, on James' account, the belief-forming process of an honest and intelligent person is constrained by "facts" and subject to "verification processes." This language may give James' readers the impression that he believed in some kind of objective truth after all, but the constraints that James acknowledges superficially mask without fundamentally mitigating the underlying subjectivism in his theory of truth because he uses words like "fact" and "verification" in a distinctively pragmatic, and therefore subjective, sense.

Assuming, then, that Chesterton has fairly—if somewhat roughly—characterized the pragmatic theory of truth, what can be said of the critique that follows? He begins by reiterating his agreement with those pragmatists who only wish to say that "apparent objective truth is not the whole matter" and that there is "an authoritative need to believe the things that are necessary to the human mind." But he warns that this insight is easily taken to an extreme that results in paradox (i.e., paradox arising from inconsistency in a given philosophy, not the positive, synthetic paradox of Chestertonian fame). For example, if the pragmatist tells us to think, not in terms of what is objectively true, but only in terms of what is "necessary to the human mind,"

15. William James, *The Meaning of Truth* (New York: Longman Green and Co., 1911); emphasis original.

he is likely to find himself attempting something that is only possible in a condition of self-deception, for "one of those necessities precisely is a belief in objective truth." Or, as Chesterton goes on to say, if the pragmatist tells an honest man "to think what he must think and never mind the Absolute," he will likely find that the Absolute is "precisely one of the things that he must think"—"must think," that is, if he hopes to derive anything of pragmatic value from his convictions. Thus, in Chesterton's view, the pragmatic philosophy, though professing to be especially practical, turns out to be especially impractical. This is because practicality is determined by the needs and desires of human beings, and human beings have a profound need and desire to believe that their convictions describe a world that transcends their own subjectivity. Thus: "Pragmatism is a matter of human needs; and one of the first of human needs is to be something more than a pragmatist."[16]

Chesterton draws out other dimensions of this paradox by comparing pragmatism to the scientific determinism that dominated the intellectual *milieu* of his day. James himself had famously argued that this was an inhuman and unlivable philosophy since he believed that free will (or, more precisely, belief in free will) is a prerequisite of meaning and moral significance in human life. Moreover, James argued that the pragmatic method is an effective weapon in the fight against scientific determinists whose arguments fail to address the pragmatic (as opposed to the "intellectualist" or "rationalistic") meaning of freedom. This is why it is surprising when Chesterton asserts that "extreme pragmatism is just as inhuman as the determinism it so powerfully attacks." He says this because he thinks that just as "The determinist . . . makes nonsense of the human sense of actual choice," the pragmatist "makes nonsense of the human sense of actual fact." Since Chesterton believed that both of these things are "necessary to the human mind," he concluded that pragmatists must, on pain of inconsistency, reject any philosophy that contradicts them—even if pragmatism (in the strong sense) is one of those philosophies. So new forms of the paradox appear: In opposition to unlivable philosophies like scientific determinism, the pragmatist espouses an equally unlivable philosophy. Moreover, the pragmatism that professes to be especially human turns out, in Chesterton's view, to be especially inhuman. All of this is another way of saying that "extreme pragmatism" is untenable because the pragmatist's own premises eventually begin to work against him. According to Chesterton, the pragmatic significance of almost any important truth involves something more than the pragmatic theory of truth allows. Thus, the pragmatic theory of

16. Chesterton, *Orthodoxy*, 31.

truth serves as both a consequence and refutation of a philosophy that is, at once, excessively pragmatic and insufficiently practical.[17]

Chesterton's critique of pragmatism is surprising, partly because the extent of sympathy it reveals, but also because, in putting it forward, Chesterton forgoes the opportunity to level a simpler and more devastating critique. He could have pointed out the Achilles' heel of all subjective theories of truth, which is that they are self-defeating and they deny the rational grounds upon which their proponents might otherwise recommend them to others. Though Chesterton makes this kind of argument in other places, he chose, in *Orthodoxy*, to take the more subtle approach of using the pragmatic method as a means of rebutting the pragmatic theory of truth. Instead of refuting pragmatism altogether, he chose to out-pragmatize the pragmatist by suggesting, paradoxically, the opposite of what he explicitly states: that a rigorous and consistent application of the pragmatic method supports, rather than undermines, belief in absolute and objective truth. We should therefore close this discussion by noting that, while it is correct to describe Chesterton as a pragmatist in the weak sense and James as a pragmatist in the strong, it may also be misleading; for if Chesterton's critique is sound, it is James, not Chesterton, who has failed to apply the pragmatic method with adequate rigor and consistency.

Despite continued disagreements about the nature of truth and the conditions of justified belief, Chesterton and James maintained a mutual respect for each other, and a mutual interest in each other's work. Though they came to different conclusions in the end, both men began from a common impulse and shared at least one major goal: that is, to make philosophy practical and put it back in service to "the common man." We should note, though, that while both men shared a desire to make philosophy practical, they did not agree on the proper means to this end. It is only a little simplistic to say that whereas James tried to show his readers that many, if not most, abstract and arcane philosophical considerations are impractical (and therefore meaningless), Chesterton tried to show his readers that seemingly abstract and arcane philosophical concerns turn out, upon examination, to be eminently practical. Put differently, Chesterton aimed to make the common man amenable to philosophy and James aimed to make philosophy amenable to the common man.

Even after their differences had come to light, James' continued interest in Chesterton's work prompted him to arrange a visit when staying in

17. Chesterton, *Orthodoxy*, 31.

England with his brother (Henry James, the famous novelist). This visit left a lasting impression on both men, and Chesterton reflected on it in more than one of his published works. In one of these reflections, Chesterton recalls that James "had just crossed the Atlantic and seemed as breezy as the sea," and that he "talked about the metabolism and the involution of values with the air of a man recounting his flirtations on the steamer."[18] Though Chesterton's primary aim in this reflection was to show the insufficiency of the pragmatist philosophy, he made a point along the way to assert and justify his conviction that James was a force for good in the modern world, despite his advocacy of a mistaken theory of truth: "I do not myself think that Pragmatism can ever stand up as a serious rival to the permanent philosophy of Truth and the Absolute," he said. "But I do think that William James did really stand up as a rattling good fighter and cleaner-up of the particular sort of solemn nonsense most current in his time. He may have only indirectly served the cause of belief in belief. But he did a lot to serve the cause of unbelief in unbelief." And this, Chesterton concludes, is "a very wholesome object."[19]

BIBLIOGRAPHY

James, William *Pragmatism: A New Name for Some Old Ways of Thinking*. N.p.: independently published, 2003.

———. *Collected Letters of William James* 2. Edited by Henry James. New York: Atlantic Monthly, 1920.

Chesterton, G. K. *The Common Man*. New York: Sheed and Ward, 1950.

———. *Orthodoxy*. Peabody, MA: Hendrickson Christian Classics, 2006.

18. Chesterton, "What Novelists Are For," in *The Common Man* (Sheed and Ward, 1950), 31.

19. Chesterton, "What Novelists Are For," 31.

Now, in our time, philosophy or religion, our theory, that is, about ultimate things, has been driven out, more or less simultaneously, from two fields which it used to occupy. General ideals used to dominate literature. They have been driven out by the cry of "art for art's sake." General ideals used to dominate politics. They have been driven out by the cry of "efficiency," which may roughly be translated as "politics for politics' sake." Persistently for the last twenty years the ideals of order or liberty have dwindled in our books; the ambitions of wit and eloquence have dwindled in our parliaments. Literature has purposely become less political; politics have purposely become less literary. General theories of the relation of things have thus been extruded from both; and we are in a position to ask, "What have we gained or lost by this extrusion? Is literature better, is politics better, for having discarded the moralist and the philosopher?"

—"Introductory Remarks on the Importance of Orthodoxy," *Heretics*

There is no such thing as education. The thing is merely a loose phrase for the passing on to others of whatever truth or virtue we happen to have ourselves. It is typical of our time that the more doubtful we are about the value of philosophy, the more certain we are about the value of education. That is to say, the more doubtful we are about whether we have any truth, the more certain we are (apparently) that we can teach it to our children.

—*Illustrated London News*, January 12, 1907

15

The Event, the Advent, and the Adventure

Philip Irving Mitchell

Paradox is so ubiquitous in G. K. Chesterton's work that a love or even tolerance of it can determine how and if one reads him. Some of Chesterton's earliest critics complained that he "perceives a thousand truths" but "no consistent body of truth," or that his reliance on paradoxes tempts to "jugglery with words" at the expense of real beauty.[1] But Chesterton argued that in a paradoxical universe, one must look for the "healthy and humane" paradox that enables playfulness and hope, and he likewise asserted that paradoxes are either "fruitful or barren" rather than strictly good or evil, for they all gesture to something of the real.[2] Chesterton asked his critics: What if paradox is less a distortion than a fitting endeavor to engage the world? With this question in mind, Hugh Kenner's famous 1947 study

1. D. J. Colson, *G. K. Chesterton: The Critical Judgments, Part I: 1900–1937* (University of Antwerp Press, 1976), 104, 105–6. Another reviewer charged *Orthodoxy* with being "intellectual bluff: it neither defends nor explains," for paradox can only assert in epigrammatic fashion (Colson, *G. K. Chesterton*, 177), while still another complained that Chesterton's method of "smart-paradox" more often distorts than measures the truth of the world (Colson, *G. K. Chesterton*, 177).

2. G. K. Chesterton, "Two Kinds of Paradox," in *The Illustrated London News, 1911–1913*. Reprinted in *The Collected Works of G. K. Chesterton* (Ignatius, 1988), 19:51–54.

described Chesterton's practice as a direct "metaphysical intuition of being" that embraced diversity and plentitude.[3] Precisely what this direct intuition is and what can be known of it will, in the following, say much about Chesterton's pursuits and why phenomenology can help unpack them.

Jean-Luc Marion has described how paradox runs counter to our usual mastery of our expectations. Paradox is not an illusion or a trick of language, but that which exceeds our standard opinions of the world.[4] A paradox is a true happening with a caveat: "Its givenness contravenes . . . what previous experience should reasonably permit us to foresee."[5] Phenomena, in short, can surpass our contextual horizons, and paradoxes recognize this surplus; they are events or, rather, advents—appearances of what we cannot otherwise know.[6] The paradoxical is only one aspect of the advent of experience. At the heart of Chesterton's work is an affirmation of the real, which in all its phenomenological mystery offers him a world worth embracing. The real is a gift, arriving from elsewhere; something that discloses itself on its own terms and need not be.[7] And yet because it *is*, it offers rich actualities to those who put themselves in a place to receive them: "The mind conquers a new province like an emperor; but only because the mind has answered the bell like a servant."[8] The familiar is strange after all; that is, full of beatitude and plentitude, a strangeness that gives itself to us yet must be believed to be received.[9] If Chesterton is correct, then an expectation and reception of adventure is a necessary humility before the eventful world and its form of advent. That is, we must accept what comes into our experience without always trying to control it through explanation. It is love and humility, not epistemic mastery, that opens the world for us to receive its splendor.

THE PHENOMENAL EVENT

In the twentieth century, Martin Heidegger was among the first to understand the phenomena of the event. For Heidegger, the event changes itself. It

3. Hugh Kenner, *Paradox in Chesterton* (Sheed and Ward, 1947), 1. See also 63, 102.

4. Jean-Luc Marion, *Being Given: Toward a Phenomenology of Givenness*, trans. Jeffrey L. Kosky (Stanford University Press, 2002), 225.

5. Marion, *Being Given*, 226.

6. Marion calls into question whether givenness needs to be limited by the horizon. See *Being Given*, 186–87, 189.

7. Marion, *Being Given*, 120, 123.

8. G. K. Chesterton, *St. Thomas Aquinas*, in *The Collected Works of G. K. Chesterton* (Ignatius, 1986), 2:536.

9. Colson, *G. K. Chesterton*, 184.

can be described as a coming to presence and as a dynamic of disclosure and withdrawal, "a self-clearing event" and "the concealment in departure."[10] Phenomenology begins with the realization that in our lived experience we do not separate out subject and object but experience them as a whole. Phenomenology, despite varied focuses and conclusions, is concerned with how the world and thought about the world arrive together in our consciousness, and so, as a philosophical discipline, phenomenology seeks to describe whatever (and however) phenomena make themselves manifest to our awareness. A phenomenologist notices that what we experience is always an *objectivity-given-to-us*, and whether in our full involvement or our involvement and resistance, "we are not only conscious, but also conscious of something other than ourselves."[11]

Describing this givenness requires the observer to step away from natural holism and observe the world as it manifests itself within experience. To do this the phenomenologist *reduces* (i.e., attempts to isolate aspects of experience for themselves). The goal of all phenomenology is not to continue in the subject-object problem but, by examining how events enter into experience, to find their unity reestablished.[12] The real, thus, demands paradoxical description, for it is that which we experience but also that which proceeds and exceeds experience, that which announces its meaning and yet defers its meaning, and thus that which can be said to make us (in, by, or with) our experience of it.

What, then, does a phenomenology of the event tell us about experience in Chesterton's works? For one, he often describes how sudden moments alter us. Near the end of *The Return of Don Quixote*, Michael Herne (the former librarian of the Seawood Abbey estate and now the deposed king of a neomedieval government) chooses to go on the road with the aristocrat Douglas Murrel. Only a few observers of the particular moment are granted its fullness as it unfolds:

> Like a revelation of lightning, in the instant before annihilating laughter came down like night, those who saw it saw a vision and a memory, bright and brittle as an instant's resurrection of the dead. The bones of the gaunt, high-featured face, the flame-like fork of the beard, the hollow and almost frantic eyes, were

10. Martin Heidegger, *The Event*, trans. Richard Rojcewicz (Indiana University Press, 2013), 128.

11. Jean-Luc Marion, *Prolegomena to Charity*, trans. Stephen E. Lewis (Fordham University Press, 2002), 72.

12. As Jean-Luc Marion notes, "We think only intentionally because to think requires leading the lived experiences of our consciousness back to the intentional object other than my consciousness" (*Prolegomena to Charity*, 73).

> in a setting that startled with recognition; rigid above the saddle of Rosinante, tall and in tattered arms he lifted that vain lance that for three hundred years has taught us nothing but to laugh at the shaking of the spear. And behind him rose a vast yawning shadow like the very vision of that leviathan of laughter; the grotesque cab like the jaws of a derisive dragon pursuing him for ever, as the vast shadow of caricature pursues our desperate dignity and beauty, hanging above him for ever threatening like the wave of the world; and over all, the lesser and lighter human spirit, not unkindly, looking down on all that is most high.
>
> And yet, though that towering and toppling appendage of absurdity was dragged behind him like an overwhelming load, for that instant of time it was erased and forgotten, in the force and appalling passion of his face.[13]

Here, Chesterton's language is charged with metaphor because the revelation exceeds what the onlookers expect, and such recognition carries with it not only laughter and absurdity, but also a lightninglike instance of confrontation—both with the hansom cab as a dragon and the passionate face of the other who is Herne. It would be a mistake to read Herne as reducible to Don Quixote or (despite his self-declared identity) Murrel to Sancho Panza; rather, the parallel *as an event* declares itself suddenly to those nearby, and its complexity is poised between awe and mockery. Such a moment embodies the struggle with meaning amidst the world, but also the ordeal of beauty which the grotesque both mimics and helps unfold, and only those who believe that Herne is something more than laughable will not dismiss this complex reality. Such an event is not then simply an example of perspective imposing a reading on a neutral world of data, nor is it entirely (if at all) under our control.

As Claude Romano points out, brute facts, by happening simultaneously to no one and therefore anyone, elude any complete casual analysis. That is, facts are abstract predictors, yet in the face of the world's contingency, facts are always subject to the unpredictable. Phenomenological events, on the other hand, are a matter of human praxis and meaning. The event is "always an event *for* someone," and as such, it challenges the self's pretensions of mastery: "It is the event that upsets the hierarchy of the agent's objectives, the configuration of his possibilities, the way in which he understands them, and himself in light of them, that is, his world as such."[14] It is not going too far to read Chesterton

13. G. K. Chesterton, *The Return of Don Quixote*, in *The Collected Works of G. K. Chesterton* (Ignatius, 1999), 8:235–36.

14. Claude Romano, *There Is: The Event and the Finitude of Appearing*, trans. Michel B. Smith (Fordham University Press, 2016), 15; emphasis original.

along such lines, for often in him, the event does exceed its supposed causes and thus reframes or redefines our expectations. For example, in addressing the miracles attributed to Francis of Assisi, Chesterton notes that attempts to portray them as nature myths, totemistic psychology, or simply the deceptions of faith healers all miss something fundamental—their event-status: "It is not so much a question of cosmic criticism about the nature of the event as of literary criticism about the nature of the story."[15] They are not only a question of historiography, but also of the ontology of experience, for the event arrives before identity, while change precedes stability: "And in the matter of history and biography, which have their place here, nothing is fixed at all. The world is a welter of the possible and impossible, and nobody knows what will be the next scientific hypothesis to some ancient superstition," that is the next possible explanation as to the testimony to past miracles.[16] Historiography, then, is adapting not only to new evidence but also to a past that has phenomenal thickness, for the events of the past reverberate into the present. In their having happened and in still happening the event discloses more than we can know and will continue to do so. Thus, the past, as *event*, is not quite past.

The Ball and the Cross concludes with such an event. When Father Michael emerges from the burning building and the fire parts in two like the parting of the Red Sea, the atheist James Turnbull sees this and eventually bows with the others as the saint passes by singing. We are not told that Turnbull converts to Catholicism, only that the intellectual world of skepticism will come to lament his turn from materialism.[17] A miracle by one set of criteria is impossible; it is an event that escapes foresight, casual predictability, empirical repeatability, or experimental control, and yet has happened. Its meaning escapes totalization.[18] When Chesterton writes that Turnbull "preferred a fact even to materialism," he has in mind not a predictable pattern which can be thereby mastered, but that which eclipses it. The ordeal of an event can be resisted, but it can also commit us, for paradoxical experience is witnessed rather than owned.[19] To be constituted a witness by the event means to both attest to it and to continually come to understand it.[20]

15. G. K. Chesterton, *St. Francis of Assisi*, in *The Collected Works of G. K. Chesterton* (Ignatius, 1986), 2:118–19.

16. Chesterton, *St. Francis of Assisi* 2:119.

17. G. K. Chesterton, *The Ball and the Cross*, in *The Collected Works of G. K. Chesterton* 7 (Ignatius, 1986), 7:257–58.

18. Jean-Luc Marion, *Revelation Comes from Elsewhere*, trans. Stephen E. Lewis and Stephanie Rumpza (Stanford University Press, 2024), 150–51.

19. Marion, *Being Given*, 216–17.

20. Marion, *Being Given*, 233.

Constitution as a witness is not limited to the miraculous. In *The Napoleon of Notting Hill*, the opposition leader James Barker's first experience of battle reveals something of the event's unpredictability and of necessary fidelity to it. That evening forces a confession from Barker: "I wasn't afraid of something happening. I was afraid of nothing ever happening—nothing ever happening for all God's eternity. . . . When something happens, it happens first, and you see it afterwards. It happens of itself, and you have nothing to do with it. It proves a dreadful thing—that there are other things besides one's self."[21] Mr. Buck, on the other hand, refuses to see the battle as having any other meaning than "reason and arithmetic," and thus rejects Adam Wayne's medievalist "atmosphere" as the event's fundamental meaning. War is about strategy—banal predictability and control, and Buck does momentarily convince Barker otherwise, that is until in the Battle of the Lamps Buck himself is taken with the energy of hand-to-hand combat. Thus, both men find themselves having to live out or deny the event's implications.

For Alain Badiou, an event is when something excluded arises and disrupts life. An explosion in circumstances, it comes forward in a context and location, yet it can have resonance for other places and times. The event exceeds mathematical predictability; it is haphazard, having neither freedom nor justification. The event emerges when we recognize it as such and those shaped by it come to interpret it, and this calls for fidelity.[22] Badiou is addressing what might be considered corporate events—large disruptions, and Barker and Buck's experience of battle has this astonishing character. Yet what about events that do not seem quite so disruptive? In the conclusion to *The Club of Queer Trades*, the "mad," retired judge, Basil Grant, is revealed to be the Club's president, and this revelatory event offers far more than it explains. In *Club*'s series of tales, Rupert Grant, Basil's brother, has each time pronounced the solution to a crime that Rupert reveals to be neither the solution nor even a crime. Most of these are explained by unusual professions—an Adventure and Romance Agency that provides mock fantasies, an arboreal house agent, a linguist determined to speak only through bodily signs, or Basil's own voluntary moral court of the heart. Again and again, Rupert learns a lighthearted lesson about modern life and the hunger for meaning, so each tale is a reverse detective story that transmutes its evidence. However, even with Basil's explanation as to why he opened a moral

21. G. K. Chesterton, *The Napoleon of Notting Hill*, in *The Collected Works of G. K. Chesterton* (Ignatius, 1991), 6:319.

22. Alain Badiou, *Being and Event*, trans. Oliver Feltman (Continuum, 2007), 174–76, 192, 195, 211. Badiou, for example, discusses Pascal's approach to the incarnation of Christ as germane to the event, for once it occurs it now excludes any former equivocalness in those prophetic sayings (*Being and Event*, 218–20).

court "for the faults that really make social life impossible,"[23] the ending does not resolve the collection's purpose, nor does it reveal all the tales as elaborate fantasies manufactured to teach Rupert or Charlie Swinburne (the narrator) some larger lesson. Rather, they and the reader are left with a surplus of possibilities, even as Basil's revelation commits them and us to exploring these.

Some of Chesterton's Father Brown stories do the same thing. In a genre designed to offer clues that can be reconstructed for the mystery's solution, Chesterton's stories often transcend explanation. We are told that the thief in "The Queer Feet" repented, but as to his confession and penance, "that is where the story ends."[24] "The Sins of Prince Sardine" concludes with Flambeau wondering if it "was all dream," and while Father Brown disagrees, it remains unsaid "whether in dissent or agnosticism." The mystery of evil is left unanswered, as is the final call of "the smell of hawthorn and of orchids."[25] In "The Sign of the Broken Sword," Father Brown's imaginative (if highly improbable) solution to a past historical mystery leaves him with an ugly dilemma—whether it is worth revealing that a local cultural hero was the foulest of villains, it is the continuing enormity of that leprous event that leaves open-ended something far greater.[26] In each case, even if the event is foremost a personal ordeal, it is never undergone as exclusively so. It is undergone with others, for others, and recognized as such by others.

EVENTS AND HERMENEUTICS

The event's excess summons a hermeneutic, and hermeneutics involves communities of interpretation, yet this shared approach is not method divorced from individual personhood. Phenomenology and hermeneutics are together an expression of freedom, for we both undergo what reconfigures the world even as we continue coming to terms with it. As Romano argues, events bear "on existence—or better said, adventure—of the one they affect or overwhelm" and this "brings us to encounter ourselves as ourselves."[27] As such, events do assume an anthropology—the *advenant*, one with the

23. G. K. Chesterton, *The Club of Queer Trades*, in *The Collected Works of G. K. Chesterton* (Ignatius, 1991), 6:212.

24. G. K. Chesterton, *Father Brown Stories, Part I*, in *The Collected Works of G. K. Chesterton* (Ignatius, 2005), 12:85, 87.

25. Chesterton, *Father Brown Stories* 12:171.

26. Chesterton, *Father Brown Stories* 12:221–22.

27. Romano, *There Is*, 219.

capacity to undergo what happens and to seek meaning.[28] Humility recognizes the passibility of human existence—our porous dependence before phenomena larger than and other than ourselves, for the world outstrips my *mineness*, yet I myself am enlarged by it. I become more by what I am not. Is such humility compatible with the notion of adventure? Chesterton throughout his career stressed seeing the world's wonder in the ordinary, which becomes extraordinary because we cannot control it: "Humility is the thing which is ever renewing the earth and the stars. . . . Humility is perpetually putting us back in the primal darkness."[29] Reality, thus, manifests its gift-nature,[30] and this summons a fitting response: "The truth is, that all genuine appreciation rests on a certain mystery of humility and almost of darkness."[31]

Chesterton held that the medieval world in particular understood this truth: He could look to Thomas Aquinas' use of *Ens* as having a fecundity, "the tree of life bowing down with a huge humility, because of the very load of its living fruitfulness," and in turn hold that Dante would recognize a capacity "to overwhelm us with the tremendous twilight."[32] Likewise, concerning Chaucer's world, Chesterton could muse, "an abyss of light, more blinding and unfathomable than any abyss of darkness" calls for gratitude, humility, and "the primeval duty of praise."[33] In all these cases, the world possesses a radiance that calls forth what Marion has described as "a liturgy of re-vision."[34]

Writing in the early twentieth century, Chesterton addressed the rivals of skeptical idealism and materialism, and held that both rendered human experience empty, for solipsism or determinism each lead to nihilism. Aquinas' stress on *Ens* ("It is nothing except itself";[35] "There *is* an Is")[35] offered Chesterton a rationale for the richness of existence, "how the mind is certain of an external object and not merely of an impression of that object."[36] It is possible to question whether phenomenology is really compatible with such Thomistic realism. Phenomenology, by its own definitions, has sought

28. Romano, *There Is*, 220.

29. G. K. Chesterton, *Heretics*, in *The Collected Works of G. K. Chesterton* (Ignatius, 1986), 1:127–28.

30. Chesterton, *Heretics* 1:207.

31. Chesterton, *Heretics* 1:69.

32. Chesterton, *St. Thomas Aquinas* 2:519.

33. G. K. Chesterton, *Chaucer*, in *The Collected Works of G. K. Chesterton* (Ignatius, 1991), 18:172–73.

34. Marion, *Being Given*, 48.

35. Chesterton, *St. Thomas Aquinas* 2:516, 518; emphasis original.

36. Chesterton, *St. Thomas Aquinas* 2:529.

to explore if metaphysics can be left to itself and has thereby focused on the act rather than metaphysical essence, on the nature of the evidential rather than the dilemma of the solipsistic.[37] It has done this ostensibly to move beyond the limitations of both idealism and materialism, and to bracket, as it were, the question of substance. For some, this would seem to trap phenomenology in subjectivism.

Nevertheless, Thomism and phenomenology need not be far apart. As Marion observes, for Aquinas, Being is other than *esse*; instead, it is "*the* incident par excellence," because it is the unpredictable happening that finally proves that the "exception becomes the rule. The event, rather than the margins of existence, is its enactment."[38] Chesterton recognized too that mutability is not a signal of subjectivity, but of the contingency of the world's fullness. "Things change because they are not complete," for only God is complete, and existence is "not sufficiently self-existent."[39] "That strangeness of things" is poetic because it is not dependent on the self and thus offers the mind more than its own projections. Reality refuses both "alternative abysses of impotence," for the mind is neither "merely receptive" nor "purely creative." It was this active and yet passible experience that drew Chesterton to Aquinas. In the union of the external world and one's open embrace of it there is "a sort of marriage. Indeed it is very truly a marriage, because it is fruitful . . . precisely because it is the combination of an adventurous mind and a strange fact."[40] Chesterton's language of marriage is not mere wordplay. Fruitfulness describes the continued renewal of the advent of the world. Thus, Chesterton avoids idealism: "He has seen grass, and will not say he has not seen grass" even when it passes away,[41] and in turn he celebrates the repeatability of the world not in its predictability, but with unending interest.[42] In *Orthodoxy* he can insist that the repeatability of phenomena is not reducible to a scientific law for it possesses both "magic" and "wonder,"[43] and he compares it to a teacher who keeps repeating the same message in hopes that dull students will finally understand, or better that "repetition in Nature may not be a mere recurrence; it may be a

37. Chesterton, *St. Thomas Aquinas* 2:517.

38. Marion, *Being Given*, 4, 18, 23–24; emphasis original.

39. Chesterton, *St. Thomas Aquinas* 2:530–33.

40. Chesterton, *St. Thomas Aquinas* 2:535–36.

41. Chesterton, *St. Thomas Aquinas* 2:537.

42. Events, after all, can take on different speeds of change. As Romano points out, they can include slow change, even so slow that they take on stability and yet are still an event (*There Is*, 216–17).

43. Chesterton, *Orthodoxy*, in *The Collected Works of G. K. Chesterton* (Ignatius, 1986), 1:253–55.

theatrical *encore*."[44] What Chesterton has in mind, then, is not a banal factual predictability, but an attentiveness that receives the reality's richness, and it is not wrong to describe this as summoning continual praise.

SUFFERING AND LOVE FROM ELSEWHERE

One of Chesterton's chief insights is that a repeatable newness which we cannot control is what makes adventure possible. Marion has borrowed the term *anamorphosis* to describe how form from elsewhere is first a lived experience involving a habituation of ourselves to it, for "one must expose oneself to the phenomenon to receive its form."[45] Thus, some preparation is necessary to receive certain events, even if only discovered in retrospect. Does such a concession, the "life of practical romance,"[46] then, undercut the excessive and unexpected nature of the event, or is an expectation of the unexpected a necessity for repeated engagement?[47] Slavoj Žižek, one of the few contemporary philosophers to explicitly draw on Chesterton, does compare this fundamental excess of the event to narrative outcomes that reconfigure our understanding. In Hegelian fashion, he also thinks they may destroy the original frame of understanding.[48] Žižek (like Badiou) seeks to account for how the unfounded, the excessive, is possible; that is how the excess can escape the either-or, even as it prepares for the new.[49] I suspect Chesterton would see Žižek as fundamentally mistaken that any new that discloses itself repeatedly in more beauties and goods has a necessary evil that enables it,[50] yet Chesterton does understand that the natural world has a wildness that can inspire anger, fear, and despair, and his own unique contribution to the problem of evil explores why adventure has possibilities

44. Chesterton, *Orthodoxy* 1:263–64.

45. Marion, *Being Given*, 123–26, 173.

46. Chesterton, *Orthodoxy* 1:213.

47. Romano defends the existential encounter of the event: "Freedom is the capacity to relate personally to what happens to us, to stand open to the critical import of the event." Availability, which is an expectation of the unexpected, is a key aspect of this. Claude Romano, *Event and Time*, trans. Stephen E. Lewis (Fordham University Press, 2014), 176, 230.

48. Slavoj Žižek, *Event: A Philosophical Journey Through a Concept* (Melville House, 2014), 11–13, 24–25.

49. Žižek, *Event*, 34. Žižek, who only partially understands (and thereby distorts) Chesterton, does admit that Chesterton is not Hegelian (*Event*, 40–42, 91–92).

50. Žižek, *Event*, 93–98. Žižek does acknowledge that Christianity is committed to *fides quaerens intellectum*—that faith like love proceeds our coming to terms with its possibilities (*Event*, 4–5).

that love may recognize, while a demand of fear for control risks obscuring their form.

The Man Who Was Thursday explores the chaotic event as the ordeal one must undergo for meaning, yet it also concludes that meaning always contains an inescapable surplus one cannot master. Gabriel Syme is a poet of order over against the anarchists of chaos, yet his experience will be that chaos is part of the mystery of things.[51] Sunday is an overwhelming, shifting surprise. Syme finds that each council member represents a wild position taken to its extreme, positions that, whether pursuing extreme idealism or extreme materialism, seem "a tree possessed by a spirit" or "a tower, perhaps, of which the very shape was wicked." Such phenomena can hardly be reduced to a subjective screen on Syme's part; rather, each supposed anarchist (who is also a policeman) becomes a disclosure of reality: "So these figures seemed to stand up, violent and unaccountable, against an ultimate horizon, visions from the verge."[52]

Yet Syme discovers that these disclosures are themselves broken refusals before a greater fullness. Chapters 10–12 unfold the absurdity of a duel in which nothing is what it seems, the philosophical police being pursued by a mob, then by the local populace, and finally by the gendarmes. "No one has any experience . . . of the Battle of Armageddon."[53] The Professor understandably compares the events to Alexander Pope's *The Dunciad* in which the world is buried by chaos and the great Anarch in an apocalyptic finale.[54] In the face of a chaotic universe full of constant disruption, all six policemen arrive "to ask one man what they mean."[55] Yet Sunday himself is impossible to pin down, refusing any stable definition:

> You want to know what I am, do you? . . . You will understand the sea, and I shall be still a riddle; you shall know what the stars are, and not know what I am. Since the beginning of the world all men have hunted me like a wolf—kings and sages, and poets and lawgivers, all the churches, and all the philosophies. But I

51. G. K. Chesterton, *The Man Who Was Thursday*, in *The Collected Works of G. K. Chesterton* (Ignatius, 1991), 6:479. At the same time, Chesterton was insistent early in his career that the overturning of the powerful, of any set system that crushes human freedom, is "the whole nature and inmost secret of the psychological adventure called man" (*Heretics* 1:83).

52. Chesterton, *Man Who Was Thursday* 6:524.

53. Chesterton, *Man Who Was Thursday* 6:512.

54. Chesterton, *Man Who Was Thursday* 6:601.

55. Chesterton, *Man Who Was Thursday* 6:605–6.

> have never been caught yet, and the skies will fall in the time I turn to bay.[56]

And even when he responds (or is this Sunday's own opening and closure?) to the chaotic complaint of Gregory and the heroic oration of Syme, he does so in a terrible expanding vision that voices Christ's words, "Can ye drink of the cup that I drink of?"[57] As an event, this too exceeds its status as an allusion. The problem for Gabriel Syme and the other philosophical police is a world where one is afraid,[58] and theirs is the failure of a hermeneutic before what the universe offers. Even when they do not understand "the backside of God" that is Sunday, they are at times brought great peace. What makes theirs a phenomenology of event is that they find that the problem of evil actually gives itself in a comic form—an absurd romp, yet if one believes in order to see, a deep assurance, even if beyond propositional explanation.

Do Chesterton's various defamiliarizations attempt to proceed, even cause that which cannot be proceeded or caused? Is to treat the universe as a quest or as an adventure to impose a horizon or to thematize that which is beyond predictability? Here, again, I think phenomenology has something to offer to Chesterton's approach—namely, love as a kind of knowing that is other than banal control. Love is the event that outstrips our attempts to master it, to understand *when* it began, or what is decided upon us, about us, or how it makes us.[59] Is not adventure and quest, then, the very shape of the appearing of love? "There is no encounter *in general*."[60] For example, does Innocent Smith in *Manalive* anticipate the gift and thereby render it no longer one? Or is he simply positioning himself to receive potential gifts? One could argue that Chesterton's "*Moor Eeffoc*,"[61] the recognition of the ordinary experience seen from a new perspective, is not a random, if serendipitous encounter but an aesthetic, moral, and spiritual exercise; a waiting for the advent of the event, which Smith repeatedly practices. He travels around the world to rediscover his love of home and family, though he does not know when that rediscovery will happen: "I have become a pilgrim to cure myself of being an exile."[62] His

56. Chesterton, *Man Who Was Thursday* 6:608.

57. Chesterton, *Man Who Was Thursday* 6:634.

58. Chesterton, *Man Who Was Thursday* 6:545.

59. Romano, *There Is*, 61–63.

60. Romano, *Event and Time*, 179; emphasis original.

61. "The motto of all effective realism . . . the masterpiece of the good realistic principle . . . that elvish kind of realism that Dickens adopted everywhere." G. K. Chesterton, *Charles Dickens*, in *The Collected Works of G. K. Chesterton* (Ignatius, 1989), 15:65.

62. G. K. Chesterton, *Manalive*, in *The Collected Works of G. K. Chesterton* (Ignatius, 2004), 7:397.

various romantic seductions of his wife are each undertaken to see anew the woman he loves. And his practice has the possibility of being such an event for others. His chasing after his hat in the wind and his willingness to go onto the roof for the view become events for others: "Their first feeling was that they had come out into eternity, and that eternity was topsy-turvydom."[63] Smith breaks into his own home to teach a radical curate the value of personal property, and he shoots at Professor Eames and Dr. Herbert Warner to bring them back to life, though it only opens Eames to gratitude and reaffirmation, while Warner "died years ago."[64] Thus, Innocent Smith cannot anticipate the exact arrival of wonder and its lessons beforehand; he can only put himself in the path of them by acts of reversal, seeing the world in unusual ways which await the hoped-for unfolding.

Adventure for Chesterton, then, is a commitment of love that allows the event to uncover itself. Love desires the other that cannot be predicted exhaustively.[65] In *The Ball and the Cross* the two protagonists experience love by commitment to love, yet also by being devoted by love. MacIan, rescued by a wealthy aristocrat who cannot sort out her own motives, holds himself "a thing sealed and devoted," though he is wrong as to what this requires of him, while Turnbull longing to repeatedly look upon the faithful Catholic Madeleine is confronted with why he will not take the host at Mass, even in disguise.[66] The same can be said of each man's growing respect and friendship for the other. They discover their love for one another only after they pledge to duel to the death. In each case, Chesterton arranges it so that the reader is aware of growing love before the characters become fully aware. Marion has described how love is manifestly another way of knowing than epistemology. We love in order to know, for charity accepts that we do not have perfect clarity.[67] Significantly, *Thursday* ends with "great unconscious gravity of a girl,"[68] as does the final historical pun of *Return*. The estate was once an abbey where men loved it, and the characters return there because one should reside where justice is loved.[69]

This conclusion is foreshadowed much earlier in *Return* when Murell returns with Dr. Hendry in the hansom cab. What Murell sees and what

63. Chesterton, *Manalive* 7:281.
64. Chesterton, *Manalive* 7:416.
65. Chesterton, *Orthodoxy* 1:337.
66. Chesterton, *Ball and the Cross* 7:134–37, 141, 164–66.
67. Marion, *Revelation*, 118–19.
68. Chesterton, *Man Who Was Thursday* 6:635.
69. Chesterton, *Return of Don Quixote* 8.241–42.

happens to Hendry's daughter is an event prepared for by love yet a love whose final arrival will only be in the beholding of God:

> The beauty that unfolded from within, like some magic flower upon the balcony, was not due altogether to the burst of sun that had struck the street. It was the most beautiful thing in the world; perhaps the only really beautiful thing in the world. It was astonishment which was lost in Eden and will return with the Beatific Vision, in astonishment so strong that it will last for ever.[70]

Astonishment before the event of love's beauty is prepared for by Murell's own actions of adventurous love, yet the event which offers itself on its own terms speaks of both Eden and New Eden. Here, perhaps one steps beyond phenomenology proper into a phenomenology of theology. Chesterton continually held that "Man cannot love mortal things. He can only love immortal things for an instant,"[71] for in the middle of adventure we are given the fullness of the eternal—something beyond the momentary that comes from elsewhere and enters the experience of love or battle or both and yet is always given in the event's (and our own) temporality. Love reverses the ego so one can be open and receive from elsewhere, and as such love then offers us a world where the event of the other is always within the possibility of *communio*. As Marion notes on theological grounds, since love is a necessity for knowing love, one believes to see, and thus one wills love well in order that one may know God.[72] Chesterton could speak highly of Athanasius' theological defense of the Trinity as "fighting for that very balance of beautiful interdependence and intimacy," which Chesterton acknowledges: "If the phrase be not misunderstood, turns even God into a Holy Family."[73] Any love is ultimately given because of the unending event of love within God. Thus, love's arrival, if it cannot be described on strictly philosophical grounds, has a shape that nevertheless reveals its fullness as beyond being.

For Chesterton, love is ultimately an event that we know by loving and being loved, not by being certain or mastering our experiences, and this love is a pledge that the world's ordinary reality is a continuous unfolding of wonder and of fertile imagination. It phenomenally pledges us as witnesses even as it also asks of us a hermeneutic of anamorphic indirection. As such it calls for both adventure and humility. Chesterton's work is a fundamental

70. Chesterton, *Return of Don Quixote* 8:149.

71. Chesterton, *Heretics* 1:95.

72. Marion, *Revelation*, 120–23.

73. G. K. Chesterton, *The Everlasting Man*, in *The Collected Works of G. K. Chesterton* (Ignatius, 1986), 2:360.

realism of the event because it is not so much a wager as a reception of what has already been given and always arrives from elsewhere than ourselves.

BIBLIOGRAPHY

Badiou, Alain. *Being and Event*. Translated by Oliver Feltman. London: Continuum, 2007.

Chesterton, G. K. *The Ball and the Cross*. In vol. 7 of *The Collected Works of G. K. Chesterton*. San Francisco: Ignatius, 1986.

———. *Charles Dickens*. In vol. 15 of *The Collected Works of G. K. Chesterton*. San Francisco: Ignatius, 1989.

———. *Chaucer*. In vol. 18 of *The Collected Works of G. K. Chesterton*. San Francisco: Ignatius, 1991.

———. *The Club of Queer Trades*. In vol. 6 of *The Collected Works of G. K. Chesterton*. San Francisco: Ignatius, 1991.

———. *Father Brown Stories, Part I*. In vol. 12 of *The Collected Works of G. K. Chesterton*. San Francisco: Ignatius, 2005.

———. *Heretics*. In vol. 1 of *The Collected Works of G. K. Chesterton*. San Francisco: Ignatius, 1986.

———. *The Man Who Was Thursday*. In vol. 6 of *The Collected Works of G. K. Chesterton*. San Francisco: Ignatius, 1991.

———. *Manalive*. In vol. 7 of *The Collected Works of G. K. Chesterton*. San Francisco: Ignatius, 2004.

———. *The Napoleon of Notting Hill*. In vol. 6 of *The Collected Works of G. K. Chesterton*. San Francisco: Ignatius, 1991.

———. *Orthodoxy*. In vol. 1 of *The Collected Works of G. K. Chesterton*. San Francisco: Ignatius, 1986.

———. *The Return of Don Quixote*. In vol. 8 of *The Collected Works of G. K. Chesterton*. San Francisco: Ignatius, 1999.

———. *St. Francis of Assisi*. In vol. 2 of *The Collected Works of G. K. Chesterton*. San Francisco: Ignatius, 1986.

———. *St. Thomas Aquinas*. In vol. 2 of *The Collected Works of G. K. Chesterton*. San Francisco: Ignatius, 1986.

———. "Two Kinds of Paradox." In *The Illustrated London News, 1911–1913*. Reprinted in vol. 19 of *The Collected Works of G. K. Chesterton*. San Francisco: Ignatius, 1988.

Colson, D. J. *G. K. Chesterton: The Critical Judgments, Part I: 1900–1937*. Antwerp: University of Antwerp Press, 1976.

Heidegger, Martin. *The Event*. Translated by Richard Rojcewicz. Bloomington: Indiana University Press, 2013.

Kenner, Hugh. *Paradox in Chesterton*. London: Sheed and Ward, 1947.

Marion, Jean-Luc. *Being Given: Toward a Phenomenology of Givenness*. Translated by Jeffrey L. Kosky. Stanford, CA: Stanford University Press, 2002.

———. *Prolegomena to Charity*. Translated by Stephen E. Lewis. New York: Fordham University Press, 2002.

———. *Revelation Comes from Elsewhere*. Translated by Stephen E. Lewis and Stephanie Rumpza. Stanford, CA: Stanford University Press, 2024.

Romano, Claude. *Event and Time*. Translated by Stephen E. Lewis. New York: Fordham University Press, 2014.

———. *There Is: The Event and the Finitude of Appearing*. Translated by Michael B. Smith. New York: Fordham University Press, 2016.

Žižek, Slavoj. *Event: A Philosophical Journey Through a Concept*. Brooklyn, NY: Melville House, 2014.

Now, if we are to glance at the philosophy of sanity, the first thing to do in the matter is to blot out one big and common mistake. There is a notion adrift everywhere that imagination, especially mystical imagination, is dangerous to man's mental balance. Poets are commonly spoken of as psychologically unreliable; and generally there is a vague association between wreathing laurels in your hair and sticking straws in it. Facts and history utterly contradict this view. Most of the very great poets have been not only sane, but extremely business-like; and if Shakespeare ever really held horses, it was because he was much the safest man to hold them. Imagination does not breed insanity. Exactly what does breed insanity is reason. Poets do not go mad; but chess-players do. Mathematicians go mad, and cashiers; but creative artists very seldom. I am not, as will be seen, in any sense attacking logic: I only say that this danger does lie in logic, not in imagination. Artistic paternity is as wholesome as physical paternity. Moreover, it is worthy of remark that when a poet really was morbid it was commonly because he had some weak spot of rationality on his brain. . . . Perhaps the strongest case of all is this: that only one great English poet went mad, Cowper. And he was definitely driven mad by logic, by the ugly and alien logic of predestination. Poetry was not the disease, but the medicine. . . . The general fact is simple. Poetry is sane because it floats easily in an infinite sea; reason seeks to cross the infinite sea, and so make it finite. The result is mental exhaustion. . . . To accept everything is an exercise, to understand everything a strain. The poet only desires exaltation and expansion, a world to stretch himself in. The poet only asks to get his head into the heavens. It is the logician who seeks to get the heavens into his head. And it is his head that splits.

—"The Maniac," *Orthodoxy*

16

Chesterton in the Dock

Kevin Belmonte

Clearly the only way to arrive at the truth is to put in evidence Mr. Chesterton's own books. . . .

He stands hereby indicted for that he has laboured well and faithfully, first to see the truth and then to tell it; for that he, being a great rhetorician, seldom uses rhetoric to obscure or to deceive; and, being a great wit, employs wit only to season wisdom and make it memorable.

How say you, Gilbert Keith Chesterton, are you guilty or not guilty?

—E. T. Raymond (1919)

Socrates was the G. K. Chesterton of his age: where should we be to-day without our Chesterton?

From this parallel further may we not learn that, if Socrates was among us to-day, showing delight in a somewhat eccentric exterior, and dosing his public with whimsical parables, he would be (if not executed) yet cruelly misunderstood, and his sovereign paradoxes unregarded.

—*Studies: An Irish Quarterly Review* (1915)

The essential weakness of the present age, as Mr. Chesterton envisages it, is really nothing less than that which distressed Socrates in fifth-century Athens. Everywhere he sees, as Socrates and Plato saw, men trying to secure for themselves and their children something whose good they cannot define.

—*The Nation* (1906)

Mr. Chesterton is a philosopher.

He himself proclaims the fact in prefacing Heretics.

—*The Harvard Monthly* (1907)

G. K. Chesterton knew the measure of one who was, and sought to be, a philosopher. Indeed, it was much as he had stated in December 1900, saying he cared deeply about the idea of bringing "a philosophical problem of some sort to knock at every man's door."[1] So, we may say, philosophy graced the inner court of Chesterton's nature. It held an abiding place for him, and he thought it should be a vital part of everyone's life. Continually, he set out reasons why his readers needed to see this—and why they should care about philosophy—"about ultimate things"[2]—as deeply as he did. A telling phrase captures this: He commended philosophy to others. And that idea opens the pages of his classic critique, *Heretics*, published in 1905: "But there are some people, nevertheless—and I am one of them—who think that the most practical and important thing about a man is still his view of the universe."[3]

Beyond this, we may encounter a poet who is also a philosopher, as here, when Chesterton penned a lovely, revealing line about the world we know, and its reasons, in 1908:

> And I have sometimes thought I heard upon the wind
> the laughter and whisper of the reeds.[4]

1. G. K. Chesterton, "Puritan and Anglican," *The Speaker: A Review of Politics, Letters, Science, and the Arts* (December 15, 1900), 301.

2. G. K. Chesterton, *Heretics* (John Lane, 1905), 16.

3. Chesterton, *Heretics*, 15. *Heretics* was published on Tuesday, June 6, 1905—per an advertisement from Chesterton's publisher, John Lane, given on pg. 678 of the June 3, 1905, issue of *The Athenaeum* magazine.

4. G. K. Chesterton, *All Things Considered* (Methuen, 1908), 29. Discerning a Johnsonian kinship in Chesterton, *The Nation* magazine stated on November 26, 1908: "He [Chesterton] is a believer . . . in Samuel Johnson," while the essays of *All Things*

Yet difficulties arise when you have a poet who is also a philosopher—for all too often the perception of a philosopher looks to someone wise, but austere—reflective, but not given to painting pictures with words, or casting them in prose that reads like verse. Chesterton's lines above are a deep and profound plea for understanding that the world we know has a Creator, and the reality that he tells stories in nature—for those with eyes to see, and ears to hear. In the beauty of the lines from Chesterton's pen lies a telling presentation of truth. Is that not the task of a philosopher, delivered though it may be with artistry?

Sometimes, also, recognition and a tip of the cap come from unexpected quarters. Writing for *The Smart Set* magazine in May 1909, H. L. Mencken loosed a bolt of wit, but one nonetheless steeped in a perception that had gained wide currency: Chesterton was a latter-day Socrates, set down in Edwardian London. Describing the sage of Fleet Street, Mencken said that "Gilbert K. Chesterton, it is plain, is getting on in the world. At the age of thirty-five he is already the Socrates of a busy grove of philosophers."[5]

But this, just now, is to run ahead on the course being pursued. We must return to the question of preliminaries. How did Chesterton step before the public, as a philosopher writing in the public square? And if we were to place Chesterton "in the dock," how could the case be made for him as a philosopher, seeking to be such from the earliest days of his writing life?

We may begin with the line above, from December 1900, when Chesterton said he cared deeply about the idea of bringing "a philosophical problem of some sort to knock at every man's door." This gets to the heart of a philosopher's purpose: to commend the love of wisdom and the pursuit of truth. Few things are more essential.

Just three months later, and writing once more in *The Speaker* magazine, Chesterton spoke of ancient Greek philosophical asceticism, of its narrowness, and stated in one passage: "But the Greeks carried their police regulation into elfland; they vetoed . . . the wild weddings of ideas, and forbade the banns of thought."[6] What was Chesterton on about here? It was an arresting and colourful riposte, meant to make the reader think. By

Considered impart "a secret feeling of intellectuality akin to that enjoyed by subscribers to the *Spectator* in the age of Anne." See pg. 527 of the November 26, 1908, issue of *The Nation* (The New York Evening Post, 1908).

5. H. L. Mencken, "Some Novels—and a Good One," in the May 1909 issue of *The Smart Set* (The Ess Ess, 1909), 159.

6. G. K. Chesterton, "A Defence of Ugly Things," a magazine essay in the March 23, 1901, issue of *The Speaker: A Review of Politics, Letters, Science, and the Arts*, 675–76.

casting imagery of a realm where one was free to ask, consider, or conclude as one was led, Chesterton saw the blight or pall that could be cast over such a realm by prohibitions on freedom of inquiry.

This distinctive reflection, focused on a revival of prohibitions on freedom of inquiry from the ancient Greeks, was all the more to the point: because in these and subsequent essays, Chesterton began to use a literary version of the Socratic method. And if Socrates had the Agora, or Athenian marketplace, Chesterton wished to have a forum in the realm of Edwardian print media. In this forum, readers were invited to a conversation with each newly published essay. It was, and would become, a recurring feature of Chesterton's presence in print. And it was a memorable preview of the content in many books to follow.[7]

The Socratic method, as defined, "involves a shared dialogue between teacher and students. The teacher leads by posing thought-provoking questions."[8] So saying, Chesterton's "Socratic method" involved a shared dialogue between an essayist and his readers. Chesterton led the way, conversationally, by posing thought-provoking questions. And, like Socrates, Chesterton was given to telling vivid, instructive parables. "The Parable of the Cave," which tells of a people whose entire existence has been spent within the confines of a cave, is perhaps the most famous parable attributed to Socrates. Beyond its firelight and shadows, they know little of the world outside. Shadows, light, ignorance—all are themes and images that stand out in the telling.

One of the more famous Chestertonian parables bears some striking similarities to this Socratic allegory:

> Suppose that a great commotion arises in the street about something, let us say a lamppost, which many influential persons desire to pull down. A grey-clad monk, who is the spirit of the Middle Ages, is approached upon the matter, and begins to say, in the arid manner of the Schoolmen, "Let us first of all consider, my brethren, the value of Light. If Light be in itself good." At this point he is somewhat excusably knocked down. All the people make a rush for the lamp-post, the lamp-post is down in ten minutes, and they go about congratulating each other on their unmediæval practicality. But as things go on they do not work out so easily. Some people have pulled the lamp-post down because they wanted the electric light; some because they

7. See *The Defendant* (1901), *Robert Browning* (1903), *Varied Types* (1903), *Heretics* (1905), *All Things Considered* (1908), and *Orthodoxy* (1908).

8. A definition given by The Institute for Learning and Teaching at Colorado State University online, at https://tilt.colostate.edu/the-socratic-method/.

> wanted old iron; some because they wanted darkness, because their deeds were evil. Some thought it not enough of a lamp-post, some too much; some acted because they wanted to smash municipal machinery; some because they wanted to smash something.

And there is war in the night, no man knowing whom he strikes.

> So, gradually and inevitably, to-day, to-morrow, or the next day, there comes back the conviction that the monk was right after all, and that all depends on what is the philosophy of Light. Only what we might have discussed under the gas-lamp, we now must discuss in the dark.[9]

Socrates and Chesterton tilled common ground in urging others to consider what lay beyond the confines imposed by narrowness of thinking (shades of the Greek asceticism and prohibitions both men knew, one from personal experience, the other from a modern resurgence of this school of thought, in the London of 1905). Stepping beyond the dim confines of "the Cave" into the world of light—a metaphor for freedom of inquiry—Socrates' parable found an Edwardian counterpart in Chesterton's parable of the conflict between light and dark, with its vivid plea for seeking the light, not rejecting or destroying the lamppost which offered light to those who kept its flame; set as it was each night against the dark of evening.

This imagery would ever remain a source of solace and hope for Chesterton, after a time of depression in his youth, amid the pervasive cultural *ennui* and despair of the 1890s—especially during his time at the Slade School of Art, when such currents in the artistic community had nearly overwhelmed him.[10] Thereafter, the cautionary wisdom and inspiration he found were given in his "Parable of the Lamppost," and in one of the most eloquent canvasses he ever painted in words:

> The idea of a crowd of human strangers turned into comrades for a journey is full of the oldest pathos and piety of human life. That profound feeling of mortal fraternity and frailty, which tells us we are indeed all in the same boat, is not the less true if expressed in the formula that we are all in the same bus. As for the idea of the lamp-post . . . the fixed beacon of the branching

9. Chesterton, *Heretics*, 23–24.

10. See the author's discussion of this in the literary biography *Defiant Joy: The Remarkable Life & Impact of G. K. Chesterton* (Thomas Nelson, 2011), 22.

> thoroughfares, the terrestrial star of the terrestrial traveller, it not only could be, but actually is, the subject of countless songs.[11]

So Chesterton was a Socrates of his age, commending good tenets of philosophy.

Still more, as if to underscore the depth of his keen interest in engaging prominent streams of contemporary philosophic thought, Chesterton penned a review of a book by G. Lowes Dickinson that also allowed the opportunity to reflect on ancient Greek philosophy. Such an exploration points to something present many times in essays and books Chesterton wrote later: a setting of ancient philosophy over and against modern practitioners of the art, noting points of commonality and contrast. Dialogues of the past, he knew, shape and many times reinfuse philosophic discourse of the present.

With Solomon he saw, forthrightly, that there is really "nothing new under the sun":

> What is the New Thought? And who thought it? This is a very mysterious matter, which has exhausted all my slender talents as an amateur detective. I know I am laying no light burden on myself and my local postman in asking such a question, for the people in movements such as this always assume that you know nothing about the movement, and proceed to tell you all about it on reams and reams of letter-paper.
>
> But this is not my difficulty. My difficulty is that I have read what is to be said about the New Thought; I have read columns and columns about it; it is the thought that I cannot find.
>
> A new thought is a very rare thing, and it would be a magnificent creature to catch.
>
> The only things I can think of that one would really call "new thoughts" would be certain celebrated jokes, certain scientific discoveries, and a few less frequent cases of a really original argument, used in an old controversy.[12]

Or, more succinctly: "The man who seeks old things will be always finding new things."[13]

In keeping with this, and as regards G. Lowes Dickinson, he said in 1901:

11. G. K. Chesterton, *The Illustrated London News* (January 13, 1917), 32.

12. G. K. Chesterton, *The Illustrated London News* (March 8, 1913), 360.

13. G. K. Chesterton, "Leviathan and the Hook," an essay on the book of Job, in *The Living Age* magazine (November 18, 1905), 443.

> In this striking Platonic dialogue Mr. Lowes Dickinson presents, in his own personality, quite apart from all logical fencing, a deep and curious problem as to the uses and limits of philosophy.
>
> He discusses the idea of good and shows that this fundamental idea may be defined variously as an instinct, a compromise, a discipline, an indulgence, a truth, an illusion, a science or an art.[14]

Meanwhile, in 1900, Chesterton had already begun to engage the philosophy of Nietzsche, Schopenhauer, and T. H. Huxley—as well as schools of thought/worldviews espoused by atheists, agnostics, and secularists. He had also written an essay entitled "The Philosophy of First Thoughts," published in a 1901 issue of *The Speaker* magazine. All these reveal him to be a "philosopher at work,"[15] engaging philosophical ideas, offering analysis, and positing alternatives. In the public square, readers throughout the British Isles, and the English-speaking world, knew Chesterton was in the flow of important conversations about ideas.

Many peers in academia, and the world of *belles lettres*, thought Chesterton a gifted modern philosopher, and gave reasons why. Here is a sampling of their estimates:

(1) Offering a trenchant critique in the January 1914 issue of *The Bookman*, poet W. B. Hooker (Yale, Class of 1902) said that Chesterton possessed "a first-rate philosophical intelligence."[16] Eleven years later, in the August 1925 issue of *The Bookman*, R. Ellis Roberts echoed Hooker's assessment when he stated Chesterton was a "modern philosophic story-teller—if Mr. Chesterton will forgive me for putting him in that category."[17] And Dr. B. E. Fernow of Yale, writing in February 1914, called Chesterton "the paradoxical philosopher" while commending him to students.[18]

14. G. K. Chesterton, "What We All Mean," a review essay in *The Speaker: A Review of Politics, Letters, Science, and the Arts* (February 16, 1901), 545.

15. A phrase coined by the author, with reference to Chesterton.

16. B. Hooker, in *The Bookman: A Magazine of Literature and Life* (January 1914), 546. William Brian Hooker (1880–946) Yale, Class of 1902, was a prominent American poet in the early twentieth century.

17. R. Ellis Roberts, in *The Bookman: A Magazine of Literature and Life* (August 1925), 258. Roberts (1879–1953), in addition to essays written for *The Bookman*, also served as literary editor of the *New Statesman* magazine.

18. As given in The Yale Graduate Advisory Board, *Yale Forest School News* (April

(2) Moving forward one hundred years to Ian Ker's acclaimed Oxford University Press study of Chesterton, the reader finds it "emphasises [his] philosophy of humour that he habitually used as a medium for comprehending and interpreting life."[19]

(3) Like Mark Twain, whom he much admired, Chesterton used wit as a means of instruction and philosophical insight. As *The National Magazine* phrased it in June 1921:

> Between Gilbert K. Chesterton, the brilliant and burly Briton who has again visited the United States, and the late Mark Twain (Samuel L. Clemens), there is some likeness. For instant vision of the humorous side of men and things, it is a toss-up which should be awarded the palm.
>
> They are twins in the possession of a serious substratum to their humor. . . .
>
> Mark Twain fixed his points—or the "moral" of his creations—with an indelible tincture of exaggeration. G. K. C. imbeds the stones of his philosophical structures in the mortar of paradox.
>
> Each in his own way is funny, but the fun reflects the "pale cast of thought."
>
> Both philosophers compel people to think while they laugh.[20]

In concert with this, and writing in 2005, biographer Ron Powers noted that "Mark Twain insisted that the secret source of humor was not joy, but sorrow. G. K. Chesterton was among those who noticed this sometimes subtle dialectic."[21] So Chesterton had written of Twain:

> He was never at a loss for a simile or a parable, and they were never, strictly speaking, nonsense. They were rather a kind of incredible sense. They were not suddenly inconsequent, like Lewis Carroll; rather they were unbearably consequent, and seemed capable of producing new consequences for ever. . . . [Mark Twain was] an unfathomably solemn man.[22]

1914), 16.

19. See the Oxford University Press overview of Ker's study at https://global.oup.com/academic/product/g-k-chesterton-9780199601288?cc=us&lang=en&.

20. See *The National Magazine*, June 1921 (Chapple, 1921), 120.

21. Ron Powers, *Mark Twain: A Life* (The Free Press, 2005), 89.

22. Powers, *Mark Twain: A Life*, 89. Chesterton said this in the Friday, April 29, 1910, issue of *T. P.'s Weekly*, 535–36.

That is the insight of one philosopher, discerning the meaning of another.

In 1918, Chesterton himself penned an essay on Stopford Brooke for *The Hibbert Journal*, a "current philosophical magazine"[23] whose essays, including Chesterton's assessment of Brooke, were featured notices in *The Philosophical Review*, a preeminent academic journal of the era.

Aside from testimonials, a brief rehearsal of lines from Chesterton's writings is illustrative of the ways he wrote as a practitioner of philosophy. Describing the need for presuppositions when commencing philosophic inquiry, Chesterton observed: "It is a good rule of philosophy when regarding an end to refer to the beginning."[24] And when it came to the importance of resolving life's great questions, he stated: "The human brain is a machine for coming to conclusions; if it cannot come to conclusions it is rusty."[25] At the same time, Chesterton offered a profound insight as to a proper understanding of reason, and the place it ought to hold in our lives: "It is idle to talk always of the alternative of reason and faith. Reason is itself a matter of faith. It is an act of faith to assert that our thoughts have any relation to reality at all."[26]

And last, space ought to be given here to *Heretics*, the book cited by *The Harvard Monthly* in 1907 as the key text in which Chesterton declared himself a philosopher. For indeed, the prose of *Heretics* is continually clothed in philosophical language and terms, as in this passage:

> When the old Liberals removed the gags from all the heresies, their idea was that religious and philosophical discoveries might thus be made. Their view was that cosmic truth was so important that everyone ought to bear independent testimony. The modern idea is that cosmic truth is so unimportant that it cannot matter what anyone says.[27]

So what kind of description, specifically, might Chesterton have applied to himself? We need look no further than this sentence, given in chapter 7 of *Heretics*: "A Christian thinker, such as Augustine or Dante, would object to this [view] because it ignores free-will which is the valour and

23. See *The Philosophical Review* 27 (Longmans, Green, 1918), 440. Edited by J. E. Creighton of the Sage School of Philosophy at Cornell, and James Seth of the University of Edinburgh, *The Philosophical Review* was one of the preeminent academic journals of its era.

24. Cited in *The G. K. Chesterton Calendar* (Palmer & Hayward, 1916), 69.

25. Chesterton, *Heretics*, 285.

26. Cited in *The G. K. Chesterton Calendar*, 47.

27. Chesterton, *Heretics*, 14.

dignity of the soul"[28] which "Christian thinkers" set upon exploring tenets of "cosmic truth." Such men, like Augustine and Dante, won Chesterton's respect and abiding reverence. Such was the kind of man he sought to be: a Socrates who looked to the lamppost—posing questions meant to help others find what he had found. That would always be his purpose, and would always guide his pen.

BIBLIOGRAPHY

Chesterton, G. K. *All Things Considered*. London: Methuen, 1908.

———. "A Defence of Ugly Things." *The Speaker: A Review of Politics, Letters, Science, and the Arts*, March 23, 1901, 675–76.

———. *The Defendant*. London: R. Brimley Johnson, 1901.

———. *Heretics*. London: John Lane, 1905.

———. *The Illustrated London News*, March 8, 1913, 360.

———. *The Illustrated London News*, January 13, 1917, 32.

———. "Leviathan and the Hook." *The Living Age*, November 18, 1905, 443.

———. *Orthodoxy*. London: John Lane, The Bodley Head, 1908.

———. "Puritan and Anglican." *The Speaker: A Review of Politics, Letters, Science, and the Arts*, December 15, 1900, 301.

———. *Robert Browning*. London: Macmillan, 1903.

———. *T. P.'s Weekly*, April 29, 1910, 535–36.

———. *Varied Types*. London: Brimley Johnson, 1903.

———. "What We All Mean." *The Speaker: A Review of Politics, Letters, Science, and the Arts*, February 16, 1901, 545.

Conor, Peter. "The Socratic Method: Fostering Critical Thinking." Institute for Learning and Teaching at Colorado State University. https://tilt.colostate.edu/the-socratic-method/.

Creighton, J. E., and James Seth, eds. *The Philosophical Review* 27. New York: Longmans, Green, 1918.

Ellis-Roberts, R. "Review." *The Bookman: A Magazine of Literature and Life*, August 1925.

The G. K. Chesterton Calendar. London: Palmer and Hayward, 1916.

Hooker, William Brian. "Review." *The Bookman: A Magazine of Literature and Life*, January 1914.

Ker, Ian. "*G. K. Chesterton*." Oxford University Press. https://global.oup.com/academic/product/g-k-chesterton-9780199601288.

Mencken, H. L. "Some Novels—and a Good One." *The Smart Set*, 1909.

Powers, Ron. *Mark Twain: A Life*. New York: The Free Press, 2005.

28. Chesterton, *Heretics*, 107.

I end where I began—at the right end. I have entered at last the gate of all good philosophy. I have come into my second childhood.

—"Authority and the Adventurer," *Orthodoxy*

www.ingramcontent.com/pod-product-compliance
Lightning Source LLC
LaVergne TN
LVHW050629100826
845148LV00011B/1790

* 9 7 9 8 3 8 5 2 3 0 9 9 0 *